THE STUDENT-CENTRED SCHOOL
ideas for practical visionaries

Donna Brandes and Paul Ginnis

Activities compiled and edited by Lindsey Hammond
Cartoons by Pat Hornsby and Martyn Briggs
Marginal 'Outfits', by Dr David E H Jones

SIMON & SCHUSTER
EDUCATION

First published in 1990 by
Basil Blackwell Ltd

Reprinted in 1992, 1993 by
Simon and Schuster Education

Simon and Schuster Education
Campus 400
Maylands Avenue
Hemel Hempstead
Herts HP2 7EZ

British Library Cataloguing in Publication Data
Brandes, Donna
   The student-centred school.
   1. Schools. Management
   I. Title II. Ginnis, Paul
   371.2

ISBN 0-7501-0428-7

Printed in Great Britain by
Redwood Books, Trowbridge

Dedications

To *Ruth Ginnis* who, by giving so much, has shared profoundly in the writing of this book.

To *Carl Rogers* who died recently, mourned by thousands of people whose lives he enriched, and whose work he inspired. Always kindly, humorous, optimistic and positive, he radiated the love upon which this work is based.

Donna wrote to him in 1986, sending a copy of *A Guide to Student-Centred Learning* and thanking him for everything... In his return letter of appreciation he wrote:

This is a time when student-centred learning certainly needs to be promoted. We are working against the trend, but such work is very important.

CONTENTS

ACKNOWLEDGEMENTS

We love writing our acknowledgements; they create wonderful feelings of appreciation and friendship.

They're also difficult to write:

- What if we forget to mention someone really important?
- What if we put them in the wrong order, and someone feels slighted?
- How can we express the full measure of our appreciation that this book is a fully collaborative effort between us, our families, our friends, our colleagues that we work with, and our colleagues out there in the field who have been writing and teaching and thinking, and providing us with inspiration?

Nevertheless, here we are, to say, THANK YOU!

To Ruth Ginnis, and to Clare, Steven, and Helen Ginnis, who gave us the time and space to do our writing, even when it wasn't easy.

To Lindsey Hammond. All that we have learned over the past four years, Lindsey has been part of, with her cheerful good humour and her unfailing energy. Lindsey and her husband Ted have supported us in every helpful way they could think of.

From Paul: To Jean Ginnis, my Mum, and to Tricia and Debbie, my not-so-little sisters, along with all the members of my wider family.

From Donna: To my wonderful sons, Bodhi and Lance Brandes, who have always been a source of strength and joy to me. To Arnold and Alice, Joc and Nat, Leonard and Merle, and all my dear family back in America, who are always so interested.

To Eva Ross and Walter Truman-Cox, who loaned us their house and their word processor to do our early writing on this book, and who offered an always-open door to Donna.

To Marion McFall, who gave us the free use of her home to write in when we started.

To Educators with whom we have had the excitement of working, who have helped us to grow and move forward in our work and our thinking, and whom we continue to respect and admire:

| David Settle | Jill Baldwin | Chris Lea |
| Kevyn Smith | Dorothy Heathcote | Tim Brighouse (thanks for the foreword) |

Ted Harvey	Ron Miller	Mike Gadsby	Stan Bailey
Francis Moran	David Lambourn	Sheila Phillips	Bill Smithson
Dorothy Hale	Kim Davies	Georgine Cooper	Diane Dodd
Ian Pickles	Allan White	Mike Foster	Tom Early
Howard Phillips	Helen Hadley	Stephen Munby	Sharon Robinson
Steve Myers	Martyn Briggs	Kären Wylie	Andy McCallum
Sunderland TVEI Support Team		Angela Garnett	David Brockie
			Warren Scott

Birmingham Staff Development Tutor Team

To our friends, because they enrich our lives and give us strength, and offer an attractive alternative to working all the time.

Dave Worlock   Becky Higgins   Peter Ward

John Gordon   David Williams

Lennie, Georgina, Christopher, Paul and Helen Bradshaw

Peter, Jill, Claire, Gareth and Paul Hollingsworth

Richard, Heather, Robbie and Amy Sattin

Diane, Tom, Molly, Frances, and Patrick Herron

Margaret, Howard, Katherine, and Rachael Phillips

Judi Ledward and Robin Hobbes

Lee Hill   Sandy Freda   Bernie Raden

Barbara Cooper and Nikola

Dick and Thea Benthin

Art and Elaine Aron

To James Nash, for his faith and patience.

To Marion Casey, for her remarkably detailed work on the manuscript.

From Paul: To Bruce Springsteen and Southside Johnny for keeping me energised and in touch.

To colleagues, besides the ones mentioned above, who contributed specific activities, either with us or on their own:

Gill Burgess, Lydia Kirby, Arnold Fairless, Joan Formosa, Cathy Barnes, Jim Simpson, Mike Anderson, Pauline Temple, Jacky West, Steven Coates, Linda Driscoll, Rosy Mackin, Brenda Pugh, Celia Banner.

FOREWORD

Every youngster has a right to attend a successful school.

This book bravely continues the quest for the educational El Dorado — a formula which will guarantee successful schools in which successful learning can happen. Its messages for practitioners and those who would wish to run successful schools are powerful; they are especially important now.

There has never been such upheaval in our country's schooling system: there is a prospective shortage of teachers and there is an agenda of reforms about which there is no sense of ownership and little joy — reforms which some may say make successful schooling less, rather than more, likely. Indeed the substance of real success is likely to be obscured by its appearance within a system designed to be governed by market forces, with all that implies for the pecking order of schools. The authors would want us to take heart from the fact that there is nothing particularly novel about that: they dissect the evidence which underscores the point that our inherited practices are all flawed with a preoccupation with failure, rather than success.

They say — and I agree with them — that it is still possible both for anyone within a school (whatever its general ethos and climate) and for any school as a whole (wheresover it may be) to translate determination into action and create havens where optimism and enjoyment guarantee every member of the school community the best chance of success. That is my most important point, and the reason why the book deserves a wide readership.

Finally, the authors and the book shout their belief that more youngsters can realise their potential and that schools can be 'OK places to be' — a phrase the authors wanted me to include as it cropped up in our conversation and represented an expression which encapsulates both the book's style and its universal message.

Tim Brighouse

1 THE CONTRACT AND THE CLIMATE

I   We will consistently recognise that each person is responsible for herself or himself.
II We will be collaborative in all respects. This involves EVERYONE working together for personal and communal enhancement, including giving and receiving feedback, joint decision making, and consistent support.
III We will be strongly committed to a policy of non-violence. We will expect everyone to live without verbal, physical, or emotional abuse.
IV Everyone in the school will be asked to view themselves as learners, including visitors.
V   We will be aiming for excellence in all aspects of learning. We are committed to holistic education, which is concerned with every dimension of human experience.
VI We are committed to the enhancement of self-esteem, through the creation of a positive learning environment.
VII We are committed to a policy of equal opportunity, which will necessarily involve a specific and proactive policy to reverse initial or continuing disadvantage.

Please take a few minutes to reflect on the Contract. Allow yourself a daydream about what it would be like to work in a school where it is in full operation—for everyone, without exception. Imagine that every person who works in this school—students, managers, teaching or non-teaching staff—is fully acquainted with its principles, and signed it before starting life at the school.

Place yourself in the school setting. How would you feel? What would be the implications—for your working life, and for the education of the students.

Your personal reaction may range from: 'Impossible!!!' . . . to . . . 'I'd really like to be there!' . . . or even . . . 'I already work in such a place!'. We ask you now to take a few minutes, turn to the 'Person-centred writings for reader-centred readers' at the back of the book, and write down your immediate reactions to the Contract . . . .

Bottom lines

The Contract represents non-negotiable bottom lines—that is, the fundamental points beyond which we are not prepared to go. It would be less than honest to pretend that they are open to discussion. They constitute our definition of student-centredness, and provide the structure for the kind of freedom which supports holistic learning. It has taken us four years of working together and with hundreds of teachers and students to become fully aware that these are the minimum rock-solid requirements for implementing the methods and maintaining the underlying values of student-centred learning.

So, a student-centred school would be based on a firm foundation of commitment to the principles outlined in the contract; these provide discipline, control, direction, comfort and safety for everyone there.

Once people have contracted to keep these ground rules, they become common property. *Beyond these fundamentals, every other decision will be effected collaboratively.*

Our vision of a student-centred school

We have a vision of what school could be like. It is a recipe made up of good things we have already seen in schools, with a dash of dreams, a hearty flavouring of creativity, a delicate taste of innovation and outrageousness, all in a basic broth of practicality. It is nourishing for everyone, and easily adaptable for anyone.

This book will spell out the recipe in as much as it *can* be spelled out, for it is a recipe to be rewritten by each new team of cooks. For now, we'd just like to offer you a taste.

To change metaphors in midstream, come and walk through one version of our school with us. Experience it through your senses, not through your analytical processes; we'll get to those later. Also, in our visionary walk we are not pretending that there no problems arising and being dealt with, or that we've arrived at a state of perfection. Things are going wrong all the time, as in any other school. Come and sense the atmosphere, see if you can feel what we feel.

You're met at the door by a girl and a boy who look about 12. They welcome you, introduce themselves, and ask who you've come to see. On your way, they stop to introduce you to the Head, who is sitting on a bench with a student and a teacher, involved in deep conversation. She nods and smiles at you, and continues listening to the student on the bench, so you say to your guides that you'll come back later.

We see splashes of colour: bright, cheerful, inviting. Colourful but hard-wearing carpets protect the floors, soften the noise, and provide easy seating. There are pictures on the walls, masterpieces by the current inhabitants of the school. Everyone, and that means *every*one, in the school has taken ownership of how the place looks, and so could point out to you one of their murals, or show you some plants they're caring for, or let you look through a kaleidoscope of simulated stained glass in one of the windows.

Every classroom is arranged differently. Also, the room we see today might look different tomorrow, because the furniture and the designers are very flexible.

People are walking around as if there is enough time to get jobs done; they seem to be busy, but without a sense of stress or hurry. Students and teachers are intermingled so that it is frequently hard to tell which is which. No one is shouting at anyone else, or exhorting them to *do* or *not do* something or other. There is conversation, but at a fireside level, and you can hear greetings, first names, laughter, questions, discussions.

In a science lab, two students are conducting an experiment, others are observing and taking notes; one student is writing the hypothesis, method and results on the board. In one room some students are gathered around the piano and we can hear them singing; in another room the school orchestra is practising, and in a third, we hear and see a rehearsal for a forthcoming dramatic event. In another room you can hear a teacher explaining the unfamiliar concept of supply and demand to a very large group of students. Down the hall a group is sitting in a circle, the teacher among them, working on a problem involving quadratic equations.

There is a general air of *purpose*; things seem to be getting done without anyone pushing or shoving. People walk from one place to another without fear or reluctance. Some may be working, others playing, others resting, or talking, but it all seems to be happening just as it should be. A student comes up to you and asks, 'Do you know where my Biology lesson is?'

Educators and students are all wearing their own individualistic clothing, though there is nothing particularly startling about most of it, although a boy and girl with matching green hair are attracting a lot of attention.

Even the lunches are client-centred... you can design your lunch according to your taste and tradition. Little is wasted, because everything is chosen. An argument breaks out at one of the tables... a plateful of chips is thrown, and there is a sudden hush. A teacher starts to get up to talk to the hurler... and he gets up and meets her in the middle of the room to work through the incident together.

The Head comes to find you, and takes you to the staff room, where she stops to add a note to a School Council Agenda posted on the wall. You have a million questions, for example, why don't the doors to various offices have names and titles on them? You ask her about it, and she says, 'Well there is no Senior Management Team any more, because we divide the responsibilities among ourselves in a different way. Many of the responsibilities are shared, and mixed groups of teachers and students carry them out.'

The Head comes with you to complete your tour of the school. There are various notices, letters, posters on the walls and notice boards; all of them are announcing or celebrating something, or covering the news of the day. None of them carry dire warnings or scoldings. Nowhere does it say: 'All visitors *must*...', or 'Students are not allowed to...'. There seems to be an assumption that people actually know how to behave *themselves*.

An enlarged copy of the Contract is on a bulletin board in the entrance hall. In many rooms you can see copies of Ground Rules and Safety Rules generated by the students.

There is a lot of movement and a lot of people, but most of it is not chaotic. There are also pools of stillness and quiet around the school. You feel that there is enough time, enough room, enough acceptance for everyone.

Again, take a minute to identify your reactions to this passage. When we've asked colleagues on courses to tell us what they think of the description, their response is usually a mixture of positives and negatives. Many tell us that it is hopelessly idealistic. Others say that it is what they want, but that it can't happen because... (then they take a deep breath and reel off an endless list).

We recognise that such a school is an ideal removed from the day-to-day realities faced by most teachers, and that moving toward this ideal seems like swimming against the tide. But our firm belief is that students, teachers and school managers, along with Governors, parents and the wider community *can* do it! A student-centred school is possible. Many of the constraints, or reasons for 'staying stuck' are internal. By this we mean that they are within the school's *modus operandi*, or within the school's people. Either way, something can be done about them. Where the constraints are externally imposed, hope can be kept alive by the way the procedures are interpreted, or at least the manner in which they are implemented; beyond this, there are various channels through which pressure for change can be exerted.

Holistic Health and Safety

By taking you on a tour through our school we tried to convey the concept of an environment where people feel safe. We don't mean overprotection, nor do we mean that we discourage taking risks, exploring, or participating; in fact, we mean to build, quite deliberately, a place where all three of these growing points can happen . . . without fear.

In practical terms we are talking about an environment that provides freedom from physical harm. The labs, the gym, the Home Economics room, the corridors, all require firm rules for safe behaviour; our experience has been that kids, even very young ones, are good at producing the necessary regulations.

Safety also means freedom from other, non-physical forms of hurt. The Contract mentions non-violence and this means more than an absence of danger. It refers to all the aspects of general safety in the learning environment that rest on the security provided by love, and unconditional positive regard. If we say to every person in the school, 'We value you for who you are'; if we bring to the school our loving hearts, our sense of humour, our ability to laugh at adversity and learn from mistakes, we can create a 'safe' climate.

> To the degree that the . . . . teacher . . . can provide this safety-creating climate of unconditional positive regard, significant learning is likely to take place.   (Rogers, 1967)

The chart on pages 7–9 sets out what a physically and emotionally safe environment could be like in various aspects of school life. You may want to complete a similar chart for your own school, and then use it to assess the areas over which you have some control, the changes you intend to make, and the current priorities for action. What is your Holistic Health and Safety Policy? The locally-managed school would be surprised at what it could do . . . if it wanted to.

Our reasons for writing this book

> Since the autumn of 1987, the focus of my professional life has changed dramatically. The cause has been my acquaintance with the book *A Guide to Student-Centred Learning*. Within two days, I had read the book, which filled me with a feeling of great excitement. I felt that I had, after eighteen years of teaching, at last found an approach which matches my own beliefs and attitudes, and above all provided a guide for effective practice.
>   (Allan White, 1988)

This statement is one of many such responses to our first book. Since writing *A Guide to Student-Centred Learning* we have spent our working lives alongside teachers, trainers and managers, in Britain and the USA, sharing in their work and exploring with them the application of people-centred principles to all areas of school life. We have been both encouraged and challenged by them, and we acknowledge the way in which these colleagues have helped us shape the thinking and practice contained in this second volume. Consequently, we feel that the ideas we present are broader and more developed than four years ago, and we have enjoyed (on the whole!) the learning processes that we've been through.

During this time, the education system in Britain has been overhauled, forcing us all into a period of major challenge and opportunity. It has taken us some time to sort out our attitudes to the reforms. Like many others, we

Figure 1.1 The safe and healthy school

SAFETY IS ....

	Students and classrooms	Teachers and staffrooms	Everyone .... The Whole School
Unconditional positive regard	Good communication; support for learning and working closely together; celebrations; sharing of talents; working and reaching for highest potential	Relationships characterised by warmth, support, caring; trust; self-disclosure; sharing of ideas and plans	Holistic education for everyone; re-balance of curriculum so that there is room for affective learning and personal development; feeling of being regarded with positive esteem; regarding others that way
Communication	Listening to each other; spontaneous conversation; no need to refer everything to the teacher; direct and open statements; sitting in circles or groups, not rows; absence of sarcasm or put-downs	Straight adult transactions; no 'games people play'; everyone free to ask for what they want and need; honest feedback; listen with respect	Direct and straight communication with everyone, no 'games'; circles and close groupings in classrooms, staffrooms, and offices; bright and positive notices around the school, no dire warnings; display of all sorts of learning activities and coming events; everyone who comes to the school is an important learner, and treated as such

	Students and classrooms	Teachers and staffrooms	Everyone .... The Whole School
Choices	Variety of tasks; working in various groups, of different sizes, and self-selected; choice of clothing, even uniform if desired; each individual enjoying maximum choice. Freedom to participate or not, no coercion	Choices of short-term tasks; working parties; duties; dress; often sharing or trading as desired, with regard to lessons, ideas, assignments; involved in policies and plans; participation in management; volunteering to participate in the life of the school; no coercion on any level	Ongoing assessment, and formative discussions of school events, decisions, policies, plans; variations in dress according to comfort and personal style; maximum choices for everyone in school, but with regard for others; freedom (and personal responsibility) for participating or not; norms are less demanding; and carry no fixed penalties for not conforming; participatory management
Trust; group-building; risk-taking	Two-way feedback (negative *and* positive) between teachers and students; warm greetings; eye-contact; guessing, estimating, arguing, sharing, disclosing, supporting, debating. Volunteering, even when not sure; confidence to explore and investigate	Sharing mistakes; asking for ideas; visiting colleagues in class; working collaboratively; sharing materials; sharing feelings; speaking positively of kids, and showing affection for them; joining with kids and colleagues in problem solving; being proactive about cutting down on griping; team teaching by choice, with planning periods built in to timetable	People telling the truth, trusting each other, feeling good about contributions to school life; people being honest, arguing, challenging, behaving with respect; open sharing of information; current issues affecting school are freely discussed; feelings are openly shared

Self-esteem	Heterogeneous grouping: no setting, no streaming. No labels. Each class chooses its name-designation. Appreciation and acknowledgement replace praise and approval. Everyone valued for their personal contributions, without comparison or competition, and each person reaching for her own potential	Self-appraisal; negotiated appraisal; peer appraisal; school counsellor available for staff, also quiet room for resting; feeling valued and looked after; resources available for staff development which is planned by staff; staff section in library	Eliminating words like 'ability', 'thick', 'remedial'. School counsellors to support everyone in the school; healthy outlets for anger; all interactions characterised by positive regard
Responsibility	Ground Rules; self discipline replaces punishment. Feeling of ownership and caring for the school, the work, and especially the people; proactive support for others	Identifying own needs for training and development; thinking of the school as centred on the kids; feeling responsible for self and well-being, and for supporting and enabling kids	Punishment replaced by contracts, agreements, counselling; school rules replaced by contracts and ground rules; awareness of language of responsibility (eg, *I can't* becomes *I won't*). Everyone sharing in policy making; campaigning for educational reform. More flexible timetable, open resources; parents and others join in maintaining attractive school; flexible use of rooms and spaces in school; everyone shares feeling of ownership of school, curriculum and policies.

have been through feelings of anger, confusion, pessimism and hope. We know how easy it is to be bitter and cynical about what seems to lie behind the recent legislation, ie:

- standardised curriculum
- standardised assessment
- non-holistic values
- Education for economic, social (and, by implication, political) purposes
- constraining of teaching styles
- relocation of power and intensification of hierarchies
- one-way accountability
- agendas determined from above
- centralised definition of 'standards' and the criteria for allocating resources
- narrow criteria for measuring the performance of students, teachers and schools
- creation of new, or wider, differences and divisions
- competition and image-consciousness

At times we have been tempted to give up and side with those who feel that it is impossibile to create a student-centred climate in such hostile conditions. In fact we have thrown away several drafts of this book which expressed strongly negative views!

Since then, however, we have come round to thinking that there are indeed many positive steps we can take, many supportive statements we can make, and many practical suggestions we can offer. As you will discover, we do not condone what we believe to be damaging aspects of the reforms, rather we feel that it is more helpful for our students, our colleagues and ourselves as teachers if we adopt a positive and creative attitude to that which is required of us. In this we join with many educators who have already worked hard to provide a humane and holistic approach to Government intentions. So, we have decided to turn our own attitudes around and to redouble our efforts on behalf of student-centred learning, which is not a passing fad, but a way forward, a strong movement which has been around for thousands of years and will continue to thrive and expand.

This book aims to:

1 Present a vision of a student-centred school where everyone—not just students, but teachers and managers too—takes responsibility for themselves and where all are enabled to reach for their potential in an holistically healthy environment;
2 Show how it is possible to move towards this vision within the state education system created by the 1988 Education Reform Act;
3 Support students, teachers, trainers and managers in becoming people-centred in their *present* circumstances, by offering practical guidelines, small steps and purpose-built activities;
4 Uplift and inspire, so that a motivation for creativity and change is generated.

We have already met dozens of teachers who would like to work in a student-centred school, and we would love to run one with them. So we are laying our cards on the table: we want some enlightened somebody (an

LEA, a University, a body of Governors, a major philanthropist) to encourage us and even to fund us in our demonstration of SCL principles in action.

Outline of the book

In the next three chapters we discuss the 'thinking behind' our approach and attempt to interpret the present education system from a student-centred point of view as well as to suggest what it can do, negatively, to both students (Chapter 3) and teachers (Chapter 4). These two chapters carry a health warning: if you already suffer from a weak heart in education, Chapters 3 and 4 could damage your health even more. You don't have to read them, you could skip them and go straight to the more positive bit.

The positive bit starts with Chapter 5 where we present a generic way of working with people of any age in any setting. The three chapters which follow are devoted to specific applications of this way of working: to students, focusing on classroom practice (Chapter 6); to teachers, focusing on professional and personal development (Chapter 7); and to everyone, focusing on participatory management and whole-school climate (Chapter 8).

It is our sincere hope that *The Student-Centred School* will stimulate professional dialogue and support a growing network of like-minded people. The 'Person-centred writings for reader-centred readers' at the back of the book is a way of making this happen. We will be delighted to hear from you.

2 THE THINKING BEHIND . . .

Hornsby.

Now we've offered you a fleeting glimpse of what a fully established student-centred school might look and feel like, we want to discuss with you some of the values, assumptions and principles which lie behind our thinking. We're now inviting you to apply those analytical processes we asked you to put on the shelf before.

Three layers of thought

To start with, please consider the following model, which is supposed to look like a cross-section of the earth's crust.

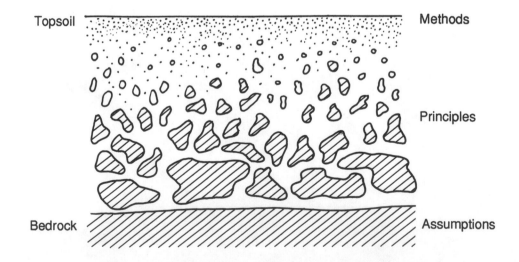

In the *topsoil* grow the observable features of our classroom and staffroom practice, such as: collaborative planning, implementing, and evaluating; group building; problem solving; choices; negotiation; experiential activity. When used properly, these approaches bear the fruit of enhanced learning and performance. To ensure a good harvest, though, these methods cannot be used superficially; rather, they will be practised as manifestations of underlying principles. An understanding and an *internalisation* of these subterranean values is required, which will demand certain skills and resources of the teacher.

The following nine principles underlie our work:

The principles	What the teacher needs
1 When we value the learner, we increase her self-esteem and her openness to learning.	listening and other interpersonal skills; an attitude of unconditional positive regard

2 The most effective learning is 'owned' by learners who are consistently regarded as responsible for themselves.	internalisation of the concepts of responsibility and ownership

3 Maximum growth of the learner occurs when she herself carries out the planning, organisation, implementation and evaluation of the learning.

a wide range of groupwork and facilitation skills; negotiation skills; assertiveness; self- and peer-assessment procedures; resource management and information handling skills

4 Much effective learning is achieved through doing.

an understanding and repertoire of experiential learning methods

5 Learning can best take place in a safe, supportive environment.

group-building skills; clear bottom lines; self-awareness; establishment of ground rules with the group

6 Learning which involves the whole person, not just the mind of the learner but the feelings also, is the deepest and most permanent.

familiarisation with confluent education methods (see page 30); ability to recognise and deal effectively with feelings in self and others; the use of drama as a learning medium

7 A learner's affective and cognitive growth are enhanced by positive interaction with other learners.

communication skills; encouragement of productive noise and movement

8 The most socially-useful learning is the learning of the process of learning, a continuing openness to experience and incorporation into oneself of the process of change.

openness, willingness to change, and honesty; an ability to recognise and value process as well as content

9 Creativity is increased in an environment marked by fun, humour, spontaneity, risk, and intuition.

knowledge and skills which encourages the appropriate use of drama, music, dance and art; a sense of humour and fun

Beneath these methods and principles is a *bedrock* of fundamental beliefs about being human, which provide a solid foundation for client-centred work and create the principles outlined above. They result in a particular attitude and a consistent approach to working with any individual or group. In fact, we hope that these values pervade all our relationships—with family, friends and colleagues:

1 A person has a willingness to change and grow (learn), indeed a desire and a need to do so, and at the same time has a resistance and a fear about changing. These two factors are equally natural and acceptable. In an environment of emotional and physical safety, inhibiting fear becomes less prominent, and the drive towards self-actualisation more prominent, providing inherent motivation for learning.

2 We can purposefully, and with integrity, adopt a stance of unconditional positive regard for a person, to which the person may, sooner or later, respond with trust. This is the basis for an effective enabling relationship.

3 The person is in charge of herself, is fully responsible for her own behaviour in the learning relationship, and can participate or not as she chooses.

4 Most human beings are capable of a wide range of behaviour, for example from the extremes of cruelty to the fullest extent of caring. People are responsible for choosing their own behaviour. Within conditions and relationships characterised by unconditional positive regard, they are more likely to choose positive behaviours and move towards virtue, excellence and harmony.

5 Human beings do not start their lives with equal opportunities, or resources, or circumstances. It is up to us, as enablers, to build an environment where we contribute at all times to the rebalancing of opportunity, the strengthening of self-esteem, the increasing of effectiveness, and the reversal of disadvantage.

We want to emphasise again that these assumptions underlie *all* our work. They apply unchanged to classroom learning, to staff development and to participatory management. Any soil is determined by the bedrock which underlies it; the rock gives rise to a particular texture, colour and chemical content . . . and so dictates what can and cannot be grown, and eventually the kind of harvest to be reaped.

Rights, constraints, and human potential

> . . . the function of education, the goal of education, the goal so far as human beings are concerned, is ultimately the self-actualisation of a person, the fully becoming human, the development of the fullest height that the human species can stand up to or that the particular individual can come to. In a less technical way, it is helping the person to become the best that he is able to become.
>
> (Maslow, 1976)

The basic assumptions of the humanistic, or holistic, or student-centred approach to education stem from a fundamental belief that all human beings, solely by virtue of being human, have both the right and the motivation to take charge of their own lives. Fulfilling this right creates the most healthy state of existence for individuals, communities, and society at large. 'Being-in-charge-of-me' is the natural state of affairs seen in infants and young children, and it is the optimum condition for learning. When people retain, or regain, charge of their own lives, individuals and communities are released to reach for their potential.

Like many educators, we are constantly inspired and excited by the potential of human beings. We celebrate the diversity of people, and the way that their view of their own possibilities is forever shifting and opening. We used to say that we wanted all people to fulfil their potential; but that is a contradiction in terms. Potential is all that a person can become, so it is never complete; it is always expanding. We can only really talk about reaching for potential. When we speak of it, we are referring to every aspect of being, and being-in-relation-to-others.

As a member of the human race, I have a natural motivation to be in charge of myself. Given positive conditions, that is, conditions of safety and support, I will *want* to acquire the understanding, skills and knowledge I need in order to achieve. So, I don't need to be pushed or pulled into my own learning. I have an inherent motivation to reach for my potential, which shows from birth in exploration, curiosity and the struggle for mastery.

> . . . . . . The single most characteristic thing about human beings is that they learn. Learning is so deeply ingrained in Man that it is almost involuntary, and thoughtful students of human behavior have even speculated that our specialization as a species is a specialization of learning.   (Bruner, 1966)

At the same time as I experience this natural motivation for my own learning and development, I also experience resistance to learning. It demands something of me; it is often painful and arduous. So, I need positive support in a way which upholds me, strengthens me and challenges me, but does not hijack my development. When this skilful facilitation is absent, or replaced by possessive controlling, constant telling or, worse still, hostility and humiliation, then my natural feelings of motivation are likely to be outweighed by my natural feelings of resistance.

Also, I do not promise to have the same high levels of motivation for learning which other people choose for me. Learning which I do not perceive to be directly relevant to my development (no matter how many other people tell me it *is* relevant) will naturally meet with greater resistance. This does not mean that I am 'less able', simply that I am unmotivated in this particular respect at this particular moment. The prescription is divorced from my natural motivation.

Clearly, these beliefs and assumptions have major implications for the way education is done. The organisation of schooling, the notion of 'curriculum' and the nature of teaching would all be overhauled if this philosophy were internalised. The education reforms we are now required to implement seem to be rooted in very different soil.

Equally clearly, these beliefs have implications for the way in which I approach my learning and my life, whether I'm a student, a teacher, a trainer, or a manager. In the face of contrary experience at school and beyond, I may need to take, and keep taking, the following two steps very consciously:

1 The first step is for me to recognise my natural right to control my own life, in other words, to acknowledge that I have the right to make and implement decisions and to determine the course of personal events, the freedom to say yes or no, and to make choices . . . Such a recognition sees

through, and resists, attempts to blackmail me emotionally. I immediately begin to feel strong and independent and 'myself'.

This is not to advocate selfish disregard for other people, even though some of our supporters, never mind our critics, suggest that this could be the logical conclusion of our thinking. Given the choice, most people want to live in healthy relationships with others, and also to take responsibility for making the world, or at least their bit of it, work better. However, arriving at this realisation, or preserving it, may not be easy; most of us live with formal systems and informal norms which erode the practice, and with it the very concept, of self-responsibility. Many people automatically:

- blame, accuse and scapegoat;
- adopt a couldn't-care-less attitude;
- accept judgements, instructions and policies from on high, quite passively;
- wait for someone else to do something;
- become fatalistic;
- remain content with their lot in life;
- grow accustomed to personal limitations: 'I can't . . .', 'I could never . . .'.

2 The second step is for me to *accept responsibility* for my own life, which speaks of the motivation to take charge; a readiness to face, and not evade consequences; to learn from mistakes; to be proactive and make things happen; a willingness to accept 'all of me as I am at the moment'; an avoidance of excuses, and of 'gaming' in relationships. Life will be characterised by an openness to learning. It amounts to a caring for, even a loving of, self.

Again, this is not selfish; it rests on a recognition that a person who is healthy and strong in body, mind, and spirit, is in a good position to give and share. Nor is it necessarily a cosy way of life; often it is less painful to pass the buck, to deceive, to hide and to pretend.

This human right—that each person has the right to be in charge of her or his own life—is, like most human rights, rarely realised in full. For many groups and individuals opportunities to exercise self-responsibility are effectively reduced and, in extreme cases, removed completely.

Some of these negating factors are *external*, such as the unequal distribution of wealth, information, authority, opportunity and resources. In other cases unjust social and institutional structures advantage some and disadvantage others. And the list goes on . . . propaganda, deliberate and forceful repression, imprisonment . . . .

Other stunting factors are internal, such as conditioning, depressed self-image, or unexpressed emotion, which undermine an individual's motivation and sense of capability.

These internal and external factors work together in subtle ways to deprive a person, or group of people, of opportunity and resources, in other words of their power and potential.

With regard to the powerful forces which shape all our lives . . . throughout this book, we could keep taking detours into describing and explaining the social, economic, and political context within which our work, and all of education, takes place. We feel under some pressure to do so, lest we be thought unaware, or worse still, unconcerned. We know full well that we work in an unjust, unequal, sexist, racist world, and our belief system challenges the status quo at its very core. If we did make all of this explicit every time, we would have a different book. Suffice it to say that, with each word we write, we know that there are many others unspoken.

Inevitably, the pursuit of student-centred values, and wanting to give people the opportunity to be in charge of their lives, would mean setting up new political, social, and economic structures. We don't describe them here, but we do think that the educational practice outlined in this volume would equip people with the personal power and social effectiveness to achieve such change. The book is deliberately visionary; it has grand implications in mind, but it is also intensely practical, and based in present reality. To get anywhere, we must start from where we are . . .

So the challenge for us is to acknowledge the urgency of the wider issues, and still focus on our main purpose here, which is to work from where circumstances are now, to be as practical as we are idealistic, and to concentrate on individuals and their immediate social interactions.

To sum up so far, we suggest the following model:

Reaching for Potential

Being in charge of me

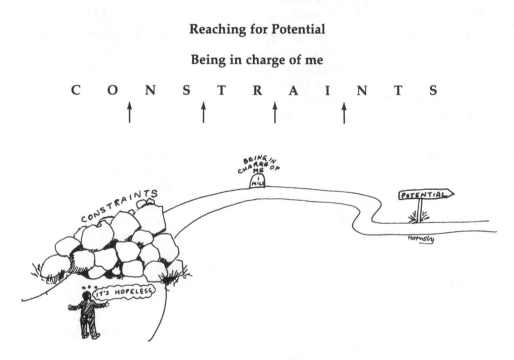

Our job as educators, as counsellors, as family members and friends (in other words as 'helpers' in the broadest sense) is to enable people to overcome their constraints. As each block is dealt with, they become more and more in charge of themselves. So, they are increasingly released to reach for their potential.

We love this quote from a TVEI student in Redbridge:

I believe a person's education is inside them, waiting to be released out with the help of a good teacher.

In order to remain true to the task, we keep six themes in sharp and constant focus in the day-to-day practicalities of our work. These themes translate the principles of our approaches into practice. They are:

1 Self-esteem   4 Resources
2 Opportunity   5 Positive support
3 Responsibility   6 Confluence

So now the model looks like this:

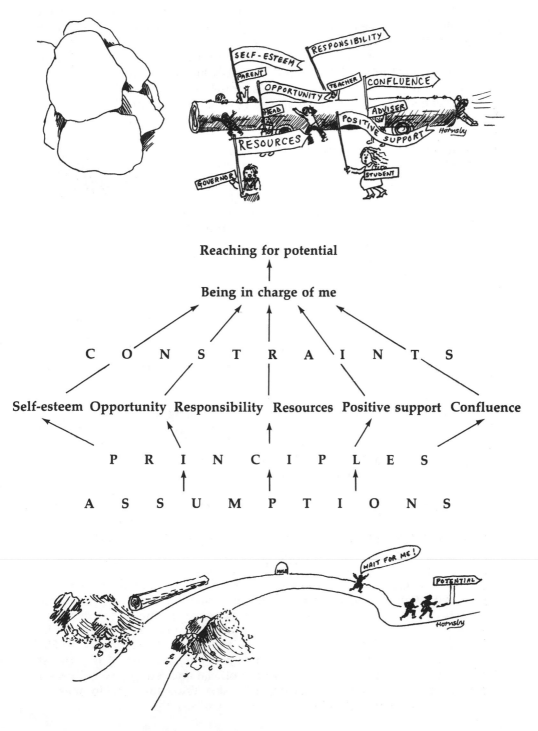

Reaching for potential

↑

Being in charge of me

C O N S T R A I N T S

Self-esteem Opportunity Responsibility Resources Positive support Confluence

P R I N C I P L E S

A S S U M P T I O N S

Let us explain each of these interrelated themes in a little more detail.

1 Self-esteem

Perhaps the major objective in this constraint-busting operation is to do away with negative self-images and to enhance self-esteem. People cannot live or learn effectively without a strong, healthy self-concept, and without caring for themselves in a positive and nurturing way. Regular school learning is almost impossible when the student has a poor self-concept.

Holding a negative self-image drains so much energy. Everyone wants to feel OK, and some people seek that feeling by looking for outside approval. Many schools and teachers—not to mention other students—are not generous with their acknowledgement. The system of reward and punishment, competition, and frequent reminders that kids are not meeting standards (many of which are based on class and culture), all create a pattern of conditional approval, where students are acceptable and smiled upon only *if*...

For the student, this usually creates feelings of intense anxiety. He or she strives for perfection, struggles to conform, and all of this channels energy away from the business of learning. A lot of time and effort go into adjusting the behaviour of self or others, so as to manoeuvre into a position of being OK. Not only is this a massive distraction and waste of effort, it can also result in serious personal damage.

Not tasting success, and therefore not receiving the acknowledgement accorded to the successful, will almost inevitably begin to erode a healthy self-image. The sources of a poor self-image will probably have come from very early experiences in the family, so that the school receives many children already in a vulnerable state. So in this sense, it is not 'the school's fault' (although teachers are frequently blamed for it). But schools on the whole do little to repair the damage, and reverse the process, instead they tend to intensify it, punishing these children for failing to conform in typical fashion. So, the school can perpetuate a condition in which a student does not experience any source of emotional nourishment, either within the family, or from friends, or indeed, from anywhere.

One further result of damaged self-concept is that personal expectations are reduced and an 'I can't' syndrome develops, which is extremely hard to turn around. Students who approach a task feeling 'I can't', don't usually succeed in that task, and instead find all sorts of alternative behaviours, which may range from trivial busy-ness, to laziness and apathy, through to downright stubbornness. Herein lies the source of underachievement, and of many unproductive confrontations between teachers and students.

Here we can also see the roots of the school's counter-culture, with its alternative methods of gaining approval, and retaining dignity. One feature of the sub-culture, where kids who are outcasts from the mainstream get together to support each other, often with great loyalty and strength, is its new pecking-order: from powerful leaders, to followers, to scapegoats. The most miserable position to endure in a school must be that of the lowest scapegoat in the pecking order of both the official and alternative cultures.

The student with low self-esteem will also find difficulty in making

relationships (thinking that no one will like him anyway). This produces yet another form of deprivation: the student is deprived of the joy of companionship, and the sense of belonging in a group situation, as well as missing out on the rich opportunities to learn from and with his peers.

So, an esteem-raising campaign is required—deliberate, constant and all-pervading.

What we are saying about self-esteem is increasingly recognised these days, and is echoed in educational literature. Few teachers can be unaware of the problem. The solution in many schools, though, is to work on self-esteem in classes on Personal, Social and Moral Education or in tutorial sessions. This is not enough. The problem is all-pervading, and demands a careful reconsideration of our school structures, of our teaching strategies in every subject, the application of sensitive assessment procedures, of the way we talk to kids, of the norms established in a school which determine the conditions we place on acceptability. We are talking about a proactive campaign to enhance the self-esteem of everyone in the school, individually and collectively.

Just try this exercise:
(Yes, we did mean right now, before you get cold feet.)

Close your eyes (After you've read this paragraph!) and think of one positive thing you can say about yourself, without any hesitation, qualification, or equivocation. No 'if's, and no 'but's, and no 'well, sometimes's. . . .

Now write it down, very large, with a thick felt pen, and hang it on the mirror that you look in every day to comb your hair. While you're combing or brushing, repeat it at least ten times.

Now, ask yourself: Did that seem easy? Was it comfortable? Did it feel 'normal'? Did it seem useful? Will you continue to do it every day, and add some new ones?

2 Opportunity

It must be clear by now how opportunity and self-esteem are closely interwoven at a personal level. Stated simply, internal opportunity is created by the student feeling 'I can' and 'I will' rather than 'I can't', or 'I won't'.

The values underlying our work demand equality of opportunity for everyone, and we support every attempt to redress imbalance and counteract injustice within the structures of education. Yet as well as the external provision of these opportunities we also want to enable people to have sufficient levels of confidence, self-belief, and pride, that they can readily make the most of them when they are offered. We want them to have a 'go-for-it' assertiveness. An emphasis on enhancing self-esteem is, in our view, a vital part of any equal opportunities programme.

The creation of a 'safe' climate is also essential. An environment which is free from physical and emotional abuse provides students with the opportunity to take part and take risks. Until it's safe for everyone to take part, then opportunity remains unequal. Often there are students (and for that matter teachers) who will get up and take risks in spite of sarcasm and possible mockery. Such strong characters are prepared to weather whatever storm might blow. But most stay locked inside the shelter of their non-participation, peering meekly at the coveted activity of others. We want to create conditions which are warm and comfortable enough for all to enjoy.

Even when a safe climate and high self-esteem are established, there's still more to do. For one reason or another, some students may be nearer the finishing post at the start, and so will achieve more quickly or more consistently than others. Again, opportunities equally offered are not equally fulfilled, so we advocate policies of positive support to overcome initial and continued disadvantage in the experience of the student, along with policies which begin to reverse the *source* of the disadvantage.

A student-centred school would be essentially democratic. At the same time it would provide strong leadership in implementing the bottom-line values. This would involve sharing power with students, parents, teachers and the community at large, all of whom could contribute to policy making, to school organisation, management, and long-term planning. The *only* restraint on this sharing of power would be when the basic philosophy was becoming distorted. The bottom lines would not be negotiable, they would not be up for election. We would need them to remain firm in order to preserve the empowering force which is the life-blood of such a school.

To give people opportunity means to give them power. Equal opportunity ultimately means the chance for equal power. We accept Handy and Aitken's (1986) definition of four types of power:

1 *Resource power*: as resources we would include money, information, equipment, facilities . . . anything external to a person which is required to achieve desired goals.
2 *Position power*: a formal role above others, which enables a person to make decisions, policies, judgements, about or on behalf of other people, and have them implemented.
3 *Expert power*: this is acquired by having particular knowledge, or wisdom, or expertise, which is in demand.
4 *Personal power*: the ability to lead, to speak, to convince, to attract . . . all the skills which, without honesty, can be construed as manipulation.

Any commitment to equal opportunity will require the equal sharing of all four types of power. This could be achieved by ensuring that:

- there will be open access to all information;
- all decisions and policies will be subject to full consultation, and anyone with an interest in the institution will be enabled to participate in the decision-making process;
- the power of veto will apply only to issues which threaten the bottom lines as expressed in the Contract (see page 1);
- through the deliberate and consistent enhancement of self-esteem, personal power, as defined above, will be increased, for both students and teachers alike;

- by engaging in an experiential process of collaboratively running the school, everyone in it will be increasing their expertise.

When this works properly, it enables people to be aware of their own potential; know what they want; assertively go for what they want; possess the personal and social skills (and will); to collaborate in pursuit of commonly-desired goals.

We believe that we will be *liberating* people through this method of education. We will be making sure that they can see other options for themselves in society besides:

feeble compliance . . . inactive dissatisfaction . . . and unproductive aggression

If everyone in the school has the chance to explore their potential to the maximum it will mean providing opportunities to be spontaneous, to pursue curiosities, to take part or not take part, to experience responsibility and ownership, to prepare themselves for whatever qualifications they seek, irrespective of any particular characteristic, or previous experience.

3 Responsibility

The third vital theme in student-centred learning is that the practical, day-to-day responsibility for learning rests where it belongs, in the hands of the learner. Assuming that the student has a healthy self-esteem, and the opportunity for learning, then the implications of students taking responsibility are radical.

In the context of school, a student being responsible for herself means

PLANNING   ORGANISING   IMPLEMENTING   EVALUATING
her own learning

The reason that it seems so hard either to understand or achieve this concept, is that most of our systems and many of the accepted attitudes in education militate against it.

The four elements of the learning process mentioned above are traditionally taken over by the teacher. For her to let go, and transfer these processes back to the students, may require a major change in attitude, language, and behaviour.

The following example illustrates these changes:

A   Customary proceedings

Teacher   The programme of study requires us to do a field trip. I've decided that the best place is the Peak District — we've been there for the past few years — so I've got all the necessary information and the worksheets for you to do. The coach will leave school at 9 o'clock next Tuesday and we will be back by 4.30 pm. Here's a letter for your parents. I would like the reply slip and a £1 deposit by Friday.

Student   What do you want us to bring? Are we allowed to . . . . . .

B Teacher beginning to share responsibility

Teacher   I want to remind you that in order for you to pass the exam, we need to do a field study.

Students   Where are we going?

Teacher   Well, I was going to find out what you thought . . . see what ideas you had.

Students   (blank looks)

Teacher   Can you think of any place we could go to study settlements, for example?

Students   (silence, looking down, up, at each other, not at her)

Teacher   (waits briefly) . . . . Well, last year we went to the Peak District . . .

Students   (brightening up) Ok, that sounds like a good idea . . . . My brother went there and said it was all right.

C A student-centred approach, once it's established

Students   We've been looking at the programme of study, because we were checking to see how far we still had to go . . . it talks about a field trip, and it's getting late in the year to plan it.

Teacher   What are you suggesting?

Students   Could we spend some time talking about it . . . the whole group?

Teacher   Well, go ahead and organise that, whenever you're ready.

The students, sitting down together, check on the requirements, and ask the teacher to explain any constraints that they might not know about. Then they use a problem-solving process to generate a plan.

In A, the teacher keeps control of the syllabus, and makes all the decisions; after all (he tells himself), he has to as the students don't have access to the necessary information. He decides on the organisation and the means of implementation (place, times, transport and communication with parents). Evaluation will probably be *his* evaluation of the students' work. These particular students do not question their passive role; in other cases, a teacher might have a much harder time getting the students to show interest, let alone enthusiasm, for his arrangements.

In B, the teacher wants to hand over at least some of the decisions to the students. But they are so used to being passive that they do not accept this responsibility. The initial silence is threatening for the teacher and she feels that she has no option but to give a lead (by suggesting a study of settlements). Again, the silence indicates to her that the students don't know what to do. Because we are not mind readers, we can't be sure of what is going on in their heads — thoughts might range from 'My brother went to the Peak District last year and it was OK', to 'I'm not sure whether she really wants me to give my opinion. I'm too shy, it'll sound silly', or 'She's probably got a firm idea of where she wants us to go anyway'. Some might not even bother to apply their minds to the question. The teacher may then say to herself 'The students don't have any ideas, I'd better give them a hand or they'll never pass this exam,' or 'I wish I could get them to speak out, but I don't know how,' so she decides to make a suggestion ('last year we went to the Peak District') which amounts to a full-scale rescue. Not surprisingly, the lifeboat is eagerly grasped and everyone climbs aboard.

In C, the teacher did not make any suggestions; he didn't need to, in fact, because the students were used to initiating and organising their own plans. This is not to say that the teacher had no role to play. If, for example, the students had not remembered the requirement for a field trip, he might soon have said: 'I want to remind you about the need for a field trip'. The students are free to ask the teacher to discuss things with them, and probably will inquire about procedures that need to be adhered to, places that have been good in the past, how to communicate with the parents, and much more.

Look back, if you will, over the three selections. For each one, ask yourself, 'Whose field trip is it?' Not, 'Who is it *for*?', but, 'Who is it *by*?' Who planned and organised it? Who was going to implement and evaluate it?

When faced with this idea of student responsibility for the first time, many teachers ask 'What's the point, what's the educational benefit of handing over responsibility to this extent?'

We want to make a couple of points about this. First, do you ever wonder, when you're teaching, why the students do what you say? It seems so strange that 30 people obey one person, who is not nearly as strong as they are collectively. Why do they pay any attention to us at all? They could dismiss our instructions and ignore our authority completely, and we would be left helpless. And yet, this happens only in the most dire circumstances. Most of the time, teachers get their own way by one means or another, and the best schools are considered to be those in which the students have accepted their assigned role to the point where they are docile and unquestioning . . . like the proverbial flock of sheep. We're not in the business of provoking student rebellion, or fuelling riots. But surely there's a place where students can think for themselves, speak for themselves, *be* themselves, and still work cooperatively and productively?

There is a difference between docility and coercion on the one hand, and cooperation on the other. The latter is a very proactive process, a reaching out to work with other people. The aforementioned sheep do not co-operate with the shepherd, they are herded, or driven. Sometimes, popular charismatic teachers are like Middle-Eastern shepherds; that is, they lead the herd from the front, and enjoy the willing surrender of their students. What we're describing is neither of these, but lively interaction between creative, assertive people.

This is surely what is meant by popular phrases like 'independent learners'. We often say these things and write them into our aims. Yet sometimes we set about creating the opposite, which is obedient passivity. Schools may promote independence and autonomy in New Wave classrooms, while taking it away within the rest of the school's systems.

Dewey said 'Children don't do what they learn, they learn what they do'. If this is true, and we believe that as a rule of thumb it is, then the idea begs two questions:

1 What *are* the students doing (in my classroom and in the whole school) that I *don't* want them to learn?
2 What *aren't* they doing that I *do* want them to learn?

Many of us want students to become shrewd decision-makers, assertive rather than aggresive negotiators, resourceful and imaginative planners, capable of collaborative as well as individual action . . . people who are self-aware, flexible, ready to support and be supported. If we want them to learn these qualities, are the students *doing* them? If they are taking responsibility for their learning in the way we suggest, then students are doing them, constantly.

Our second point is about the nature of responsibility. When we read, hear or say things like: 'We aim to develop teaching styles which enable students to take more responsibility for their learning.' or 'How can we make students more responsible? What can we do to give students more responsibility?' We realise that this language of giving and taking responsibility does not really communicate the concept we are trying to unwrap here. What we believe is that you cannot *give* someone responsibility, at least not for themselves. They've already got it.

Clare, a four-year-old, does not always do what her parents say. Over the past two years, this has caused some lively discussion in the household. Watching her run down the street ahead of us, on the way to the park the other day, we could see that she wanted to be off on her own; she stopped at the corner only because she knew she would be in deep trouble if she didn't. She explored the park and studied the stream, fairly flew up and down the climbing frames, pushed her own swing, and made her own choices. All that she did demonstrated that she wanted to be in charge of herself, and when we didn't interfere, in the safety of the park, her sense of personal responsibility was unmistakeable to us all. Steven, her one-year-old brother, was racing after her, at a speed only limited by his short legs and frequent tumbles; his persistence in aiming to get where he wanted to go was nothing short of inspiring. In fact, this innate urge to be *in charge of me*, is so strong in small children that it is what keeps parents on the tightrope between appreciating the free growth of body, mind, and spirit as their children get older, and ensuring their safety and social competence. (Not to mention the parents' need to feel in control!)

People *are* in charge of themselves, and little kids show it. Another way of looking at it is to recognise that we are not able to govern another person's mind, short of the most drastic measures. People have been known to withstand torture, hypnosis and brainwashing in order to preserve their beliefs and ideas. It is not possible to force a person to accept something or learn it, if they choose not to internalise it. You can compel someone's overt attention; you can get people to write things down, read things out, look at the blackboard and gaze at the latest in visual aids or technology, *but* no-one can force anyone to engage their mind. This is a choice, which only the mind itself can make.

If we take this to its logical conclusion, then no one can teach anyone anything. The responsibility for learning is naturally and intrinsically with the learner. This responsibility can neither be taken away nor given back.

We think this is the key to education; and most of the problems of motivation that teachers face arise from ignoring this concept.

We've talked about people being responsible for their own learning, and their own behaviour; what we haven't mentioned is that they are already responsible for their own feelings. Just as you are.

This recently happened to Ruth:

Due to the demand for Biology GCSE, the LVR group is timetabled to have lessons in the lecture room. Understandably, this room is also popular for showing videos (as it has good blackout facility), and for putting two or three groups of students together (as it has a large seating capacity). I had just settled down to my first lesson when the door flew open and a class appeared expecting to watch a video with their teacher. My class packed up and restarted in the room which the other class had vacated. Ten minutes later the bell rang for the middle of the double lesson and, you guessed, a class which was timetabled for that room was waiting at the door. Yet another room change for us, and another start to the lesson. The same thing happened the following week, and so . . . .'

If you were Ruth what would you do with your anger?

We are suggesting that you have some options; that this is where the element of responsibility comes in. You now can choose whether to have a tantrum; say 'That's fine', and take your class and your temper to another room; or go to the Deputy Head to complain that your arrangements have been messed up—again. Or, you can choose to let your anger slip away, seeing that it is not really appropriate to act upon it.

Many people are in the habit of excusing their behaviour by blaming their emotions: 'I couldn't help it, I saw red!', 'If you do that again, I won't be responsible for my actions'. 'It was a crime of passion'. Though it's a hard line to take, we believe that the choice and the responsibility are always there. It's not a popular view:

'You made me love you, I didn't want to do it, I didn't want to do it . . .'
'I can't help falling in love with you . . . .'
'You drive me crazy . . .' . . . and so many more.

We're not generally used to taking full responsibility for our own feelings. Of course, there are some disadvantages to being so very responsible, for instance, we then have to admit to being wrong sometimes. We have to own up to our mistakes, and not blame circumstances or other people. We also have to acknowledge the things we do well, and accept that we have some strengths and talents. For example, how many people do you know who can accept positive comments about themselves, and do it with grace? Can you accept both negative and positive feedback yourself? It's easy to see how we get into the habit of disowning—owning is hard work.

And so we come back to building self-esteem. This means learning to like ourselves, warts and all, while at the same time working to change the things with which we're not satisfied. Personal responsibility leads to being responsible for the kind of person we are . . . and are becoming.

4 Resources

We can sum up our views for now (though we will come back to this topic in Chapter 6) by saying that, in order to enable everyone to reach for their potential, we will want them to have *access* to *adequate, appropriate* resourses. Healthy self-esteem, genuine opportunity and a willingness to take responsibility must be in place, but learning attempts are thwarted without the resources which will enable people to achieve the desired goals.

We're not just talking about providing learning materials, but also of human resources and community resources, in the widest sense. Also, we want to equip students with the information-handling skills which will enable them to select appropriate resources and use them effectively.

5 Positive support

In breaching our walls of constraint and reaching for potential, each of us relies on the positive support of others. Nourishing relationships among students and teachers create a sense of emotional security and have a significant impact on self-esteem.

The most enabling quality that one person can display to another is unconditional positive regard, a phrase which describes the clean, non-possessive, non-manipulative attitude which seeks the growth and empowerment of the other. UPR is the launch-pad for successful individual endeavour, and is the foundation stone for genuine collaboration. A school which allows UPR to be the final check, is a school infused with trust.

So what would a teacher who felt unconditional positive regard for the students actually be doing?

To start with, she would *like*, even love, the students. She would have a willingness to be available, a sense of selflessness (which does not mean she doesn't have ego needs, but that she is getting them met in a healthy way and doesn't need constant approval and praise from the kids). She would be neither submissive nor subordinate, nor superior, but aligned with the students in following their endeavours and achieving the goals of the school. The mutual support system would make it much easier for people to take risks.

This may sound a bit angelic and disembodied, because we are describing an attitude. But all the activities, strategies, plans that we are establishing in a student-centred school are based on this one inspiring, but demanding, value.

6 Confluence

The late 1960s spawned the term 'confluent education'. It came out of the work of George Brown and other humanistic educators of the time, who felt that education should incorporate the flowing together, or *confluence*, of affective and cognitive learning. The idea was (and is) that since we all of us think and feel at the same time, there is no reason to ignore emotions and pretend they don't exist while people are in school.

It is educationally and politically popular just now to talk about 'educating the whole person'. If we really want to go beyond mere lip-service in accomplishing that, then we have to be proactive in making learning more confluent.

We ought to be educating students—and staff—to understand their own feelings and those of other people, and to know how to deal with them. Especially strong feelings, which inevitably arise in schools, and which are usually ignored or repressed. We're not talking about 'baring our souls' in the classroom. What we mean is that students could learn how to express anger in a constructive way, instead of fighting; they could know how to communicate about their fears and disappointments, instead of having to cover them up; to share successes and failures, instead of hiding their triumph or their worries; and to listen to each other, instead of having to grow a hard shell. Teachers could do the same, with each other, and even with students, instead of maintaining an inhuman silence about the very things that matter most to us.

We ought to be developing intuitive powers, and helping students to accept the validity of their feelings, and at least to examine, value, and trust, what their intuition tells them, if not always to act upon it immediately. Music, art and drama provide opportunity for confluent responses, and students ought to be encouraged to recognise and enjoy these. This is a way of knowing which is as meaningful as cognitive knowledge, a way of viewing experience which is valid in its own right.

We must also address the affective content of the curriculum. There are two levels of emotional reactions to subject matter: first, we have our own feelings of enjoyment, excitement, or distaste about the learning we're doing. Second, the very fabric of an academic subject is rich with emotional meaning. History is stirring, or dead; maths is beautiful in its symmetry, or cruelly boring; science is relevant to every aspect of human life, or dessicated before it is taught and remote from our every day lives.

It's no good saying we have no time for this sort of activity; if we don't encourage affective learning along with the cognitive, we are wasting our time anyway; people only learn well when their feelings are engaged.

Why all this philosophising?

In our staff development work, we usually find that we are given a very short time to work with any group of teachers, except in rare cases. In those brief encounters, the teachers are often desperately demanding practical ideas and voicing their doubts and fears about student-centred learning. So it is only rarely that we are able to build solid, in-depth, understandings about the thinking behind our work.

Of course this is not only personally frustrating, but often fairly destructive, as teachers are left with rudimentary, and often mistaken concepts of what student-centred learning is really about. So here, with the luxury of choosing our words, and saying what we want to say, however forcefully we want to say it, we have seized the opportunity to lay some deep and firm foundations.

3 A CHILD CAN'T LEARN ANYTHING WITH A BRICK TIED ROUND HIS NECK

Our education service is as much a system of constraint as it is a system of opportunity. We have argued that the purpose of education is to release people to reach for their potential, and that the prerequisite is to enable them to overcome both internal and external constraints which stop them being in charge of themselves in the fullest sense. Our question is, does the present education system contribute to the construction or demolition of those constraints? Does your school? Does your teaching? Does the Education Reform Act? . . .

Damage

A parent told us: 'A few weeks after Lena started school, we had terrible trouble. Every morning was the same; she never wanted to leave the house. It was a battle getting her through the school gate, and she would cling to me all the way down the corridor. I would leave her fighting back the tears, just inside the classroom door, turned away by the teacher's 'She'll be all right'. I felt sick at heart, and I thought I was doing this for her own good. What else could I do, anyway? She has to go to school.

As I crossed the playground, Lena would come running after me, screaming, 'Mummy, Mummy!', so each time I would struggle back with her to the classroom. I really was at a loss . . . it couldn't be just about being separated from me, because she was already quite used to that. She'd gone through play-group and nursery, was used to baby sitters and staying with Grandma. Besides, this didn't happen when she first started school, not until the middle of October.

The whole thing went on for about three weeks, after which Lena seemed to settle down. After talking to other parents, I found that this wasn't·uncommon. What Lena said about her own feelings was, that she was "scared of Mrs Q."

In the case of Lena, Mrs Q responded positively to the mother's talks with her about Lena's difficulty; she really paid attention—first to what was said, and then to Lena herself. Many Heads and members of staff are aware, and do their best to help children make the transition into school life, and from primary into secondary, and even through to the entry into further or higher education.

Sometimes, though, individual teachers do create emotional havoc through their lack of care, or their lack of skill, or—more often—through a harsh philosophy of what school ought to be about. But the problem doesn't lie just with the staff. It is inherent in the system of schooling as we know it.

For many children, entering school is accompanied by high levels of anxiety. We would argue that continued life in school is accompanied by high levels of *suppressed* anxiety. Non-acceptance of school is often seen in the first weeks of a young child's school career, and then seems to disappear. But in most cases it hasn't really vanished, it has just been squashed down, so that it comes squeezing out in other ways: shyness, adaptive behaviour, compliance, truancy, ganging, vandalism, disrespect for teachers and managers. As we have said, a counter-culture usually develops, wherein safety, support, and above all, dignity, are gained from peers. Achievement happens in a new context.

.....the pupils set up an *alternative* means of achieving dignity and status by turning the school's dignity system upside down. In the opposition's counter-culture, dignity and status are earned by active hostility to school and teachers, whenever this is possible. The teachers contribute to this alternative system, paradoxically, by trying to subvert it, for whenever a teacher seeks to undermine it, he provides the opposition with yet a further opportunity of achieving status in the alternative system. The counter-culture requires and depends for its existence upon teachers' attempts to eradicate it.   (Hargreaves, 1982)

Let's talk about a so-called 'good' school we visited recently.

We came into the fourth year English class, to do a series of lessons on advertising, alongside their usual teacher. The students were seated quietly in rows, hands on desks, all dressed alike; they stood up when we came in, heads down, eyes sneaking up to peer at us. We told them who we were, and what we were doing there. We enquired whether they wanted to ask us any questions about ourselves, or what we might do with them. Silence.

So, we asked them to tell us their names, and one thing about themselves. Everyone 'passed' when it came to the personal information. And just speaking the names created embarrassment, blushing, barely audible voices, and it was clear that not everyone had heard all the first names before.

Trying to get a spark of interest going, we asked them to work in pairs, and we went out of the room, leaving them to write down questions that they'd like to ask us; when we came back in, each pair had three or four questions on paper. They seemed terrified to read them out. Again, the snickers, blushes, glances, coughs. We asked ourselves what all this fear was about.

Later when we knew them better, we asked them and they told us it was: fear of being laughed at, fear of getting it wrong, fear of the sharp tongues of their peers and the teacher.

Gradually, over several weeks, the lessons warmed up, but it was hard work!

To us, the nervous behaviour of these students is almost more frightening than rebellious, aggressive, indifferent behaviour would be. Both indicate damage to children.

> .... What is most surprising of all is how much fear there is in school.... Most children in school are very scared. Like good soldiers, they control their fears, live with them, and adjust to them. But the trouble is....the adjustments children make to their fears are almost wholly bad, destructive of their intelligence and capacity.   (Holt, 1964)

The factors in school that produce adaptive behaviour and negative behaviour are the same. They are:

1 Reward and punishment
2 De-personalisation
3 Assessment and streaming
4 The set curriculum
5 Inaccessibility

1 Reward and punishment

The behaviour control and the quality control mechanisms in most schools spring from ill-understood and badly applied principles of behaviourism. Undesirable behaviour is noticed and punished; acceptable behaviour is taken for granted and often ignored. The reward is: 'We won't punish you.' This system of negative reinforcement still dominates the ethos of many a school.

Much has been said about the limitations of negative reinforcement. Many schools are becoming increasingly aware of the need to change their emphasis; and so they bolster their systems of positive reinforcement: merit awards, Headteacher's stamps, writing only positive comments on students' work. This seems better, confrontations decrease and the atmosphere generally improves, but what we are actually seeing is a process of extrinsic rewards for good behaviour.

Children quickly learn how to please, and that is what produces adaptive behaviour. They behave 'well' to please someone else, often out of fear of *dis*pleasure. This robs them of the intrinsic good feelings that come from understanding what *feels* right to them. It follows that moral development is nil; the yardstick for right and wrong, good and bad, is the teacher's approval. It operates in exactly the same way as the teacher's disapproval, both attempt to motivate extrinsically.

> Almost all children possess what have come to be called 'intrinsic' motives for learning. An intrinsic motive is one which does not depend upon reward which lies outside the activity it impels. Reward inheres in the successful termination of that activity, or even in the activity itself.... However pleasant such external reward might be, and however much we might come to depend upon it, the external reward is something added.   (Bruner, 1966)

And so the shift from negative to positive reinforcement is only another way of getting the same results by similar means. Outward behaviour may change, but no personal growth has occurred.

Back to the negative side, beyond the official sanctions there are even subtler forms of punishment:

- showing students up in front of the class
- an ever-so-witty sarcastic sense of humour
- dismissive responses to students' work
- setting kids tasks at which the teacher knows they will fail
- deliberately calling on students who are 'unprepared', just to catch them out

There is a whole range of mannerisms, gestures and comments, which have the effect of denigrating or dismissing a student.

We came across this snippet in the *Chicago Sun Times*, referring to a school in Texas:

> Four fifth- and sixth-graders—three boys and one girl—were required to either carry bricks in their hands or hang them from their necks last month, for repeatedly forgetting to take supplies from one class to another. The Superintendent commented: 'It was not a punishment. It was a gimmick.... we needed some type of reminder.'
>   'A child can't learn anything with a brick tied around his neck,' said the Grandmother of one of the boys.
> (Sun Times, May 20, 1988)

The end result of punishment of any kind is to lower self-concept, which it does in a variety of ways. It robs children of their delicacy and their sensitivity; a tough protective shell is formed, so that more and harder punishment is required in order to maintain control. We're not saying that people don't need to be tough at times; the kind of appropriate strength that protects one from harsh circumstances comes from inner confidence. The kind of self-protecting barricade that we'd like to do away with is built by fear: fear of embarrassment, rejection, shame. This two-way barricade can be effective in keeping harm out in some cases, but at the same time it blocks opportunities for love, and other forms of emotional nourishment. The barrier also keeps in creative and honest self-expression. Fear of communicating, expressing feelings, asking for what is wanted, generally 'being yourself', can easily be seen in the adult population. The barricade, when built at a formative age, is very hard to take down.

This process is most unjust when students and teachers are subject to rejection solely because of *who they are*. What happens to students whose cultural norms, language, beliefs, habits, and values are at variance with those of the establishment? Or to those who are female, male, too fat, too thin, too dirty, too clever, not 'clever' enough? School is not just a prison to some of these people, it is a place of torture where, every day, it is *not* OK to 'be me'.

A concluding thought:

> Nothing will change for the better until educators and others understand that stimulus/response theory . . . is wrong. . . . There are a plethora of discipline programmes on the market these days, but all of them are based on stimulus/response psychology — on doing something TO the student . . . For students who want to behave these small stimuli serve as reminders that they are out of order, but for students whose needs are not being satisfied, they are useless. Our jails are filled with people who have been disciplined up to their ears — and, because most of them are lonely and powerless, they continue to commit crimes.
>
> (Glasser, 1987)

2 De-personalisation

There are some unquestioned practices in school which rob children of their individuality and specialness. We herd them around from place to place, in lines. Walking from A to B is considered perilous or potentially mischievous, and so kids are expected not to be able to do it without running, smashing or destroying.

We stop them from wearing the familiar, comfortable, individualised clothes that they like to wear outside of school. Of course, we know that having an established set of clothes removes the often difficult decision about what to wear in the morning to keep up with the adolescent Joneses. It can relieve parents of stressful shopping trips, where fashion clashes with parental common sense and the family budget is stretched to the limit. As an adjective, 'uniform' means: 'alike throughout, or at all times' (Chambers Dictionary, 1972). School uniform has been regarded as a social leveller, erasing some of the visual aspects of class distinction. One questionable benefit of uniform is that pupils are instantly recognisable, especially when they are truanting in the town centre, or mucking around on the buses. Uniform is considered a time-honoured British tradition—'All the best schools have one'. Some American state schools now see uniform as a way to enhance their prestige. The students are eager for the novelty and the image. All the usual arguments for uniform are expressed by parents and teachers in an American school district trying out uniforms for the first time:

> 'So far, these uniforms have brought a sense of pride and purpose among our students. They feel a sense of identity with the school.'
> 'I don't know about money for a vacation, but we now have enough money for the gas and electric bills.'
> 'My daughter loves it, because she doesn't have to worry about what she's going to wear in the morning.'
> 'I'm not saying uniforms are going to do away with discipline problems, but I think it's going to help.'
> 'The kids are just marvelous. They are more subdued. Happily subdued.' (*Chicago Tribune*, 30 September, 1987)

But (you knew this *but* was coming, didn't you?) We have reservations about the *real* reasons behind school uniforms. Uniform helps teachers feel more in command of their ranks, since it obliterates the expression of personal taste or fashion. And often you can *still* tell the advantaged from the disadvantaged by the shabbiness of the latter's uniform. It places blatant emphasis on conformity, preparing the kids for the idea of being bossed around, being part of the faceless rank and file. It removes the responsibility for dressing appropriately for the weather or the occasion.

The 'us them' conflict is frequently fought on the battlefield of school uniform, as teachers struggle, sometimes denying their own better judgement, to enforce trivial rules about socks and trainers, ties and outdoor coats. Teachers may fight with their colleagues in staff meetings about whether the rules are being enforced properly by Mr Slack. The issue of school uniform often assumes a symbolic importance far beyond its value in the business of education.

The school surroundings, too, can be de-personalising. Leaking roofs; boarded windows; peeling paint; desks that are too small; broken chairs, made of metal and scraping on the bare wooden floor; grim and demoralising colours (where there is any colour at all, that is). What message does this send to our students and to our staff?

It is another form of saying we don't care. The result is that performance suffers; the care-less environment does not encourage ownership or self-respect. There is little motivation to look after an environment which is already neglected. We punish kids for doing to the school what (in some cases) the authorities do to it anyway.

It is simply not good enough to say that we do not have the money to do anything about this. Of course there is no money left when we get near the bottom of the priority list. More than anything else, this is an indication of just how much or how little people matter in our society. Just a small reduction in the spending on weapons of annihilation would decorate every school in the country to a humane standard.

We add to the dehumanising effect by the very way we run the place:

- taking registers
- the reporting system
- constant policing and checking
- using surnames
- locking pupils out at break and dinnertimes
- the bells
- huge classes
- the timetable with tiny snatches of time for each lesson
- not even knowing who is who when it comes to report cards.

(Can you supply a few more?)

3 Assessment and streaming

Formal assessment creates a 'danger zone' because of its enormous power to shape a person's self-concept.

Assessment is necessary. Learners need to know how they are doing. They need to assess as they go along, to prevent their work from becoming circuitous, or deviant from the path of long-term targets. This kind of assessment is formative and can be done by the learner in conjunction with others. What we feel is overdone, and yet deeply rooted in the system, is the compulsion to do assessment *to* students, to assess them externally, often by setting up mechanisms which compare and categorise student performances, and present information about students in a packaged and labelled form to others.

The intentions of the national assessment procedures originally laid down by TGAT (Task Group on Assessment and Recording) take us away from the excesses of norm-referencing, subjective teachers' judgements, predictive testing and meaningless grades. These do not have a place in a student-centred approach. We support the move towards assessment which is formative, integrated into the learning process and based on commonly-understood criteria.

The more students are involved in their own assessment the more student-centred the process becomes. TGAT, in the first of its *Three Supplementary Reports* (1988) recognised the value of students assessing themselves:

> ... pupils' powers of self-assessment may be developed and utilised, and they could also serve to improve the quality of the assessment evidence ...

The Report immediately sounds a note of caution:

> We stress, however, that the value to the pupil of the national assessment process is to give a guide about progress which has external reference and validity. If negotiation could alter the result, this value would be lost, and public confidence in national assessment distributions would be put at risk. (para. 18)

It seems as though the drive to compare and to determine 'normal' standards cannot, in the names of validity and credibility, be given up. A student's (and a school's, and a teacher's) performance will be set in the context of everyone else's performance. This breeds competition, the usual crude notion of 'ability', and even cruder notions of productivity and cost-effectiveness. The student-centred intentions of the assessment arrangements can easily become lost.

Even within this system, though, there is a way of keeping the student at the heart. The student-centred teacher can establish a process of negotiated assessment based on external feedback which we outline in Chapter 6. For now, we'll look at the negative side of the assessment coin.

Whenever assessment is not directly *for* and *by* the learner, problems seem to start. Status is given to assessment carried out by an assessor other than the student through a formal, or even informal, process. It is accepted, believed, even desperately sought after, especially by the students themselves. We instil in them the need to know, and to care deeply about, what others think of their achievements. As a result, students can easily take their 'results' as final descriptions of who they are and what they can do. We want a student to say to himself: 'I don't know how to add fractions yet, so I've got some work to do.' *not* 'I'm a person who can never do fractions.'

The judgemental aspect of external assessment tends to damage self-esteem, and create a very sticky label which may remain attached to the student throughout his school career and beyond. Setting and streaming intensify the labelling process, so that students are seen as 'better than', 'not as good as' or 'not good enough'. Even in mixed-ability groupings, which are certainly preferable in our view, teachers can continue to apply the labels in their own minds. Labels create expectations, both high and low, resulting respectively in the well-documented Pygmalion and Frankenstein effects.

> 'What is perhaps most interesting about the Pygmalion and Frankenstein effects is that they are not the products of some mysterious telepathic communication between teacher and pupil. Rather, teachers behave differently when they expect great things from a student than they do when they expect something less. Among other things, teachers who expect a student to do well work harder at teaching the student, and induce the student to work harder at learning. In other words, self-fulfilling prophecies occur in the classroom, because the teacher's expectations set off a chain of behaviour that makes it likely the expectation — positive or negative — will be fulfilled.'
> (Paul Chance, *Psychology Today*, April 1988)

There is little respite for kids as parents often tend to gear their expectations to the labels attached by school.

Frequent external assessment usually results in students being motivated by the need for external validation, rather than by the satisfaction of achieving excellence *per se*. There is a vast difference in emotional health between a student who is feeling OK and enjoying the pushing and stretching process of learning for her own satisfaction, and the one who is striving to be *seen* to be OK, to 'have made it', in the eyes of others.

We want to make four points with regard to the effect of external assessment on self-concept.

1 More potent, we suggest, than the expectations of either parents or teachers, is the expectation of self. The system can breed perfectionism, an obsession with getting things right all the time. At the other end of that

spectrum is the fear of never getting it quite right, quite good enough, so that there is never the feeling of complete satisfaction with self. After feeling *I'm not OK* for some time, any motivation for improvement can easily disappear.

'If you're labelled a failure, you take it to heart, and believe it so much that you don't put in the effort to prove otherwise.'   (Fourth Year student)

A shadow is cast over later life, so we hear adults saying:

'I'm terrible at maths, always was, I always leave the accounts to Andrew.'
'It's no use trying to explain electric circuits to me, I was never any good at Physics.'

These ideas about oneself, once established, often remain firmly stuck. It takes great effort for these old tapes to be erased, and new ones recorded, so that people can be released to develop whatever skills they want. There are thousands of adults who don't sing, don't draw, don't dance, don't *read*, because they were told, or they interpreted the subtle signals in school as saying, that they didn't do it right, or never did it well enough.

2 Another spin-off of this system is that it is extremely difficult for many adults to hear anything positive about themselves; appreciation or compliments tend to create blushes, denials, awkwardness, rather than pleasure. Adults are well practised in handling negative strokes, but they have had little experience in absorbing positive ones. A simple remark like:

'You look lovely in that dress.'
'I appreciate your talent at the piano.'

can cause consternation and embarrassment. Although this is often the public response, inwardly the comments may be cherished, or even exaggerated out of proportion; the sensation is so rare, in fact, that some adults just don't know how to handle it and have to be re-accustomed to receiving positive feedback.

3 People come to value the skills that the tests and assessments value, and to devalue their other qualities, relationships and talents—all the things that are never measured formally. People who come from a very academic education may have to start learning essential life skills when it is almost too late. There comes a time in everyone's life when interpersonal skills, sensitivity, and communication matter a lot, so that there may be a good deal of catching up to do.

4 External assessment becomes a habit; we become accustomed to receiving the judgements of the Experts and accepting them without question. We place ourselves, submissively, in the hands of the teacher, the doctor, the employer, the lawyer, the accountant, the politician and the Prime Minister; they all know more about what is good for us than we know ourselves. This has obvious and massive social implications. Assertiveness training is now popular on both sides of the Atlantic. Many adults want to unlearn their meek habits, repair the damage that school has done to them, and begin to stand up for their own opinions and rights.

4 The set curriculum

> In a research study, newly-weaned babies were allowed to feed themselves with whatever they liked from a wide range of wholesome foods . . . The babies loved it. At first, they tended to sample everything. Then they settled down to a small selection of foods. But they all occasionally went on eating jags. Five eggs at one meal. Or even a large drink of Cod Liver Oil. None of the children had an upset stomach as a result of this diet. An analysis of their 36,000 meals showed that each infant had balanced its diet perfectly.   (Open University, 1977, p 147)

The babies in question were not given chocolate, sweets, meat pies, or ice lollies.

We are suggesting that, if students were allowed to retain the freedom of curricular choice within a healthy range of opportunities, they would eventually choose a menu that was broad, balanced, coherent, and differentiated. Most notions of curriculum do not share this basic trust in students' choices.

Like the food researchers, we would not offer unhealthy fare, such as violence or pornography. We believe that, left to itself, without any external conditioning, the organism will choose what is healthy for its own growth. But by the time kids reach us in school, a lot of influences have been at work. They already have a lot of information about what parents and other authorities think is good for them and what is forbidden fruit. They are already capable of choosing to please, or, conversely, choosing in order to rebel.

> .... I have a grandchild, whom I've been watching with great fascination. This child has taken me back, to memories of my children as babies, thirty years ago. I learned that if I wanted to know what was good for them, I should let them tell me, for instance, when it was time to go to sleep, whether they would eat this or that, whether to play with one game or another. This yielding, let-be attitude is difficult to describe, and harder to practice. It's difficult to give up our manipulation, control, intrusion. We know that we attempt to master nature, rather than yielding to it, or being harmonious with it. We do not always recognize this same approach in dealing with people.
>   (Maslow, 1976)

The creation of a National Curriculum contrasts sharply with this attitude to learning and teaching. We recognise the NC's benefits in terms of continuity and progression, and share its belief in every student's entitlement to a full programme of learning opportunities. Also, we know many students who actively enjoy the set menu; they have no mind to question the choices made on their behalf. But we also know, personally, students who find their prescribed curriculum unmotivating and irrelevant, removed from the reality of their present experience and perceived future. Or they find it too harsh and uncompromising . . . or too discriminating, unsympathetically driving wedges between learners who would otherwise be equals.

When learning intentions are set without consulting the learner, the student can feel . . .

> There is something I don't know
>   that I am supposed to know.
> I don't know *what* it is I don't know
>   and yet I'm supposed to know,
> and I feel I look stupid
>   if I seem both not to know it
>   and not know *what* it is I don't know.
> Therefore, I pretend I know it.
>   This is nerve-racking.
>   since I don't know what I must pretend to know.
> Therefore, I pretend to know everything.
>
> I feel you know what I'm supposed to know
> but you can't tell me what it is
> because you don't know that I don't know what it is.
>
> You may know what I don't know, but not
>   that I don't know it,
> and I can't tell you. So you will have to tell me everything.
>
> (*Knots*, by R. D. Laing)

When there are no choices and the student has no say, then the student cannot learn to take responsibility for herself; and there is a diminishing effect on self-esteem.

We believe that the following equation sums up the problem:

$$\text{increased prescription} = \text{increased damage}$$

This damage can take many forms:

- some students come to see learning as inevitably joyless;
- some fall into the 'I-don't-know-what's-good-for-me (but you do)' syndrome;
- some people spend their whole lives *waiting* to be told what to do or give the right answer to a difficult decision, and will often put up with a dissatisfying status quo, rather than take a risk, or go for what they want;
- indecisiveness and nervousness under pressure, through little experience of real, high-stake decision-making;
- some people come to think that learning can only take place in school and be received from teachers; after school, it stops;
- some people have difficulty making the transfer of skills and learnings from one subject to another, or from school to their lives outside school;
- it sometimes comes to seem that certain kinds of learning are more important, and bear more status, than others: for example, being a Housewife is not as important as being a Doctor;
- the social and political stupefaction which results from the presentation of unquestioning, official truth;
- the virtual deification of experts, and the consequent reluctance of people to believe in their own personal and co-operative power.

What's more, making kids attempt topics which are deemed good for them, but for which they have no intrinsic motivation, is a recipe for confrontation and teacher stress. Teachers feel bound to *cover* all the requirements, and so will not, and feel they cannot, take the exciting detours that open up naturally in class discussion or students' interest.

> I have a negative reaction to teaching. Why? I think it is because it raises all the wrong questions. As soon as we focus on teaching, the question arises, 'What shall we teach?' What, from our superior vantage point, does the other person need to know? This raises the ridiculous question of coverage. What shall the course cover?...... This notion of coverage is based on the assumption that what is taught is what is learned; what is presented is what is assimilated. I know of no other assumption so obviously untrue. One does not need research to provide evidence that this is false. One only needs to talk with a few students.
>
> (Rogers, 1983)

Inevitably, the set curriculum places emphasis on knowledge and skills that are easily described, assessed ... and taught. They are the safe and 'useful' ones. It appears more difficult to prescribe affective development—the intelligence of feeling—and consequently, the so-called 'balanced curriculum' ends up balancing only a thin slice of human experience.

> The one element most curriculum programs lack is that they do not teach anything about being a person: communication, handling our upsets, making our relationships work, self-expression.
> (Steve Myers, Principal of Travelling School, Santa Cruz, California)

Where other elements are included, they are often given low status, and little opportunity for full exploration—for example a 20 minute tutorial period given over to the whole range of personal development and social interaction. (Now you name a few.)

Adrian Greeves tells the story of an infant, Alice, whose parents separate, and who comes to terms with it all by 'writing' time-consuming stories. He concludes:

The courage and invention of her storytelling enabled her to remake herself, and her case, therefore, is a model of how a receptive education can aid growth... What does, I think, follow from Alice's stories, is that room must be left for the vital parts of education which are not open to assessment. Schools must keep alive a pride in such triumphs of the spirit as don't signify in the register of marks... Otherwise the Alices in our schools will emerge as dumbly literate wrecks. (The *Guardian*, 10 January 1989)

5 Inaccessibility

This really happened:

We were running a course on student-centred learning, and the issue of racism had come up. Some of the white people in the group were resisting the idea that student-centred learning did not really tackle the problems of racism and unequal opportunities.

So a black teacher, we'll call her Rahinder, asked us if she could teach the course the following week.

When we came in the next time, she sat us down in rows, and since we were used to sitting in a circle, we were immediately aware of her superior position, standing over us in the front. She began to speak in a language unknown by any of us; although some words were vaguely familiar, and others we could take in context. Most of what she said we did not understand.

There was an almost palpable reaction of embarrassment, hostility and resentment building up. *We didn't know what she was talking about!* What did she want us to do? It wasn't clear. She told us she wanted us to learn the poem she was handing out, and we could start by reading it aloud. We stared at the page... it was in that same language, most of it completely foreign. We struggled, we began whispering and helping each other. We really wanted to do as she asked, we were working at it. She shouted at us to be quiet, she moved us apart. Some people sat looking down at the floor, she prodded them to get back to work. It was hard to know what she was so angry about, we were all doing our best, weren't we?

In the experience, we felt like children at a loss: there was nothing else that we could do, because we were trying. We felt set up for failure, and she was impatient with our floundering. If it had gone on, lesson after lesson, day after day, month after month.... well, what would have happened?

As teachers, we woke up to some pretty challenging facts about ourselves. We realised how, well-meaning though we might be, we make learning inaccessible to some students, and keep them from reaching for their potential. Before this happened, we had imagined that our guidelines and ground rules for SCL were appropriate for everyone, and dealt adequately with individual differences. Now we realised for the first time how frustrated, lost, and hurt, students must feel as they struggle to operate in the language of the teacher and the textbook, when it's not their own. We understood the need to provide much more language support so that students could achieve proficiency in the required language. Not only this, we appreciated the place of the Mother Tongue in school.

Finally, we saw how students might resent the teacher's power, and fear her displeasure—and how both might come to be taken as direct personal attacks.

Language is central to be learning process. With it we can either contribute to, or counteract, the constraints which prevent students from reaching for their potential. If the language of the teacher, the resource materials and the business of the school is inappropriate, we reinforce in the students an 'I can't' assumption. They develop their own ways of coping: they pretend, or bluff, or imitate; they give in or give up; they openly or ingeniously invent avoidance behaviours. We have come to recognise that racism pervades our education system; it is so obvious that it's almost invisible to the untrained eye. Using inaccessible language is only one example.

There are many other ways in which we create inaccessibility in school:

1 We deny students access to us, the teachers, as people. We:
   • often react, rather than listen
   • sometimes suspect, rather than accept and trust
   • rarely disclose much about our own lives and feelings
   As a consequence, they:
   • may see 'Us and Them'
   • may suspect and mistrust our motives
   • sometimes don't believe we really care
2 We often block off access to other learners, so kids may think:
   'I ought to be able to do all my work on my own.'
   'There's something wrong if I need help.'
   'It would be cheating if I talked to my friend, in class, about this work.'
3 We don't usually give students access to information or decisions about school matters, so they may well think:
   'I do not have the right to make my own choices.'
   'I have no authority, no status.'
   'I must accept what They decide.'
4 Students don't usually have access to support when they want and need it, so they may come to feel:
   'I must not expect support from friends or teachers.'
   'I have no right to demand . . .'
In many cases, students don't have access to resources in the school. Cupboards and doors are locked, equipment is not seen to belong to them; they cannot simply go and get a video recorder to use in a lesson. So the message received can be:
   'I'm not trustworthy, I'm not mature.'
   'I will inevitably cause some trouble, or break the machine, or do it wrong.'
   'These are teaching resources, not learning resources.'
These messages reinforce the idea that: 'It's not my school, it's Theirs.'
5 We often discourage students from having access to their own emotions.

> We contribute to the growing child's isolation and loneliness
> whenever we, in effect, tell him that we do not wish to know how
> he feels. Yet there is much in the school life of both boys and girls
> that would make even the sturdiest child express intense emotion,
> if the pressures against it were not so strong. In some schools, it
> is true, there is much gaiety and laughter, but painful emotions

are often squelched. At the elementary school level, for example, millions of children feel the sting of failure, the lash of sarcasm, and the pain of rejection. There are thousands who, week after week, know the torture of helpless rage. If all these children, and others who encounter countless hurts—some deliberately and maliciously imposed, some that arise in the natural course of life's struggle—if all these were free to cry, as well they might, there would often be a flood of tears at school. But such signs of distress would be unseemly. It is better, for the sake of decency and order, to keep up a pretence that all is well. And by a strange irony, which persists in our culture, from a more primitive time, it is more appropriate, if one is deeply moved, to show it through signs of anger (sarcastic laughter for example) than through grief and affection. An outpouring of feeling would be frightening to teachers, who have rigidly schooled themselves never to let the hurts and tender emotions of their own lives show in public.

(Jersild, 1955)

So what happens as we deny children full access to their emotions? They come to think that only a very narrow range is 'normal'. As a result:

- Many people have a hard struggle even to accept that their stronger emotions are healthy and acceptable; not to mention knowing how to deal with them.
- In personal relationships, many people pull back from listening and communicating about strong feelings, because they simply don't know *how* to respond.
- We create a whole range of devices so that we don't have to deal with the wider range of emotions.

Some kids go around feeling intensely lonely because they have no one to talk to about their hidden feelings. They often make up for this by seeming withdrawn, or by appearing brave. There is no mechanism for them to be themselves with all the strength of feeling that they have.

The system is most unjust when all five forms of access discussed above are offered unevenly, unequally, on the basis of some random criterion such as: favouritism; colour; gender; ability; appearance.

Transmitting these messages of inadequacy and inaccessibility at school is just the start; kids then take them and apply them to the rest of their lives.

> ... I now accept that many of our 'problems' are really childhood difficulties that we failed to resolve when we were young, and now carry around with us in our adult lives.'
>
> (Skynner and Cleese, 1984)

Everything we've discussed in this chapter seems to lead us to this point: that much of our current practice, reformed as it now is, conspires to stop our students from being, holistically and fully, who they are, and from becoming who they can be.

4 THE LONELINESS OF THE DISTANCED TEACHER

Of course, we realise that many teachers are extremely happy in their jobs, that they love teaching, respond well to children, experience career satisfaction, and can honestly say that they *never* feel lonely while working.

However, research (eg Lortie, 1975, and many others) shows that many other teachers experience everything from occasional boredom and frustration to deep feelings of isolation, which may eventually cause problems with their own mental health, or make them opt to leave the profession. We ourselves know many disillusioned teachers, who are either presently seeking jobs in other fields, or threatening, or planning to do so. There is even a group called 'The Escape Committee', which exists to aid teachers who want to leave the profession; it publishes a monthly newsletter which'encourages teachers to leave, and gives them practical tips on finding new jobs. We are inclined to believe that much of the negative emotion stems from an experience of loneliness which prevents teachers from feeling deeply satisfied in their work.

It is a rare human being who has not experienced loneliness at some time in her life. It can vary in intensity from a mild, momentary experience to a desperate and destructive long-term issue. Loneliness is not just an emotional sensation, it is a highly complex psychological phenomenon. We will not attempt to analyse loneliness at that sort of level here, but to look at it as it affects teachers in their professional lives.

> It is commonplace to observe that human beings are inherently and thoroughly social. We are gregarious and group-living creatures and apparently this has always been so. A great deal of research has confirmed and extended the commonsense view of the pervasive and critical nature of social relationships in human experience. One example is research on the construct of loneliness, defined as the psychological state that occurs when one's network of casual and intimate relationships is either smaller or less satisfying than one desires. Whether one is involved in a friendship, a parent-child interaction, or a love affair, the important issues are likely to be: does the relationship work, does it meet one's needs, in short, is it satisfying? The goal of any study of loneliness is to gain insight into the dynamics of personal relationships by focussing on the origins and consequences of interpersonal dissatisfaction.
>
> (Duck and Perlman, eds. 1985, pp. 221–222)

We find the phrase 'interpersonal dissatisfaction' very accurate. While it is unlikely that a teacher, surrounded by students and colleagues during the day could *be* isolated or unfrequented, he could certainly *feel* dissatisfied, or feel that his professional relationships are not working. We would suggest that a great many teachers do, in fact, experience this kind of dissatisfaction, and that they therefore feel *unnecessarily* alone in their jobs. They may feel at a distance from the very people they see every day and so feel unfulfilled and insecure. Or it may be that conditions are at least tolerable and 'satisfactory', yet there is a suspicion, even a conviction, that fuller, more enriching and more human relationships can be had in the job.

In this chapter we will examine ways in which the system allows, creates, and perpetuates this kind of loneliness, or interpersonal dissatisfaction. In Chapters 7 and 8, we look at ways in which the methods we advocate can reduce the problem.

Teachers' experience of loneliness

I remember many times feeling anxious about all I had to do, and not knowing how to do most of it; feeling very threatened by deadlines and standards which I had to meet. There was no way out, there was no-one to do it but me. I felt completely thrown onto my own resources, which were stretched to the limit; at times I felt pushed beyond the limit, and yet in a way these were the times of growth. A number of people said nice, reassuring, empty things, yet I never sensed a genuine understanding of how I felt, far less any real assistance. Some people would have been prepared to help, but the structure of the system would not allow it; they had no time either, and were often sinking too!

This young teacher's expression of helplessness and anxiety epitomises for us the loneliness which great numbers of teachers feel. The sense of isolation may take various forms and have different causes, yet the problem is the same.

Many teachers picture themselves inside a box. They are alone, in a defended position, surrounded on all sides by people who want to criticise them . . . or ignore them . . . or attack them . . . or change them from without. Because they frequently use behaviour which distances them from the students, they receive no comfort or support from that quarter either — the kids are outside the box as well.

I had a dream one night, about three months after starting work in a new school. I dreamt that I was in my house; and my family were asleep, or in the dream were somewhere else, I can't remember which. I dreamt that I got up and went downstairs, and suddenly it was daylight. The curtains were open, but I was very conscious that the doors and windows were tightly shut. It was rather like being in a sealed container. Gradually, I became aware of a few kids from my new school approaching the house, and I was determined not to let them in. They were joined by their friends, and eventually a great number were pressing themselves against the doors and windows. I can remember feeling two conflicting feelings . . . on the one hand a sense of panic, lest they should get in, and on the other, a sense of security because I knew they couldn't . . . or wouldn't. This dream troubled me so much, that the next morning I went to see the Headteacher about it.   (A Head of Department)

Other teachers report dreams like the following:

I dreamt that I was getting ready to go to school, getting dressed, seeing to my children, packing our lunches. Someone was waiting outside to drive me to work, but as soon as I came out of the house, he drove away. I went back in, and went through the process of getting ready again, and search as I might, I could not find the keys for my classroom. All the while, I could see through the window that the car was outside again, waiting. This cycle was repeated several times . . . the feeling was that I just *could not* get to school, I couldn't get there . . . I had visions of the children running wild, the Headmistress raging at me, people getting hurt . . . I ran outside and shouted at the driver, but he drove away again. I was in tears . . .   (A young teacher)

We are not attempting to psychoanalyse these dreams. For us, they symbolise the anxieties teachers may feel in their beleaguered position, feelings of panic and frustration, of not having the 'keys', of not being able to 'get there', and also of avoiding the demands of being too close to the students.

What is it about the system which creates and maintains these deep feelings of isolation and anxiety? Many school norms, both overt and covert, have the effect of distancing teachers from one another. They include:

1 Time and space
2 Hierarchical organisation
3 Staying separate
4 The energy drain
5 Loneliness at the top.

1 Time and space

I remember my constant awareness of time . . . being in time; on time; out of time; right time; wrong time; break time; coffee time; lunch time; gaining time; saving time; losing time; time off; time out; time and time and time again. Each evening as I drove westward back along the motorway, I was compelled to watch the sun sink, and in every moment it mocked my inability to use its day to the full. Each teaching period was summoned by bells, sentenced without trial, ripped off, and dumped in the litter bin . . . The Red Queen cried 'Faster!' and, looking around, I saw that I was in the same place as before. 'If you want to get anywhere else, you must run twice as fast as that!'

(Notes from a colleague, David Lambourn,
when he was a mature student-teacher)

Schools establish norms about the use of time; in most schools, the timetable is constructed from unquestioned assumptions, and you might as easily shift them as move the walls in the building. The timetable has great impact on the ethos of the school; it determines the when and the where and why of the contacts between people. Teachers are physically separated from each other for most of the working day. Rarely are teachers given the time to plan, teach, and evaluate together. Breaks and lunchtimes are packed with official duties and personal business. In the age of Directed Time, however, scheduled meeting time has increased, and as far as bringing colleagues together is concerned, this may be a step in the right direction.

However, much of the Directed Time we come across seems to be taken up with *business*: departmental meetings, staff meetings, pastoral meetings, all of which are usually compulsory, which undermines the possible benefits. Probably in most schools there still will not be time allocated for teachers simply to talk together when and how *they* want to.

> There is much in the school situation that cuts teachers off from one another. What goes on in the name of discussion, faculty meetings, committee meetings, and the like, often does not bring people emotionally together, but keeps them emotionally apart. Everything may be discussed solely on an intellectual and logical level. Even though there are individual teachers who try to break the ice, seeking to reach out to others, and asking others to reach out to them, there usually are many who keep a nice distance.
>
> (Jersild, 1955, p. 71)

Talking is always at a price. If you do take, steal, borrow the time to talk to other teachers, there's always something else that simply does not get done. Also, if you do grab the time, often there is no-one else around to talk to, because they've all got their heads down in the staff room, or it's the end of the day and they've gone home, racing to do their errands on the way. It is a cruel and unnecessary form of punishment that there is always such a rushed feeling about every aspect of school; it's as if we're all on a treadmill. We can't get off, and the bell keeps urging us on. We found, in working with mature teachers in particular, that they were longing for the opportunity to *talk* to their colleagues about their work. This one luxury was the greatest advantage of in-service training opportunities.

> Most schools consist of cubicles in which individual teachers work alone, removed from contact with colleagues. Because of tight scheduling, time is rarely available in sufficient quantity to permit intensive interaction among teachers during the regular school day. Support groups, collegial evaluation and supervision of rookies by veteran teachers, professional development, all demand substantial investments of time.   (Duke, 1984)

2 Hierarchical organisation

Most schools are organised hierarchically. Within the system as it exists, there are positive reasons for setting up and maintaining hierarchies. They provide lines of management and communication, which, at their best, enable the efficient execution of tasks. Influential positions of responsibility and decision making are filled by appropriately experienced and trained personnel. Weighty matters are in capable hands. Increased responsibility, and with it increased salary, provides status and constitutes the reward for diligence and effectiveness.

On the negative side, not everyone who has earned these rewards actually receives them. There is a very narrow turnstile of promotion to pass through, and though many have the qualifications to arrive at the top, only a few actually make it. Conversely, there is the well-known Peter principle: 'In a hierarchy, every employee tends to rise to his level of incompetence.' That is, when you're good at your job, you get promoted, and that keeps happening until you get to the job that you cannot fully do; and there you stay.

Hierarchies divide responsibilities and functions, and in that way they divide people on an unequal basis. As there is little access to each others' tasks, there is little sense of common ownership. Instead there is secrecy, suspicion and a typical 'management/workers' scenario. Hierarchies encourage a disowning of problems and their solutions among the 'rank and file'; they don't tap the full reservoir of resources and talent and creativity across the *whole* staff. What often happens is that a few people *struggle* towards the solving of a particular problem, and then the same people have to expend a massive amount of energy in implementing a policy and foisting it upon people who have no stake in it. These few people at the top are flattened with exhaustion, and other people at the bottom are frustrated because they are not getting in on the action. What a crazy waste!

'As I haven't had anything to do with the decisions, I am not responsible.' 'It's their job, it's their fault.' 'Leave it to them, they can sort it out.' All those phrases of disownership tend to reflect an attitude where you almost want to make it difficult for those above you, just because they are above you and they deserve it, and anyway it's a way of getting your own back. The power of non-cooperation is just about the only one left.

It takes a very strong person, full of integrity, not to abuse power once she has it. In the interests of saving time, or of stopping the buck, (which may start out as good intentions) a top-person can so easily take on the mantle of petty authority, having the last word — the first and only word, in some cases — on absolutely everything.

The way hierarchies put people down (when viewed from the bottom), and their burdensomeness (when viewed from the top), result in people feeling overworked, undervalued and unsupported. People are often left feeling badly about themselves and about others.

Formality is another enforcer of relative status. In the name of respect, or professionalism, schools often maintain a good deal of etiquette which reinforces the distance between colleagues. For example:

• staff dress

- addressing colleagues, or being addressed, by surnames. In some schools being on first-name terms with senior members of staff is seen as a real privilege and a clear sign of approval . . . and perhaps results in disapproval from peers.
- meetings run from behind desks, always chaired by the head of department, year etc.
- the Headteacher knocking before coming into the staffroom — an indicator of how her position in relation to other colleagues is perceived.

Hierarchies usually create separation and loneliness at a functional and at an emotional level. The constraints created by hierarchies combine to keep most teachers from taking charge of themselves, and from reaching for their highest potential.

This (helping someone reach for their potential) is not easy . . . . teachers and other kinds of professionals suffer from having been inducted into a mastering, manipulating, controlling outlook toward nature, toward people, . . . Helping is actually a very, very difficult thing to do. Frequently, the best thing to do by way of helping other people is to keep your hands off. Stay out of the way . . . One thing is clear — I can report this empirically — the best helpers of other people are the most highly-evolved, healthiest, strongest, most fully-developed people. Therefore, if you want to help others, clearly one part of your job is to become a better person. The better person you are, the less neurotic you are, the less need you have to manage.

(Maslow, 1974)

3 Staying separate

We have described a picture of schools where colleagues are emotionally distant, even in those cases where they work closely on a professional level. There is usually an air of formality, and a taboo on personal disclosure.

'If these people knew what I was really like, what would they think of me?' 'I mustn't let my colleagues know that... I'm not married to the woman I live with... I've been married before... I go to a—place of worship... I don't believe... I used to be... I'm famous for...'

In short, we sometimes withhold from our colleagues everything which is at the heart of our personalities. We become the people we think we have to be in order to be accepted, then we turn round and teach the kids to do the same. It seems as though people are not free to be themselves.

We both remember times when we've struggled to keep our minds on professional tasks, when we had the most pressing personal concerns... a child ill at home, or a difficult decision to make, a sense of bereavement or a disrupted relationship. Sometimes the 'excess emotional baggage' could be something joyful: an anticipated birth, a party that evening, or a brand new love interest. In other words, the real stuff of life, the stuff that it's not professional to talk about in school.

Think about this in terms of the appliances in your house. Imagine how fast the electricity meter spins when the washing machine, dryer, television, electric fire, fridge, hair dryer, cooker, and the microwave are all on at the same time. Then, what happens when you come along and plug in the Hoover?

If those things are shared, then less energy goes in to staving them off, replaying the mental tapes, making the exciting plans, or generally avoiding what is really going on inside. Having our feelings and thoughts listened to often enables us to let go of them. Then there is more energy to give to the job, which in turn can seem less draining. The same is true of the kids, and of the boss at the top of the hierarchical tree.

Is this how you sometimes feel when you come to work in the morning ... just one more output and you'll blow all the fuses?

Time management is a well-accepted managerial concept—how about emotional management? What can you unplug? What can you set aside, for now at least, knowing you can plug it in later when there are not so many demands on the supply? Where can you let off some of the excess energy by talking to someone?

We wish schools were places in which we could 'tell the truth', avoid lies and pretence and pseudo-politeness, stay away from sarcasm and communicate with honesty.

We want to teach this directly, and model it as well. We want to establish a climate where there are *no consequences* for telling the truth; that is, no disciplinary procedures, no grievances, no punishments of any kind. We want the climate of the school to *encourage* people to be themselves.

4 The Energy Drain

Hargreaves (1978) says

> Other professionals get tired; teachers become exhausted... This exhaustion is exacerbated by the high degree of professional isolation among teachers. By this I do not mean that teachers lack friends. I refer rather to the non-supportive relationships among teachers, which leaves each one to solve his own problems.

Teachers are constantly putting out energy, but this is seldom replenished by those around them. Think about your own issues. Which of the factors below drain your energy away?

soul-destroying environment   academic pressures too high

being unpopular with colleagues

the promotion race   writing reports

feeling responsible for the kids' behaviour and their assessments

marking   creating own resources (due to underfunding)

oversized classes   fear of failure

diffusion of roles   new documents

dingy, dirty, noisy, demoralising surroundings

peer-group pressure to conform   trying to please senior colleagues

imposed change   the us-them struggle

fighting emotions

Add a few of your own.

Do you feel exhausted at the end of the working day? Is it true that '.... this exhaustion breeds an out-of-school apathy, by which teachers are too drained of energy to follow up their interests...' (Hargreaves, 1978).

What is it that's taking the life out of you?

The problem is not that teachers work very, very hard (a lot of people really *like* to work hard) it is that the huge amounts of outgoing energy are not being replaced with incoming positive energy. The resulting sense of emptiness is what contributes to the loneliness.

The 'energy drain' is unnecessary, not because jobs don't have to be done, but because there are sources of energy which often remain untapped, or are reduced to a trickle.

We believe that *everybody* needs to receive positive strokes in order to do a job properly, with enthusiasm and satisfaction. We all need to have the energy that goes out replenished with positive energy coming in.

Now, on the positive side, make a list of the ways in which *you* are replenished and restored in your school.

5 Loneliness at the Top

Here, we draw on one senior manager's experience of loneliness at the top of an educational hierarchy. Philip Jackson recalls the time when he was Director of the University of Chicago Laboratory Schools:

> . . . as I look back on it, one of the chief residues of my own administrative experience is the memory of having felt alone, not in the simple sense of being by myself, without companions, but in the deeper psychological sense of being apart from others.

He puts his finger on six sources of 'administrative isolation':

- Suddenly, I felt visible in a way that was quite unfamiliar to me. . . . I had a self-conscious feeling of *being onstage*, as it were, almost all of the time.

- The infrequency of *big decisions* . . . does not diminish their discomfort when they do occur. At such moments the feeling of aloneness intensifies.

- An unexpected source of my overall feeling of separation derived from my possession of *confidential information*. The funny thing about this kind of knowledge, I discovered, is that it brings you closer to the few while separating you from the many.

- Also, there was the isolation that comes from *criticism*. . . . In fact, it was the pretending to be unruffled by the brickbats hurled my way that served to reinforce the other forms of psychological padding that were gradually stuffed, as it were, between my true feelings and their public expression.

- There is also the more serious kind of *pretending* when the administrator is called upon to exude a degree of confidence he truly does not feel. . . . The maintenance of a facade of interest and politeness was also required when fulfilling the several social functions associated with the administrative role.

- Finally, there is the separation that *busyness* itself produces ... the sheer press of events squeezes out intimacy and relaxed casualness from situations where they might otherwise be enjoyed.

(Jackson, 1977)

Many Headteachers tell us that this is their experience too. Most of them go on to say how they fear it getting worse. They sense the gulf between themselves and their teaching colleagues widening, as the implications of local management and staff appraisal unfold.

Each one of these virtually universal factors is exaggerated by the speed and volume of change required by the 1988 Education Reform Act. The flood of documents explaining the new legislation in glorious detail demands reading-time, understanding-time and implementing-time. The whirl of new practice creates its own set of emotions, ranging from the positive (but rare) 'I can't wait to get stuck in', to more familiar variations on the themes of panic and threat.

Imposed change is often felt, by those to whom it is done, to imply criticism. This, linked with negative media images and the absence of negotiating rights, keeps forcing the morale of even the most resiliant teachers downwards. Market forces divide us, the pressure to succeed according to criteria which we may not even believe in, is becoming economically irresistible.

Now, more than ever, is the time for creating supportive, nourishing procedures at every level. Individual schools and central LEA services are having to readjust; some are undertaking radical restructuring. This provides an unprecedented opportunity to address the emotional, as well as the cost-effective, running of our institutions. The Education Reform Act, for all its intentions, did not, in our view, hit the nail of effectiveness on the head. Loneliness, in its various forms, debilitates. The antidotes to loneliness and, consequently, the keys to effectiveness, high standards and the rest, lie in self-esteem, closeness and ownership.

The 'etching' overleaf portrays a teacher under siege; it is violent and dramatic. It takes all the possible components of stress, and piles them together so that the teacher's survival seems doubtful. Many of these factors, *taken individually*, are not threatening. They are certainly not intended to be so. But join them all together, and they look overwhelming.

Do you ever feel beleaguered like this?

5 A WAY OF WORKING

In this chapter we intend to start turning our philosophy into practice by outlining strategies which can reverse the damage done to students and teachers, and can, when practised consistently, enable individuals and groups to overcome their constraints and reach for their potential.

We describe this way of working as a set of facilitation skills which, we propose, are applicable to all aspects of life in a student-centred school. The specific application of these skills to classroom teaching, professional development, school community and management are dealt with in the following three chapters. Here they are presented in general terms.

These methods, refined through years of experience, address issues which are always pressing for educators, such as: motivation, underachievement, discipline, satisfaction, interaction. They are as workable and necessary under the conditions of the Education Reform Act as they ever were before.

It will be easy to see how these strategies are based on the six interrelated themes discusssed in Chapter 2: self-esteem; opportunity; responsibility; resources; positive support and confluence.

To *facilitate* means 'To make easy, to promote, to help forward' (*Concise Oxford Dictionary*, 1964). A good facilitator makes things easy for everyone . . . except herself! A group which functions effectively is like a well-tended garden; it is the product of hard work, and needs constant attention. If the gardener simply sits and admires her handiwork, essential maintenance doesn't get done. If she takes a vacation, weeds grow, the edges become overgrown, plants which had started to bloom may wither, and fruit may not be harvested.

As far as we're concerned, the facilitator has a well-defined and very demanding job, and in fact will probably be the most tired person in the class or meeting at the end. The task not only requires constant concentration, but also a high degree of self-discipline. We view facilitation as a particular style of leadership, one which takes you, at times, out of the front position and places you alongside, or even slightly behind, the group members. We use the words 'facilitator' and 'leader' interchangeably.

The student-centred facilitator chooses, moment by moment (and this is the real skill), the best way to:

- transfer responsibility to the group;
- support the group in achieving its own aims, both corporate and individual;
- help everyone to understand the group process—what is happening at every level within the group at any time;
- stay true to herself, while putting the group first;
- maintain the Ground Rules.

These five intentions, in our view, make a facilitator student-centred. Unpolluted by her personal investments, these intentions will guide the leader to make appropriate responses. The speed and accuracy with which these

choices are made depend on intuition, which in turn is built upon disposition, training and experience.

Choices, choices, and more choices

A range of options opens up to a person-centred facilitator as he considers
how to get started with a new group. The issues are to do with *how much*
responsibility is handed over to the group and the *pace* of the transfer. We
find it helpful to indulge in another metaphor. Compare the facilitator's
choices with a visit to the swimming pool.

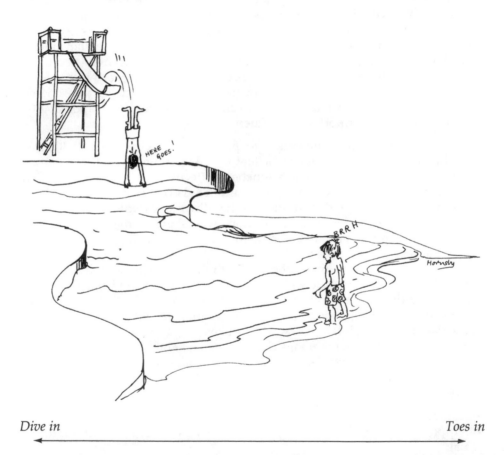

Dive in   *Toes in*

A toes-in approach would involve the facilitator in a cautious and measured
sharing of responsibility, perhaps by consulting the group while still doing
the planning for them, or by offering limited, rather than open, choices.

If the facilitator chooses to dive in, he will assume the group to be fully
responsible for itself. He will consistently enable the group to do its own
planning, organising, implementing and evaluating with his support, but
without his throwing them a lifebelt.

Factors which guide this choice may include:

- the facilitator's personality, training and experience;
- the make-up of the group;
- the time allowed for the work;
- the reason for the group's existence;
- the external constraints.

There is no need for the group to flounder or for you to drown. You can choose a point of entry in each situation that is easy and comfortable for you and which will work for the group. We will consider facilitation strategies at three depths in the pool: toes-in; waist-deep and deep-end.

1 Toes-in

As options for getting started if you just want to stick your toes in, we present 'Toes-in Tips':

1 Sit down with the group.
2 Improve your own communication skills with the group by avoiding sarcasm, and by telling the truth.
3 Be more ready to acknowledge contributions and achievement, avoid putting people down.
4 Begin to offer choices.
5 Sit with the group, and use strategies to break down barriers, and to start building a safe climate.
6 Learn, teach, and use listening skills.
7 Decide on and declare your bottom lines (the points beyond which you are not willing to move).
8 Begin to concentrate on raising self-esteem.
9 Begin to shape up some ground rules, with your groups.
10 Teach the skills of giving and receiving feedback.
11 Encourage people to take risks, learn from mistakes, try new things.
12 Deepen discussions; enable people to explore what they *really* think and feel, *not* what they think will please you.
13 Encourage people to drop old ideas about themselves, (known in the trade as 'old tapes'). Suggest that they stop saying: 'I always fail at maths', 'I failed my driving test four times. I'll never be able to drive' and start saying: 'I *used to be* terrible at maths', 'I *used to think* I could never drive a car.'
14 Ask questions to which you do not know the answer, or to which there are many possible answers; encourage lateral thinking, argument, multiple options, divergent viewpoints.
15 Trust the group yourself: 'Nothing can go wrong here, because together we can sort out anything.'
16 Throw some salt and pepper into the pot . . . keep your sense of humour.
17 Encourage creativity, spontaneity, and humour in others. Value unpredictability.
18 Freshen up your own thinking: *read, visit, observe, talk, share with colleagues!*
19 Do what it takes to feel centred and open in the group—for instance,

take some deep breaths, wait a minute, laugh at yourself, share your feelings, remember whatever it is, it's not the end of the world.

20 Be yourself! There's no point pretending to be someone you're not.

All of these 20 tips can be practiced without changing anything but your own behaviour and attitudes.

We want to explain seven of these points a little more fully.

1 Sit down with the group

Avoid setting up a physical separation between *you* and *them*. In the classroom, when negotiating or evaluating work, in the staffroom at staff meetings or in working groups, closer relationships may be generated if you do away with the barrier of the desk and the model of the leader standing at the front. These may be replaced with a circle. The circle defines a place where listening, concentration on the group's activities, and equality, are naturally encouraged. Eye contact is possible, no-one is looking at the back of someone's head. Distracting behaviour is easily noticed, and active participation tends to replace daydreaming and dozing.

Beyond these factors, the circle has a symbolic power of it's own. It is 'our place', hopefully and deliberately, our safe place. Sitting there, people can be together and say what they think and feel on an equal basis. There tends to be a feeling of enclosed completion. It may take some time to erase the traditional patterns, so that the teacher is willingly included as a member of the group. Likewise, in the context of staff and management meetings, it may take some time to erase the feeling of hierarchy. So, even when there is not room for a complete circle, almost any arrangement is better than serried ranks with the leader at the front.

2 Listening skills

Listening is a primary force in building good relationships. Not being heard can be devastating; it discourages people from participating, suppresses ideas, and, most destructively, gives the message: 'You aren't worth listening to.' Feelings, creativity, intellectual potential, can all be turned inward and locked away, if your words fall on deaf ears.

Teachers will probably understand this very well. Nothing seems to enrage a teacher more than students not paying attention: 'Will you *listen* to me!!!' 'What did I just say? You weren't listening, were you?' And yet, in some classrooms, teachers hardly ever give the gift of *their* undivided attention to what students are saying to them. Teachers often complain that school management, LEA, and Government don't listen to or take account of their opinions; in many cases, they're not even asked for them in the first place. Although teachers may feel this way, ironically, there are those who don't make the link and recognise how important this must be for the students too.

Listening doesn't have to be painful. We see it as an interval, a time when you can suspend judgement, agreement, advice, accuracy, and opinion. All of those can come later, maybe just a few minutes later. Listening time can be peaceful and restful; you don't have to do anything else at all, just sit there and take it in.

Think back to the last time you tried to tell someone something and were frustrated by the response they gave you. What was it about the way they responded that frustrated you? What clues did they give you that they weren't getting the message you were trying to put across?

We've been amazed in the course of our work to discover that most people don't know how to listen to each other. (Even when they know how to they often choose not to.) Often when people profess to be listening they are doing one (or more) of the following:

- rehearsing their next response
- reacting to what you've said
- coming up with analogies
- coming up with examples
- agreeing
- edging towards the door
- being bored
- falling asleep
- making approving sounds (mmming)
- making disapproving sounds (clucking)
- looking directly at you with that slight glaze over their eyes.
- fiddling
- sympathising
- waiting to get a word in
- trying to get a word in
- disagreeing
- looking at their watch
- being shocked
- competing
- pretending to listen
- nodding

List a few of your own—be merciless.

Some ideas we have found useful in developing our listening skills are:

'I know I can't fake real listening.'

'Other people can sense when I'm not *really* willing to be there *really* listening to them.'

'I can send the little voice in my head on holiday temporarily, and when that's gone there is nothing in my mind opposing what the other person is trying to tell me.'

'I know that I'll get a chance *later* to say my piece/stick my oar in/stir the pudding/train the vine/give advice/tell jokes/gossip/devise analogies/make my shopping list/sympathise or any of the million other things I might come up with during the conversation session other than just listening.'

'Without being a mind-reader, the speaker can usually tell when I'm doing any of these things—besides *I* know that I'm not listening properly.'

Two other points it is useful to remember—if you have any space left in your mind after that—are:

1 There are times when you don't *feel* like communicating. You don't want
to talk, you want to be quiet; you don't want to talk to *that* person, you
feel like cutting off; you're angry with that person, so angry or upset that
you forget all the theories and skills you've ever learnt (just when they
might be most useful). In fact, you're *sick* of communicating. And that's
ALL RIGHT!

2 It's very easy to have the theory clear-cut when you're calm and in charge
or yourself. It's in the intense moment that the skills seem to fly out of the
window and all you're left with is a burning need to 'win', to 'be right', to
'sort things out' or to make things 'all right'.

Once you feel confident about your improved listening skills (which, by the
way, you may actually have to be trained in to do properly) you can pass
them on to the students. When a whole class knows how to listen, you can
expect to see the following:

- students can talk to each other across the circle without referring everything to and through the teacher

- the concept of Right and Wrong begins to disappear and exploration is
encouraged
- students can debate, argue, discuss about academic content, without the
intervention of the teacher, both in the circle and in small groups
- conflicts can be resolved and negative feelings dealt with very quickly, in
such a way that students can then concentrate on their work more
effectively
- students can get used to listening to the teacher as well, in a new and
more accepting manner

3 Do away with put-downs

While being listened to is a great builder of self-esteem, being put down is
the greatest destroyer. We call put-downs 'Killer statements', because they
kill trust and self-esteem.

Some teachers use sarcasm as a deadly weapon; they take unfair advantage of their authority and their often superior 'wit' to taunt students, and
make them feel small so that they stay in their place. It is an effective way of

bringing someone down a peg or two. Personal dimunition is the reverse of personal growth. How cowardly it is to sharpen your razor tongue on someone who can't fight back without disastrous consequences. Fear of the teacher's tongue helps to ensure students' passivity, which is essential, if instructions are to be unquestioningly obeyed.

Withering ridicule can also be non-verbal... the glaring eyes, the pointing, wagging finger; shaking, pushing, sweeping people aside as you strut down the corridor, deliberately turning your back to show disapproval. These are all body language games designed to shrink self-esteem. It is unlikely that students will feel safe to explore, experiment, take risks, 'have a go', or be honest about their feelings, weaknesses and progress if such destructive verbal and non-verbal behaviour prevails.

We know we are speaking strongly about this; we find it difficult to dilute the strength of our feelings. For us, it is a matter of human dignity. People often say to us that we're over the top on this point, that we make too much of it. 'You're soft, you're oversensitive'. 'It's good training for later on in life; kids need to be toughened up. Everyone knows we're only kidding anyway.' 'It's our way of showing how affectionate we are.'

Maybe... maybe. But the responses we get when talking in depth with people in training and counselling settings indicate that a lot of damage is done through 'well-meant' comments. What we believe these so-called 'toughening' remarks actually do is not strengthen people from the inside out, but create a soft core of insecurity, and self-doubt. People tell us, after they've done without sarcasm for a while, that previously they always wondered what their friends and teachers really thought about them. There's risk involved in sarcasm, as the deliverer cannot be sure that the comment will not hurt.... deeply; put-downs have a way of hanging around in our minds to kick us when we are down. For us, it's too big a gamble; in any case, sarcasm is the opposite of the direct communication we are advocating.

4 Purposefully raise self-esteem

Games and activities designed to raise self-esteem are plentiful. The greatest impact on self-esteem, though, is made by genuine ownership, by a dignifying environment and by the way you *are* with your students. All the same, games do have an important place, especially in reversing negative trends and initiating the process of esteem-repair if it's needed.

5 Give and receive feedback

The whole group will need to learn the dual skills of giving and receiving feedback; these are foundations for all sorts of assessment. This is a highly-developed skill, and people usually need extensive training in it; but it is so essential to group building processes, that we feel we must introduce it here, even in the 'Toes in' stage. To be used effectively, it carries with it an assumption of 'I'm OK, You're OK! So the facilitator needs to feel confident in himself, and in letting other people be themselves. It also requires a sort of mutual independence; it's a grown-up relationship.

Feedback is given, as far as humanly possible, without judgement and criticism, and is meant to be received that way. It can be positive or negative.

Judgement: 'You look really nice in those socks.'
Feedback: 'I've been noticing your socks . . . I really like the way they fit.'

Characteristics of feedback are:

- It's done with Unconditional Positive Regard
- It is information about something you've noticed or are feeling about another person.
- It is offered, using 'I' statements, (not 'You are' statements)
- It is not pushed or hammered home.
- It's up to the other person to take it or leave it.
- It is not a demand or an expectation that the other person should change . . . there are no 'shoulds', 'oughts', or 'musts', and no subtle intonations which convey underlying messages.

Example of feedback: 'I have something that I'd like to say, if you'd like to hear it . . . . (yes) . . . . I want you to know that I'm not criticising you. I just noticed that you have interrupted a number of different people in the group this morning.'

The main purpose of feedback is to enable people to get into the habit of *not* witholding their feelings but of sharing them instead. Both positive and negative feedback can be hard to give or receive. Positive feedback is not the same as praise, just as negative feedback is not the same as judgements.

The person hearing the feedback takes it in, if he wants to, and examines it. Having examined it, he neither hits himself on the head with it, nor pats himself on the back. Instead, he uses it to decide whether he wants to change his own attitudes or behaviour in some way.

Giving and hearing feedback goes hand-in-hand with a process of building a realistic self-concept. Newcomers to this skill could perhaps be warned that some people will grab at feedback, looking for validation, and others will slough it off, feeling that they need to protect themselves. A light touch is necessary.

6 Debrief activities

We would always recommend that activities be debriefed—a process of sharing feedback within the group. Debriefing is a vital part of the learning process, enabling the group to increasingly take responsibility for itself. The following notes were drawn up by The Student-Centred Learning Support Group, Monkwearmouth College, Sunderland.

> A *Purpose of debriefing*: it is hard to overemphasise the importance of providing for a structured period for reflecting on the activity. It allows for the following:
>> analysis of what happened
>> self-reflection and self-analysis
>> drawing out the lessons to be learned
>> relating the outcome to the original aims
>> drawing out new points
>> deducing ways of improving skills
>> reinforcing skills
>> drawing out links with other situations, and with existing knowledge
>> planning future development
>
> B *Stages of debriefing*: there is a fairly straightforward logic to debriefing an activity, which can be outlined as follows (with some appropriate questions).
>> I Get the facts: What happened? What did you notice? How did it go? What did you feel?
>> II Analysis and evaluation: What helped/hindered? What made things happen as they did? What did we do well? What did we learn? How far did the activity fulfil its aims? What improvements can we suggest? What did you like/ dislike? What did we get out of it?
>> III Future planning: What was good about what we did that we want to keep? What do we want to practice/improve? What else do we need to know or do in this field?

7 Set reviewable Ground Rules

Once debriefing has become a regular occurrence, it will probably be the right time to establish a firm set of Ground Rules. These will be based on:

- the leader's bottom lines which are fixed and made explicit to the group;
- the components of the group experience which the group regards as essential for effective working.

More and more we are becoming aware of, and spelling out, the difference between negotiable and non-negotiable Ground Rules. It is extremely important not to pretend that anything goes, when it patently does not. The values and principles outlined in Chapter 2 are the framework for stated, non-negotiable standards. The effective facilitator will make those explicit. She can then proceed, without manipulation and with integrity, to encourage the group to establish the other rules by which they want to operate in a given situation.

The necessity for establishing working Ground Rules, and the kind of skill that this requires, is one of the reasons for being dogmatic and saying that *leaderless* groups do not work.

By now, it's *almost* unnecessary to say that these points apply just as much to the staff-manager and staff-trainer relationships as they do to that between teacher and students.

In all of that, you may have noticed, there was no mention of *getting on with the work*.

We find that it usually pays dividends to spend time on establishing a positive climate for group work. In order to do this we set aside, for an initial period, whatever tasks there are in terms of 'content'. This is as true of meetings of staff, governors, parents, advisors, as it is of lessons. The business is then achieved much more efficiently, thus making up the time spent on creating the climate.

Some people, however, are not willing to make this initial investment of time. They feel that they must begin with the work straight away. So, here are some 'Toes-immersing' tips for starting out with the work.

1 Begin to view the programme of study, or the agenda, as a set of problems to solve. Offer members of the group the choice of where to start.
2 Suggest approaches which require people to work collaboratively; eliminate competition.
3 Have students work on components of a topic, so that they need to report back to each other to make the whole. This breaking off and coming back process is equally useful for researching issues in business meetings. For example, it can be used to clarify issues, examine options, develop arguments for debate, and predict the various implications of a decision.
4 Utilise the full resources of the group, by capitalising on prior knowledge and experience.
5 Encourage peer tutoring and peer evaluation.
6 Plan the work so that there is maximum investigation and minimum lecturing.
7 Introduce an affective side to any topic. Encourage the expression of personal feelings and shared experiences.
8 Use drama as a learning medium.
9 Let group members decide how the outcomes are to be communicated to others.
10 Do as much of the work as possible by stretching the school walls: go out, have visitors in, write to pertinent people.
11 On a prescribed topic, arrange for a wide range of resources to be available, and let the group members decide what they want to use.
12 Re-evaluate your time structures; do as much as you can to allow room for:

spontaneity	exciting detours
unpredictability	jokes, laughter

13 Learn to ask questions that evoke divergent answers, that are open-ended, that allow for thought and creativity, rather than predictable responses.

14 Wherever possible reduce the significance of right and wrong. As facilitator, don't play the role of arbiter; encourage group members to make their own judgements, to debate, check, test and prove for themselves.

We want to make it clear that the above suggestions are part of the 'Toes in' stage, and therefore are only the *beginnings* of being student-centred.

Waist deep

Once you are in up to your middle, you can comfortably swim back and forth along the continuum, taking smaller or larger risks depending upon the state of your own courage, and the progress of the group. Some subtle attitude changes may have begun to develop, and also some firmer ones. Let's review some of the 'deepening' methods you could use.

1 Ask them

A new habit to get into: every time you want to sort something out, or lie awake at night wondering what to do about a problem at school, or give an answer, or come to the rescue . . . .*stop*! Count to ten. Ask yourself if you've given the class/group/staff/team/student a chance to put their minds to it. Who else, apart from you, is affected by, or has an interest in, the problem? If, in this sense, it belongs to other people as well, have you *asked them* what they want to do? How will anyone recognise their responsibility, if you keep sorting out everything for them?

We're not saying that this is easy! One snag is that what matters to the leader often does not matter at all to the group; if the leader owns a problem and starts out to discuss it, he may find that no one cares but him. Here are two examples:

1 The group may not be working well together, and may be suffering from sabotage or apathy. The leader sees it as a serious problem, but 'asking them' evokes a shrugging of the shoulders. The group is stuck. (Remember, a traditional teacher often faces the same dilemma.) There are no sanctions or punishments, and there are no easy answers. The leader can continue telling the truth about the benefits of improving the climate, as he sees them; he can remind them about the Ground Rules; and he can ask the group to suspend their current practice, and allow themselves to experience something fresh, and then assess it.

Beyond all this, he can assert his rights as a member of the group: 'I'm here too, and I don't like what's happening. We're on the same side, here let's find a way for all of us to be satisfied. We're stuck right now, even if you're not admitting it at the moment. I'm not prepared to go on discussing things when people aren't paying attention to each other, and not caring about each other's feelings, and then not being willing to face up to it. What I'm going to do is keep on confronting you with it. But I think we could solve it together, if we put our minds to it.'

Sometimes, we have to move back along the continuum for a while, and just get on with the curriculum or agenda. Often the group members will object to this, and actually then want to sort out the problem. If not, we can always come back to it much later.

We don't ever want to be manipulative; we do see it as the facilitator's most vital function to keep the Ground Rules going, and keep handing over responsibility, so he may have to be very persistent.

2 In classrooms when the kids are disowning the curriculum, or when staff are not interested in sorting out their own professional development opportunities ... in other words, when the leader is trying to accomplish a task that the group doesn't care about ... what are the leader's choices?

To avoid manipulation, again, all he can do is 'tell the truth': 'We are all on the same side, and want to keep it that way. I feel in sympathy with you, and we still have to work this out. If we had a choice, we might not be dealing with this issue, but we don't have that option. Let's find a way to get on with it together.'

The leader has a responsibility to remind the group what the consequences may be if they don't handle the matter. Sometimes there is a big risk involved, and the stakes are very high. There are conflicting interests for the person-centred leader; on the one hand the leader doesn't want to develop the kind of dependence that will come if he rescues them. They will 'achieve', but only by leaning heavily on the leader: next time, they will only 'achieve' by leaning heavily again. Consequently, little personal growth occurs. The other side is that the leader wants the best for them, wants them to achieve the maximum, and not in any way to be disadvantaged in relation to their peers. So, he's liable to feel uncomfortable about letting them flounder when the stakes are high, for example, when it comes to assessments.

The student-centred leader will be constantly working to raise the groups' awareness of their own responsibility in the many cases where the stakes are not that high, they are not official and public, and they are not going to affect their future opportunities ... the day-to-day life decisions in school. So then, when it does come to the higher stakes, the group members will be in a state of readiness to take responsibility. One of subtle skills of facilitation is to know when to help and when not to; a very flexible, and *not* a hard-line approach.

If the facilitator is really feeling unconditional positive regard, that will be the foundation of willingness on the part of the group, to take responsibility.

2 Problem solving

This means carrying 'Ask them' a step further, and improving the efficiency of the process. It is a good idea to spend a bit of time on problem-solving strategies. There are various models, with various vocabularies, but with the same basic framework:

1 Define the problem, work out whose problem it is.
2 Discuss all the ins and outs of it, gathering information.
3 Brainstorm for solutions.
4 Choose a solution to try.
5 After there has been time to try it, evaluate that solution.
6 Back to the drawing board, if necessary, or congratulate yourselves on a problem well solved!

Once learned, the structures can be used for tackling attainment targets, staff agenda items, financial management, or whatever problems the group has to face. The investment of initial 'training' is therefore well worth the time you spend on it at the beginning. But that is not the main point; we want to stress that the primary aim is to continue the handing over of responsibility to the group members.

Once again, we'd like to remind you and ourselves that we teachers often underestimate what the students can do.

3 Telling the truth

Remember, in this context, truth is not the absence of lies, truth is a deep sharing of your own feelings and ideas. At the heart of most relationship problems, on both a personal and institutional level, is a failure to *tell the truth*, either to ourselves or to others. We are not talking about baring your soul and revealing embarrassing details and secrets but about facing up to what you really think and feel with regard to the matter presently at hand.

The other side of telling the truth is *being heard*, which is why we always emphasise listening skills. In building the safety required for the nurturing of truth telling, the facilitator has to start by telling the truth herself, and listening to others... In other words, she must model the behaviour that she wants the group to develop.

For a school to be fully person-centred, the whole school community has to be heard, and has to be hearing truths which may be difficult to receive. We have to ensure that we hear from all those with an investment in the school, whatever their status; from minorities as well as majorities; from those unaccustomed to public communication, as well as from the confident experts.

Coming back to the group leader: she has to develop the skill of telling the truth to herself, which will mean:

- being in touch, knowing the feelings are there and recognising them;
- clarifying and looking more closely at them;
- articulating the feelings to herself, not pretending;
- telling the group how she's feeling and what she's thinking.

All four of these stages are about owning the feelings as mine, and speaking for myself. This process may be rapid, or it may take time, and it may require the person to go back and say 'I now understand what I was feeling, and I want to share with you what I meant when I said...'

Another side of telling the truth is when the facilitator is acting as mirror to the group, explaining what she is noticing, and observing. The mirror does not judge, remember, it only reflects... you alone make the judgements about what the mirror tells you.

4 Looking at our language

The process of handing over responsibility can be helped along by slight but important changes in language which remove the concepts of permission and approval, and substitute concepts of ownership and and self-reliance.
1 Experiment with replacing the following phrases by using the ones in brackets:

If you're good, I'll let you... (Would you like to...?)
I couldn't mark your papers last night because... (I didn't mark...)
I couldn't help noticing... (I noticed)
You've got my permission to... (I'll support you in your decision to...)
I think you should... (Have you thought about...)
You make me feel... (I feel)
This always happens to me... (I do this a lot)

2 Encourage the kids to substitute 'can't' with 'won't' in sentences like:
I can't do my homework tonight.
I can't be on time in the morning.
I can't sing.

3 Look what happens when we stop using the word 'Why'. Many teachers use the word 'why' in a nonproductive, even damaging, way. It is a rhetorical question. There is no right answer to questions like:
Why are you late?
Why didn't you do your homework?

The statement behind the question is assumed (by the student) to be 'You are wrong to have done/not done this'. The 'why' usually produces a defensive answer, an excuse, or a lie, and it offers an opportunity to avoid responsibility.

Take 'Why aren't you listening?' Usually it feels too risky to tell the truth, which might be 'I am bored to tears by what you're saying'. Few teachers would accept this as a reasonable answer. So, the truth is not often told, instead students either exercise their creativity in coming up with a 'persuasive' answer, or mumble 'I dunno'.

Instead of asking a 'why' question, we suggest making an 'I' statement like 'I really want you to listen to this'. In fact, in most cases we recommend reducing the number of questions which require right answers and substituting the statement behind the question.

4 Confront people when they talk about 'trying'.

The word 'try' often expresses a weak intention. People often use it to excuse themselves, as in 'I tried to reach you...' It also provides a convenient loop hole, as in 'I'll try to see you when I'm in London' or 'I'll try to get your reference written tomorrow'. It can be a sign of people not accepting full responsibility for their actions and intentions. For 'try', substitute 'I'll let you know by Friday if I'm going to see you in London' and 'I've got six things to do this evening. Your reference is number 5 on the list. If I don't do it tonight, I'll do it tomorrow.'

5 This is a little point, *and* it matters; see what happens if you change 'but' to 'and', in most sentences.

When the first half of a sentence is followed by 'but' (or its cousins however, yet, ...) its value tends to be cancelled out. For example:

'I'd like to go to lunch with you, *but* I have to mark these papers.'

'I'd like to allow you to stay in at break time *and* I'm not going to because I can't be here and the school policy is not to leave you alone.'

'I'm glad you've finished your homework *and* now I'd like you to make a final copy for your folder.'

6 Personalise and own statements, using 'I' rather than 'one', 'they', 'it':

'I'd like to know what you think about...'

'I want you to...'

'I'm feeling worried about...'

You and your students can practise all this using games and role play, until the way of thinking and talking becomes part of your natural patterns. The aim is to enhance self-esteem, and encourage personal responsibility, not to catch each other out, nor to be critical or pedantic.

5 Feedback becoming challenge

In our earlier section, feedback was used to replace negative criticism and praise. Now we want to look at feedback as a replacement for telling-off and punishing. Since these last two are not part of the repertoire of a student-centred facilitator, *challenging* is the appropriate initial response when someone's behaviour is sabotaging themselves or the group.

I don't like it when you attack people that way; I'm sure you're feeling very angry right now, but if you want... to hear what you're telling him, you need to say it so that he doesn't have to defend himself from your attack.

or, on an in-service course:

> *That remark sounded racist to me . . . . is that what you really meant to say? . . . . .*
> *It is? Well, then I want to tell you that I find that offensive, and I think we need to*
> *spend some time discussing it.*

or, in a classroom where two students are fighting:

> *Stop it, now!* (Pulling them apart) *I'm not going to let you do that to each other*
> *in here. I'll help you sort it out another way.*

The facilitator is not value-free, and there are explicit bottom lines and Ground Rules. The challenge, when those bottom lines are transgressed, is strong, but not delivered in the form of a judgement. The facilitator drives a wedge between the behaviour, which is not being valued, and the person, who is still being valued. A judgement de-values the person along with the behaviour, eg *You are a bad boy for fighting like that.*

You maybe think we're sounding too saintly, perhaps you want to ask us *'Don't you ever shout, or lose your temper completely?'* The answer is, of course, 'yes'. Sometimes it feels really good to scream or go over the top. And of course that can work, up to a point.

What we want to avoid is labelling a person, and so closing the door on their potential to want to change. So when we can stay calm enough, we select responses that stop the behaviour while preserving the person's integrity.

A challenge is more effective if it comes from someone else in the group, not the facilitator, and in a well-established group this may well happen. But it's the facilitator's job to make sure the challenge is given and heard, *or* that an opportunity is given for the group to reflect on whether they want to do something about it.

We'd like to help people get into a position where challenges lead to growth. Good facilitators develop a sensitivity and a sense of timing which tells them when they can trust a person to bounce back and take a challenge in his stride. Again, a mark of a good facilitator is being able to find the balance between over-protecting group members, and being too hard on them.

So . . . what would a group look like if it were Waist Deep, at this median position on the continuum?

Through a consistent policy of *Asking them*, and *Telling the truth*, the facilitator has enabled the group to take much more responsibility for planning and organising their work, which they are doing more collaboratively, and which they are evaluating at a formative and summative level. Communication is more open, and not always directed through the leader; people are trusting each other with feelings and opinions, and with delegated tasks; and the general climate is more positive.

Deep end

What we have done so far is to describe a gradual entry—yet not without its risks! However, a facilitator might have reasons for choosing a more radical way of starting.

The leader might, for instance, say to the group (preferably at the beginning of a course or year):

'The way I want us to work together may be different from the ways you are used to. It will mean that you become involved in the planning, organisation and evaluation of the goals and achievements of this group. We will need to create a very safe environment, so that you know you are free to say what you think and feel without being put down or ignored. So let's just get clear about what it is we want to accomplish.'

It is impossible to predict what might happen from this point on. The leader might simply create an opportunity for the participants to speak. She may do a round of 'What do you want from this group?' She might list with the group the requirements and constraints which exist.

At this time, she may encounter a great deal of resistance. GOOD! Student-centred learning is not about compliance. The causes of the resistance could be:

- rebellion (arguing against the leader may be automatic anyway)
- apathy
- confusion (not grasping, yet, what it's all about)
- considered refusal (We know what you mean, we've been through it before, and it is too hard for us.)
- or, most of all, a healthy desire to understand why things are suddenly changing.

So how do we handle this initial resistance? The way we would do it is to negotiate, to keep explaining, to point out or draw out the possible advantages. We might ask for a temporary 'suspension of disbelief'; '*Are you willing to try it for this first period of time and see how you like it?*'

You might well ask us, 'But what do I do if the resistance persists?' If this is the case, the leader seems to have at least two options:

1 The facilitator may choose to go back to a more traditional style for a while. He may then start at the shallow end and proceed more gradually to introduce student-centred learning with the group. He may even choose to give up, and try again with a different group, having meanwhile gone to look for further support and training for himself.
2 To stay at the deep end. This would mean that the leader would make it clear that she is not going to take responsibility for the group's learning or achievement, and would consistently refuse to rescue them. A lot of skill may be needed in handling the opting out, the anger, the criticism, the chaos which might ensue. All of this may help the group to arrive very quickly at a deep understanding of what it is for each of us in this group to be responsible. This is a radical position. We have done it and lived to tell the tale. It runs counter to the normal practices of school life.

The facilitator who is operating this way may need to be very strong in the staffroom as well as in the classroom. Yet in the end, it might have been a very efficient way of raising awareness, and of getting to the other end, where people really do take responsibility, not just play around with it. A radical beginning can sometimes produce a radical result. What you might have then is an extremely strong, cooperative group, with the accompanying rise in self-esteem for each individual.

There are also sets of skills which can be learned, developed, and polished, and which we believe should be part of a facilitator's training.

1 Depersonalising criticism

There is no need for the facilitator to see criticism or negative comments as abuse being heaped upon herself. She can learn to disassociate herself, to see that the responsibility for the bad feelings lies in the other person, not in her. A difficult task, but definitely learnable.

2 Handling discomfort

We have frequently heard group members say, 'I was really uncomfortable when you did that exercise last night'. They say it as if they mean, 'You shouldn't have done it, that was a bad thing to do'. One of our unvoiced responses to 'I feel uncomfortable' is, *great*! We don't usually say it, because it sounds tough and uncaring. What we mean by it is that most people expect to feel uncomfortable to some degree when they try on and walk around in a new pair of shoes. A new car needs running in, and a new set of dentures may click and clack. Discomfort is natural and therefore not seen as bad. With new behaviours, new feelings, new ways of working, it is also healthy to feel uncomfortable. It *stretches* you, you are experiencing something on a different level, perhaps, than ever before.

So, when we hear about discomfort from a group member, we simply acknowledge it, do active listening while they tell us about it, ask them what they would like to do differently next time. Usually, this dissolves the problem. We want to remind the group members that unless they state their feelings and take responsibility for them, we do not know what they are experiencing; so, we must give them opportunities to tell us, even though it may seem unpleasant or disheartening at the time.

3 Consensus and dissension

Most group leaders have experienced the frustration of working hard with a group to negotiate a decision (say, on agenda setting) reaching consensus, and then having one or two dissenters saying they don't like it. They have a perfect right to say it, we know, but we still feel impatient, or even defeated at times in that dilemma. Once again, we would ask the group how they want to handle the stalemate. Or, we would make an agreement in advance that having allowed ample time for discussion, we will take a vote and then stick with a majority decision.

Often in a group one person will take the stance of a rebel or a maverick. If we reject these 'loners', we are losing a major opportunity for helping group members to use lateral thinking, to see polarities and paradoxes. The loners have a lesson for us about conformity. We find that if we really listen, not only are they disarmed (since there is no longer any need to be aggressive) they often have something really valuable to tell us that we never thought of before.

4 Continuous assessment

Having once stated that people in the group are responsible for making their wishes, and their concerns, known to all of us, we then leave that up to them. At the same time, we are engaged in a continuous formative assessment, asking at intervals how things are going, checking that people are indeed getting what they want. We give frequent opportunities for group members to make process comments, and always allow time for de-briefing or evaluation at the end of a session.

Self-assessment with feedback from other group members and the leader replaces external evaluation.

5 Intervention

When leading a group, whether the occasion is a meeting, a lesson or a course, the facilitator sees an ever-changing landscape unfold before her. She chooses her responses: *when* to intervene, *how* to intervene, or perhaps *not* to intervene at all. The levels of observation and listening, rapid assessment and choosing, the required range of intervention skills, make facilitation a highly complex and advanced activity. Much of the experienced facilitator's thinking is done at an intuitive level. (By the way, we define intuition as intelligence which is speeded up so that it's possible to get from A to F without having to stop at B, C, D, and E.)

An analogy:... Driving a car demands, simultaneously, rapid assessment of situations, swift responses, and the co-ordination of various skills. Learning to drive is usually marked by bumps, jerks, gratings and stallings, making those early journeys slow and uncomfortable as the driver struggles to achieve co-ordination and competence. With experience, though, comes the confidence to go faster, try more complicated manoeuvres, venture into unfamiliar territory... and the ride is less painful for the passengers. Sooner or later, depending in part on the driver's character, driving becomes second nature and before long she's cruising along on 'auto-pilot'.

Likewise, the complicated business of facilitation can be learned, given a humanistic disposition, adequate training... and time. Then, experience enhances intuition making the process smoother and safer for the participants.

When working with a group, the facilitator will want to operate in a 'gear' which frees her to concentrate, operate intuitively and make the appropriate responses. So, she will need to be aware of her own feelings, but not necessarily to state them the minute she notices them. Consider the following example:

A group member, in a discussion, expresses a strong opinion against working mothers. The facilitator's mind flashes to a memory of a time when her own children were small and she was the sole support. Because of her position in the group, her response is influential to what happens next. Some of her choices:

1 'I am feeling upset because I myself was supporting my children, alone, and felt I had no option but to go to work... So I have personal feelings and opinions about this issue, but perhaps we can get into this later. I'm just saying this because I felt it strongly... now I can let it go.' (Honest sharing, in order to clear her concentration.)

2 'How can you say that? You don't have any idea what it's like to be a working mother! I remember when blah blah blah blah...' (Hijacking the group's attention.)

3 She can go on with the group process, but be distracted by thinking about her feelings. (Covering up.)

4 She could escalate her upset, and get into a 'mood' about it, and then sulk, withdraw, only half listen. (Private indulgence.)

5 If the statement is about a matter which, for this facilitator, is below her bottom lines (for example, it could be a sexist or racist issue) she may want to stop the process and make a personal comment like: 'For me, this statement is below the line.' Or, she may want to open the issue up for group discussion. (Purposeful detour.)

6 'Wait a minute, you dumb jerk! If you don't shut up, I'll . . .' (Personally satisfying, but destructive to the dumb jerk.)
7 She could inwardly identify her feelings, and then set them aside to be talked about later, or to be dissolved for the time being. (Self-discipline.)

An experienced and well-trained facilitator also knows when to 'push'—perhaps confronting someone who is hiding from himself. This can be done in a strong and gentle manner: 'Have you thought about looking at it this way?' 'Is what you're doing now working for you?' 'Think about this, and see if it makes any sense.'

And again, the seasoned facilitator knows when *not* to push—to let go of her own judgements and investments, and leave the group member to sort herself out. Making this particular choice can be very risky; it means finding a balance between getting in the way, and not bothering at all.

Do not underestimate the level of strength and skill needed to stay afloat at the deep end. One major risk is that there is just no telling how long it might take. Other risks include the possibility of severe criticism from colleagues, because it seems as though the targets are not being attained. Kids might be getting awkward in other lessons, so that colleagues see their authority being undermined by what you're doing; you become the enemy. What's happening is that you are pursuing very different educational aims which are not likely to be understood, never mind accepted.

Group building and maintenance

What else is an experienced facilitator doing *all the time* with a group, no matter where he's chosen to enter the swimming pool?

1 Helping the group to get together, in the first instance, and then helping them get *back* together each time they meet. This is technically called re-entry. Perhaps he might use a round, or a warm-up exercise, or just a simple welcome. This period in the group's meeting serves several purposes. First, it is part of the leader's job to infuse the meeting with an element of humour, of lightness. This is not just for cosiness; humour makes it possible to achieve tasks more effectively, because of the relationship between fun and the release of creative intelligence.

   Between meetings, the group members will have been active in many other groups... classes, teams, staff groups, other working or social groups, families. It is useful to spend some re-entry time recapturing the flavour of what it is like to be in *this* group together. Trust-building exercises which work towards sharing or self-disclosure, or which enable people to talk in pairs, or to greet each other, help to re-establish the climate of safety.

2 The facilitator, if no one else does it, may need to help the group establish its goals for the present session, or figure out where they left off and where they are going next.

3 At first it may be up to the facilitator to enable the group to get started on its tasks, and the way this is done will depend on where the group is in the swimming pool. The facilitator will also probably be the one to suggest using drama, role play, lateral thinking and so on, and, in general, to encourage the group to devise experiential ways of working.

4 When something happens, like sabotage, apathy, someone raising an objection, then the facilitator may stop the process, if no one else does, and enable the group to look at what's going on. This may involve some repair of the group climate through discussion and conflict-resolution. This is not the same as saying that everything has to be nice, or that all cracks must be smoothed over. What we are saying is that there is something to be learned from everything that happens in the group, and the facilitator is usually the one to decide whether to stop and reflect.

   This doesn't only apply when something negative is happening. The facilitator has the responsibility for introducing process comments, and bringing out the affective domain unless someone else does it. Debriefing, or reflecting at the end of an activity or a session trains everyone in the habit of turning any experience into learning.

5 At the end, the facilitator has the responsibility to make sure that the time doesn't just 'run out' or 'fizzle out'. A closing activity, or at least a few minutes of reflection, leaves the group with a sense of completion.

Wanted: a skilful facilitator

It seems extremely ironic that in most colleges, teacher training does not include courses about the facilitation skills we've just been describing, even though they are essential for effective leadership. We would not for one moment deny that personal qualities such as integrity, intelligence, humour, warmth, and respect, are *essential* for teachers in the first place. It would be wonderful if these characteristics could be tested and approved by groups of students before the teaching certificate is awarded.

But there are also sets of skills which can be learned, developed, and polished, and which we believe should be part of the training of teachers, managers, governors and advisors.

The ultimate facilitating skill is one that is really hard to describe; it is called *being yourself*. You, with all your ideas, feelings, humour, worries, warts and all, are an equal, but vital, group member. The more congruent, genuine, and open you are, the more trust there will be among all the participants.

This equation is one that is up to you to balance; you are the model, even when you are handing over responsibility to the group!

6 A WAY OF WORKING...WITH STUDENTS

The way teachers work with students is now influenced by, but not determined by, the National Curriculum. Despite its size and status, this Curriculum still leaves a great deal to teachers' professional judgement: methodology, resources, classroom organisation, schemes of work, time-tabling of subjects, grouping of students.... Teachers will bring their own attitudes and practical teaching philosophies to the national requirements and so create their own distinctive interpretations.

What's more, the National Curriculum can never be the total curriculum. All the other things that happen in schools, through the unique chemistry of each classroom, in corridors, on the playground, in assemblies, in relationships, in school rules and norms—contribute to the total learning experience of the student.

In other words there is a vast area, central to students' learning, which has not been, and cannot be, legislated for. This offers teachers a lot of room for manoeuvre. Although many may regard the total package of the Education Reform Act as foe rather than friend of the student-centred philosophy, it can (even at its worst) be seen as a stimulant to radical reappraisal and creativity, simply by its demand for change on a major scale.

Focusing on the freedoms and opportunities, rather than the constraints, of the 'new age', we intend, in this chapter, to describe a student-centred approach which:

- covers that central area untouched by the legislation yet of constant significance to teachers, including motivation, discipline and classroom interaction;
- suggests ways of handling the requirements of the National Curriculum: Attainment Targets, Programmes of Study and assessment arrangements.

Mind you, we have to confess that it has been a challenge to us to remain optimistic, energetic and true to our principles when faced with certain aspects of the legislation. We have already explained some of the tensions, as we see them, between student-centred learning and the National Curriculum, for example:

student choice	*v*	prescription
holistic education	*v*	emphasis on knowledge and skills
assessment for-and-by-self	*v*	assessment for-and-by-others
reference to own targets	*v*	reference to national norms
directed by student's negotiated needs	*v*	directed by what third parties say students ought to know, do and understand
education for the student's own purpose and potential	*v*	education for social, cultural, economic purposes
collaboration	*v*	competition

We do not wish to underplay the strength of conflict in this tug-o'-war between different educational philosophies. We want to find a way of creating and sustaining a student-centred approach even in an environment which does not nurture our underlying values. We begin with Ground Rules as they provide the foundation and framework for effective work with any group.

1 Ground rules and bottom lines

Ground rules are a set of agreements, negotiated between the facilitator and the group, designed to create that safe and positive learning environment. We want to suggest that ground rules in all aspects of school life have both negotiable and non-negotiable aspects.

It has taken us a long time to acknowledge to ourselves that our student-centredness is based on immovable premises about what will work, and what is morally acceptable to us, in creating a learning environment. Within the context of enabling students to take responsibility for themselves, we are not going to betray our own absolutes. So we see one of our major roles, as facilitators at any level of school life, as holding firm on the bottom lines. Furthermore, the teacher can't be student-centred when she is not being true to herself.

There are two steps in establishing the non-negotiable features of ground rules. The first is that the teacher comes to recognise her own bottom lines . . . . the boundaries beyond which she is not willing to go. She makes these foundations explicit to herself. The bottom lines express deeply-held values, plus a range of practical considerations: 'I won't have you hitting each other' 'I won't have you doing that experiment without your goggles'.

The second step is to make these bottom lines clear to the students, very early on in the climate-building phase of the relationship. If these steps are missing, the teacher may begin to experience emotional dissonance. What she is saying and doing is getting further and further away from what she is really feeling and believing.

To be fair, sometimes you might not discover all of your bottom lines right away, but will stumble across them as the work develops. In that case, we would suggest that you could come clean about the re-discovery, and begin re-negotiation about it. (This is not to be confused with the teacher arbitrarily changing the rules any time she feels like it.)

You might find it a useful exercise to draw a window like that below. The line across the centre is movable. It represents the difference between what is negotiable in the classroom (the top portion) and what is definitely not (the bottom portion). You decide where the line is to be drawn, and what issues you will write in above and below it. You will be able to see that it doesn't matter how many actual words go below the line; what matters is how much negotiating space the kids can have, without you robbing yourself of your own integrity.

We are filling one in as an example. Yours will almost certainly look different.

(Negotiable)

- -

No punishment   **No one gets hurt (emotionally or physically)**

**I will take a stand against anything —
structures, comments, or attitudes —
which puts people down**

(Non-negotiable)

When you have drawn this model for yourself, and filled in your bottom lines, you have an opportunity to accept yourself as you really are. Whatever you need to have as non-negotiable ground rules, it is best to be honest about them *now*.

Bottom lines are still student-centred. The student-centred teacher sets out proactively and deliberately to change students' minds when they have attitudes that put other people down. We intend to establish a safe and accepting climate, if we can possibly do it. We know we can't do it by telling people to be trusting and trustworthy. We know that we cannot teach anyone anything, or change anyone. People *choose* whether or not to learn or change. We also know we have a lot of power here in our classroom; we trust ourselves not to abuse it. In the classroom we can ask the students first of all to experience non-violence, safety and equality of opportunity, and *then* formalise the way they want to be and work together on the basis of this experience. In this way we introduce them to the negotiable and non-negotiable issues.

This may be interpreted as a piece of sheer manipulation. It is true that we are clear about what we want, and we put a lot of energy into getting it to happen. The antidote to manipulation, in our eyes at least, is honesty; so all along we will be telling the truth about what we stand for, and exactly what we are doing. We ask for feedback, for discussion, for candid opinions.

Crunch question: What is a student-centred path through a situation where the teacher is commited to certain Bottom Lines which are, even after weeks of work, still not being owned and operated by the kids?

A real-life example:

A class of second years, comprising 2/3 boys, 1/3 girls. The boys dominated open discussion, they volunteered readily, they were physically and verbally more overpowering than the girls; they either ignored, or insulted the girls. They pushed to the front all the time, they shoved the girls aside as they grabbed resources or displayed their work. In class, the girls were, on the whole, quiet and still. They showed enthusiasm and energy when they were working together in girls' groups, on tasks which didn't demand any contact with boys.

The teacher had laid out her Bottom Line about equal opportunities for everyone, and had spent a lot of time talking about it, raising the issue again and again in class, even setting the syllabus aside at times, because it was so important to her.

She felt she had to provide the girls with an opportunity to tell her how they were feeling about all this. It took a while for the truth and the anger to come out; this only happened because the teacher handled the issue very delicately, sensitively, and confidentially with the girls. Meanwhile, the teacher was STILL consistently and persistently talking about the issue in class, and working to get the whole group to own it as a problem, and to generate solutions.

As a result, the teacher took the following actions:

1 She positively discriminated in favour of the girls by, on occasions, allowing only girls' comments in discussion, choosing girl volunteers before boys, making sure the girls had first pick of options and resources.
2 She gave very obvious signals of acknowledgement to girls' contributions.
3 She explained to the whole group why she was doing all of this, and asked for comments. The boys had a lot to say, of course, about how unfair it was, and how angry they now were. Time was set aside to deal with it.
4 As it was an English class, she chose a short story and a novel which highlighted the issue in a removed setting, and, in discussion, brought out the points about sexism.
5 The teacher provided further support and encouragement for the girls, meeting with them as a support group every week, and giving generously of her time.

Three months later, and the bottom lines were still not being owned by the boys, and the girls were now expecting the teacher to continue to take responsibility for them.

She became aware that in insisting on her Bottom Lines, she was working against strongly ingrained habits, and attitudes, with little reinforcement for what she was trying to do, in the rest of their lives.

Now, what further options, (not necessarily answers!) can we supply? The teacher could:

1 Separate the boys and girls, and get another teacher to work with one group, while she works with the other. The aim would be to provide a safe place for airing feelings; each group could plan a lesson for the other, or plan a surprise, or take each other on a visit.
2 Do some assertiveness training, so that the girls become less meek and the boys grow to be less aggressive.
3 Use art, drama, dance and music as ways in to more serious exploration.
4 Use role play to act out situations where constructive and destructive behaviours are compared. Use values clarification techniques to make the issues, individual responses and future options for change glaringly obvious.
5 Move along the continuum, stop flogging the dead horse, do more telling and instructing, and get on with the syllabus.
6 Now add some of your own.

When a teacher is passionate about certain values, she is going to have to be very assertive. Sometimes she will simply have to lay down the law. We now feel, that if we had been handling this situation, we would have intervened strongly, much earlier. Once the behaviour is dealt with, we can take the spotlight off that issue, get on with other business, and later return to the issue from a much stronger position.

The factor that maintains the integrity of the student-centred teacher is remaining *unconditional* in her regard for *everyone* in the class. She may feel angry, she may feel that some people in the class don't deserve her regard, because of the unjust way in which they're behaving. If the issue is sexism, and she is a woman who deplores such attitudes, it may be asking for superhuman effort to ask her to withhold retaliation. But attack won't get her what she wants, because it will devalue someone else in the process, and will block the possibility of change in that individual. Genuine change will be converted into compliant conformity, at best.

2 The curriculum

There is lots of elbow room within the requirements of the National Curriculum. Experiential, investigative and collaborative approaches can be used; in many cases they are encouraged and in some cases they are required. Integration of subjects, thematic approaches and topic work are expected in Key Stages One and Two, and are entirely possible in Key Stages Three and Four, given sufficient creativity and optimism, despite the pressure of expectations and Standard Assessment Tasks for subject-specific teaching in the secondary phase. The high public profile of Attainment Targets and Levels of Attainment need not constrain teaching methods or deter us from using the full continuum of styles, although it is easy to see why some teachers are less willing to take risks, given the competitive implications of the assessment procedures.

One of the great advantages of the National Curriculum is the availability of the documentation. Students and parents have ready access to the information about Attainment Targets and Programmes of Study. This openness, if welcomed and handled skilfully, can form the basis of negotiation and collaboration. We have a framework for talk with parents and with students.

It is possible for students to take ownership of the National Curriculum. They can be supported in understanding the targets, programmes and assessment procedures. Then they can work together with the teacher to plan and organise the learning that is required of them. In this respect, our approach to the National Curriculum is no different from our approach to any other imposed syllabus. Many teachers, including ourselves, are well experienced at pursuing student-centred approaches within the constraints of an examination syllabus or departmental syllabus which they do not have the power to change.

We do understand, though, that teachers are more vulnerable than ever, when they want to leave the straight and narrow. We want them to be familiar with student-centred methods, and begin to feel comfortable and skilful in using them when and where they are appropriate. These are not the times for people to jump in at the deep end of the continuum, without feeling both confident and competent.

The traditional delivery system for learning used to look like this:

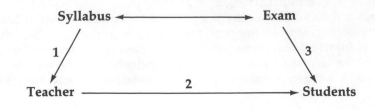

Without changing much, it now looks like this:

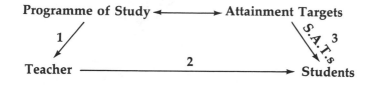

In our view, it is possible to be student-centred in the following way:

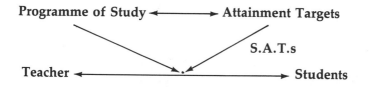

The change in the model represents the handing over of ownership to the student, so that he feels in charge of Attainment Targets and Programmes of Study. In order to do this, the teacher will be supporting him in: first, understanding them; second, feeling responsible for them; third, being able to master them; and fourth, evaluating his work against the targets. Part of being student-centred will be to work with the whole *group* of students so that it is natural to give and receive support, and to use each other, and the teacher, as resources.

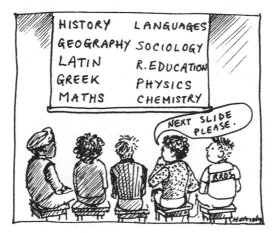

Since there seems to be so much emotion and risk involved, we recommend that the teacher, first of all, considers her own interaction with the Programmes of Study, so that she clarifies her feelings before deciding how to proceed.

We offer below a chance to look at the possible thinking and feeling that might be happening:

'I'm a SC teacher, and I've just received the National Curriculum in my subject. Knowing that I'll want to deal with it in a SC manner, I'll make some time to address it in some depth.

1 I'll look through it.

2 **Thinking**

analysing content.....................................

recognising structures, aims,
   objectives ....

selecting out the absolute
essentials ....

Feeling

worrying about
'covering' it all

feeling angry at being
so restricted

in conflict about
how the Programme
fits with SCL

3 I'll acknowledge my reactions to myself, and remind myself not to panic.

4 The first encounter has been between me and the programme of study.
   Now, I'll bury the document under the carpet, for the moment, and erase it's restraining influence, if any. I'll try to imagine having no external exams or any other pressures, only my own internal ones, and I'll list the concepts or skills that I would feel are absolutely necessary in terms of the students' holistic learning (my bottom lines of learning). (*Aside*: we want to acknowledge that this part of the exercise is extremely difficult to do! And worth doing.)

5 I'll draw myself a diagram:

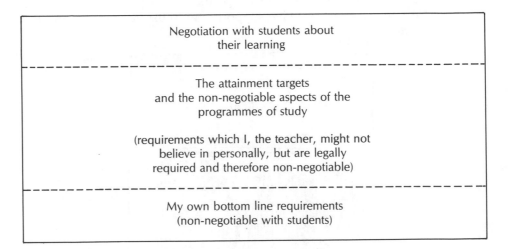

Negotiation with students about
their learning

- -

The attainment targets
and the non-negotiable aspects of the
programmes of study

(requirements which I, the teacher, might not
believe in personally, but are legally
required and therefore non-negotiable)

- -

My own bottom line requirements
(non-negotiable with students)

There may be places where the targets and programmes overlap with my own requirements, and in these cases, I am at peace with the curriculum.
   Starting at the bottom, I'll fill in my own diagram.
   Now I'll feel very clear in my mind, about the relationship between the curriculum and myself. And I still have to feel prepared for the second encounter: me-and-the-curriculum with the students. My own bottom lines are not negotiable, and I will begin by explaining them to the class. I will show them the national requirements and discuss these Targets and Programmes with the whole class. Then I'll Tell them the Truth about the choices remaining to them, as I see them, and open up the discussion to their thoughts and reactions. We can then work together on the hows, the whens and the who's, and maximise all the choices available.
   So, together we work through a process of examining and reacting to the whole syllabus, working out our strategies.

Handing over responsibility

Here is one example of how I might work it through with the students, so that they can come to take responsibility for the curriculum and feel that it is really theirs. This is only true to the extent that I believe it myself, and can hand it over to them.

Going through this process presumes that we have already done some preliminary work on communicating truthfully with one another, building a degree of trust, and establishing Ground Rules. In this example, we will leave all the possible disruptions aside, so as to have an overview of the whole process with a group which already functions well.

Caveat: *Please, please remember that the following is not prescriptive . . . we just want you to understand a possible way of being student-centred in this situation.* Let's say we're dealing with Science . . .

I Exploring motivation

Me	I'd like us to think about why we're all here. I imagine there are a lot of different reasons and motives for being in this class . . . Anyone want to tell us why you came here?
Student	My parents made me.
Me	(writing it up) OK, what do you think they had in mind?
Student	They want me to be a Doctor . . . . . I'm not so sure myself.
Me	OK . . . who else?
Student	I couldn't get into Tech I, so I was told to come here.
Me	This wasn't your first or second choice . . . .
Student	No, I couldn't care less.
Student	I chose it. I like studying about animals . . . . I want to be a vet or something in that line.

We continue this discussion until everyone who wants to has had the chance to say something, or until it gets boring. In this step, we have more insight into the levels of motivation . . . all of us . . . and we accept how things are at the moment.)

   Me   What I notice is that some of us want to be here, chose to be here; some of us are indifferent; and some really don't want to be in this class. That's perfectly all right with me, as a starting place, and I'm not going to try to sell it to you just now. When we start really getting into this subject, I'm hoping that we'll be able to find ways to make it really fun and alive and interesting for everyone. We'll all have to use our imaginations and creativity to make that happen . . . . I also want you to know that I believe everyone here can complete this course successfully, if you want to.

II Understanding the requirements

I will have done some preliminary work, or had it done if the facilities are available, getting several copies of the Science Curriculum for students to pass around and look at, and extracting relevant segments for our age group and attainment levels. (I might have done this by putting them on computer, or having it typed out on cards, or in folders.)

Now, I'll begin the process of sharing ownership with the students. I'll say something like:

This (holding up the folder) is the National Curriculum for Science. Let's spend five minutes discussing what it means to have a National Curriculum . . . Discussion follows . . .

I think it's really important that you understand the Grand Plan, as well as just our bit of it. So, later, I'd like you to look over the few copies of the whole curriculum which I have here, so you'll know what it consists of, and how it looks. Then we can discuss the range and size of the whole thing, and how you feel about it.

For now, I've reproduced all the parts that are relevant to us, and I'm providing each of you with a folder which has all the Attainment Targets and Programmes of Study available for you this year. These will belong to you, and you will be able to make some choices about how, and when, and with whom, you want to work.

Dear reader   If you are worrying about the time and work behind this process, can we just ask you to look out for the amount of learning that is happening . . . with regard to language, concept clarification, overview of the subject; these three will contribute to a much more efficient way of working in the future.

And, we hope, a lot will change in your relationship with the students, so that you will be In It Together, and the students will feel more in charge of their work.

We're sitting in a tight-ish group around the flip chart or board. In each step, I'll be recording their responses . . . all of them.

III Exploring prior knowledge

Me	Let's look at the Attainment Targets, we'll leave the Programme of Study and come to that later. I suggest that we concentrate on Targets 1, 2 and 3 first. I'd like to know how much you already know about these Attainment Targets, whether you've been through some of this before, whether you've already attained some of them. Let's start by asking, 'What's familiar to you here?'
Student	Living things, we all know something about living things. I've got a microscope at home . . .
Me	What do you study with your microscope?
Student	Pond water. I saw some amoebas last week.
Me	Anyone know what Tricia is talking about.
Student	Yeah . . . . amoebas are tiny, only one cell . . . . there's other ones too, but I can't think what they're called.
Student	Micro-organisms . . . I've done all this last year.
Me	Don't worry . . . you won't have to do everything twice. We'll work it out. What else does anyone think will be in the syllabus? . . . .

(And so on; again, until it is milked of usefulness. By now, everyone has an inkling of how much they already know, and they are beginning to speak the language.)

IV Predicting

Me	This is the Programme of Study. It tells us what we have to learn to climb up to these Attainment Targets. There is a lot in it to choose from, and there are some things that it requires, and some things that I myself wouldn't feel good about leaving out. What are some of the things you think might be in it? (The students are brainstorming their various ideas)

V Looking at the programme of study

Me	Good, there were a lot of good ideas there. Now, I'd like you to have a look through it . . . just a preliminary one, and then we'll talk about it. (They have a chance to skim through it, and talk to their neighbours)
Me	What do you notice as you look through it?
Student	I've done an awful lot of it before . . .
Me	That's fine, you won't have to repeat anything.
Student	A lot of what we said in the brainstorm is in there.
Me	Yes, you seemed to know what's needed, without anyone telling you. Anyone else?
Student	I can't read it. There are too many difficult words.
Me	Thanks for telling me . . . we'll find a way to deal with that.

Student   Send her to remedial class.

Me   Hey! . . . . I'll just remind you about our agreement not to put each other down. I'm glad Ilinora told me that, and we'll have to think what to do about it, and see what she wants to do.

(Not everyone is joining in this process. Maybe some people have said nothing. Maybe a lot of them . . .)

Me   Those of you who haven't said anything yet, may I just remind you that this is your work we're talking about . . . whatever we decide, you're agreeing to it by staying silent now. Maybe we could do a round of ideas in a minute. Anything else before we do that?

Student   There's just too much. We'll never get through it in time.

Me   I'll have to acknowledge that there certainly is a lot to do. Have another look and see if you can find ways to break it up into digestible lumps.

(And so on, until a lot of the things they've noticed are recorded, and they have now started to be aware of the structures within the unit, and to see that it can be broken down.)

VI Exploring and accepting feelings, offering reassurance

Me   I'd like to hear how you're feeling about it now

Student   How come you're showing us these papers . . . I don't want to bother with all this stuff, its too hard to understand.

Me   Anyone got an answer for that?

Student   Well, it's not you that has to learn it, it's us . . . . . .

Me   I'm glad you realise that! Any other feelings about it?

Student   I think it will be really boring.

Me   What do you want to do about that?

Student   (long silence) . . . I guess I could do something to make it interesting, like make a video or something. Could I?

Student   I think THIS is boring, what we're doing now. Can't we get started?

Me   Don't look now, but we've started, this is it. We'll take another step now, and see if we can find ways to make this fun and master the knowledge and skills at the same time. It's yours, how do you want to do this?

VII Planning together

This is the point where I would remind about our bottom lines, as I see them, sum up what we've agreed is and is not negotiable, ask again for comments and feelings, and begin to take the step of looking for creative ways to 'cover' the curriculum. If I think some things *must* come first, developmentally, I'll have to come clean about it.

In doing a round of suggestions, students will usually come up with ideas about small groups, mastering and then sharing different concepts, projects worked on through committees, graphic representations, drama, and lots more. I, as the teacher, get to say what I think too. Many people may still be Passing.

The process of handing over will not stop here, of course. It will continue. Day after day we'll be taking steps back, and steps forward. I will have to be very determined to support, and not rescue or take over.

Handling a topic: conservation

To begin with, you may not be willing to risk sharing responsibility for the Programme of Study in its entirely with the students. Instead, you want to try a student-centred approach to just one topic. We are imagining 'Conservation' as an integrated study, fulfilling requirements in both the Science and the Humanities Programmes.

After each section ask yourself:

What's happening here?

What's the teacher doing?

1 One powerful way to begin a lesson is with a direct experience of the theme. Within the classroom, the group could:

- agree to pool their lunch money and work out the best way to feed everyone using only half the total;
- have had a very limited supply of paper on which to do the final assignment of the previous module;
- have a certain number of tokens and engage in a discussion — having agreed that a token is surrendered with every contribution and when tokens are spent, they have to be silent and not leave the circle or sabotage the activity.

When the time limit is reached, the discussion that follows could include some of these questions:

a) How did you feel when you ran out of tokens?

b) Was it more important to conserve your tokens or say what you wanted to say at the time?

c) What would you do if you knew that you were not going to get any more tokens as long as you live?

Encourage the students to ask each other questions.

A quicker, but perhaps less powerful, way in would be to start a discussion about spending, squandering and conserving in the students' own lives.

What's happening here? What's the teacher doing?

2 Ask the group to brainstorm or work in pairs to make lists of issues about conservation in their homes, their communities, and in the world. At this point students may want to scan the week's papers, access information in the resource centre, check a point with another teacher and so on.

What's happening here? What's the teacher doing?

3 Set up a value continuum with the whole group which has as its extremes:

I always squander everything ⟵──────⟶ I always save everything

Get everyone to place themselves along the continuum and give their reasons for being there. Then divide the group in half numerically, and ask them to try to convince each other to change sides. Finally, ask them who they might be, in the present, or in history, who would be having this argument.

What's happening here? What's the teacher doing?

4 Focus on one of the answers given, and start a drama about the conflict between the two sides. As the drama develops, the group may need to have a deeper sense of who each of them are, and so many want to discuss their individual roles. They may want to make artifacts, or to do some other activities which would help to build belief. Perhaps a trip to

the resource centre would be in order, to find stimulus material or to research the issue in greater depth. Students may find that they need more information in order to carry on the drama.

What's happening here? What's the teacher doing?

5 The drama would now be used to highlight the basic issues in conservation. To enable this, the teacher might stop the action and ask questions of the group, or of individuals. She might intervene in role, or prime one of the students to do so. With further experience and training, students may make interventions and create new tensions themselves.

What's happening here? What's the teacher doing?

6 Now the students will be asked to decide how they will pursue the topic of conservation. They will plan together and make contracts.

A richer curriculum

Sometimes we ask teachers what they wish they had learned when they were in school. We hear all kinds of answers, like, 'I wish I could fix the Hoover when it breaks down every other day or so,' or 'I wish I knew how to talk to my 15 year old son.' They suggest a whole range of expertise that would help them deal with life's little problems and frustrations, develop their own talents and skills, and use their creativity to support successful relationships.

Creativity and problem solving go together. We want students to be able to *do* things that they want to do when they leave school, including practical things like repairing a toaster, and aesthetic things like creating a fine sculpture. We also want them to be able to do the very difficult jobs in a marriage or family, like listening, accepting, resolving conflicts.

We can hear our readers protesting 'There isn't time for that when we have to cover the curriculum!' And we wholeheartedly agree. There isn't time to 'cover' each of these areas separately . . . . so how can we expect our students to learn all this?

We have a three-level response:

1 A lot can be done by paying attention to learning through Process — the *way* the prescribed curriculum is delivered.
2 Schools can regard themselves as places for holistic learning, and encourage a lot of learning beyond the NC. If the school sees itself as a centre for learning in the community, many creative activities can be happening outside of school time, although we would prefer this to happen as part of the normal timetable, perhaps through one flexible, voluntary and open afternoon per week. The Governors, through their curriculum statement, have a great influence on the total curriculum of the school.
3 As educators, we must continue to fight against prescriptive measures: we can talk to parents, we can communicate wherever there is opportunity, to people with influence and people without. We can write, we can talk, we can vote . . . we can share ideas with each other, we can join forces and put our weight behind existing campaigns, invite people to see alternative good practice, inform ourselves, and inspire ourselves.

3 Working to a contract

The very word 'contract' has many different meanings; here we are using it to mean an agreement, either with one's self, or with another person, perhaps the teacher or a peer.

We make contracts with ourselves informally. What we want to get done next weekend; when our next diet will start. Sometimes we make them more formally, as in New Year's Resolutions. How strong are these commitments? There's a sort of acceptable weakness about these self-promises sometimes . . . . it's almost a bonus if they're kept. The kind of contract we're describing here *expresses firm intention*.

To make sure that a contract can be fulfilled, it is essential to set a realistic target. This is one reason for negotiating with a teacher or peer. It works both ways; we might otherwise be *over-* or *under-* ambitious.

The teacher will have some experience to bring to the contracting procedure; a knowledge of resources, shortcuts, reminders about the requirements and about the bottom lines of learning.

Negotiating a contract is likely to include a discussion of consequences. There is no question of punishment if the agreement is not kept, but there will almost certainly be consequences of one sort or another . . . a group task incomplete, others left waiting, part of the syllabus only partially understood, not to mention feelings of frustration, disappointment and embarrassment. To avoid anxiety about these consequences, and perhaps the fear of other results that may be lurking ('Could she possibly mean that there really are no punishments?') a very honest discussion must happen before the contract is implemented.

A note of caution here. We sometimes see teachers using contracts manipulatively, as a very subtle, even cheerful, threat. Or, more dangerously, the contracts are all Sugar and Spice, as long as they're kept. But if they're not, especially consistently not kept, then the teacher's idea of student responsibility is really tested. If a teacher has an investment in the contract being kept, this must be stated at the outset, to avoid sudden explosions of anger that has been building up; anger that could seem like betrayal to the student. We would suggest that if you want to hand over responsibility, you'll have to hand over this investment as well.

The student owns the responsibility and the consequences
The contract is written, signed, and counter-signed, all to strengthen the intent and to make sure that there are specific and recognisable outcomes.

A learning contract is a plan; one that the student designs, and agrees to follow and complete. It is a map for the work to come. But more than that, its fulfilment relies on *the student's* integrity and firmness of intent.

Initially, of course, a contract looks to the future; the student sets his own aims, plans, ideas for working, and also the deadlines and time frame of the work.

Then, in the present tense, the contract is formative. It allows the student to ask: 'How am I doing? Am I meeting my aims, my deadlines?' 'What have I left out; do I need to speed up?' 'How do I feel about the quality of my work?'

When the contract is complete, the student looks back over the work and asks 'Did I?' And so the contract is a reference point for summative assessment, with regard to that task.

Students and teachers may also want to make personal contracts, at various times, which are about changes in relationships, or habits, or behaviour which does not work. In the same way as in the learning contract, writing down these intentions helps to strengthen determination and provide checkpoints along the way.

4 Assessment

We've always believed that assessment is a natural and integral part of the educational process. Like everyone else, in the wake of the Education Reform Act, we will witness for years to come the unravelling of a new system, and scramble to catch up with all its implications.

If we could do it our way, the process of assessment would be interactive and spontaneous. All the time, the facilitator would be aiming to help learners clarify where they are now and where they want to go to, to understand future possibilities and decide when and how targets will be achieved.

What makes assessment student-centred is the fact that it is *owned* by the student; the assessment of the learner and the learning is done *by* the learner, based on feedback from various sources, not *by* an external assessor, whether a teacher, a Board, or whatever. The student-centred teacher's job is to support and insist upon a clear and effective formative look at what the learner knows and can do, and what is possible from this moment on.

Children and adults alike seem to engage, naturally, in an informal assessment of themselves. This natural drive for assessment comes first of all from the vital need that we all have to be affirmed, to know that *I am OK*. Secondly, our motivation to grow and develop asks 'What comes next?' and 'What is it that isn't working?'. Ideally, there is a delicate balance between the affirmation and the growth points. If there is too much affirmation, perhaps there isn't enough self-challenge. On the other hand, if there is too much doubting, not enough affirming, the development can be blocked by anxiety.

Without any external feedback, this self-evaluation founders, because it is starved of enough relevant information. When a feedback famine persists, it can lead to various forms of damage. For example, we probably all know the kind of person who is forever asking 'Is this OK?' 'Am I doing this right?' 'Do you think I'm doing the right thing?' Such a person is desperate for feedback. On the other hand, we've probably also met the one who flatly refuses to look at herself at all; she doesn't want to receive feedback, or learn about herself, and will determinedly bury her head in the sand!

In order for the natural self-assessment process to continue in a healthy state, we believe that there must be a degree of external information. What happens in most forms of assessment, time and again, is that the information is delivered from the external source *in an inappropriate form*. That is, it comes in the form of a judgement, whether negative or positive. When this occurs, especially persistently in a child's early life, it can interfere with that natural balance between affirmation and goal formation. Two results are that people re-form their self-images in the light of those judgements; and that they may start to depend on other people's assessment of them.

This blocks learning. It's like putting on a set of blinkers so that students can no longer see who they are, or assess what they are doing, or know where to go next, without being told by an outside person. The only learning which can then occur is that which is determined by, or likely to earn the approval of, an external assessor.

By contrast, what we're aiming for in a student-centred school is to produce a healthy environment which provides external and non-judgemental feedback, and enhances the natural self-evaluating process.

When a person has become used to receiving and processing direct feedback, of the nurturing variety, and is well practised in the art of self-assessment, then he is likely to be in a strong position to handle opinions and judgements about him from less sensitive sources. He will know how to use those opinions and judgements as evidence; not to have to swallow them whole, but to process them and use them in a formative and healthy way. We see this as a vital preparation for remaining strong, capable, and self directed, in a world full of: hidden agendas, unpredictable reactions and unsolicited judgements.

An example of student-centred assessment

Student-centred assessment is rigorous in that it challenges; it is also fun, in that it is done creatively. The student is asked to take account of all the sources of information that would allow an accurate picture of her achievement to be constructed; this will include feedback from peers, teachers and assessment tasks, along with an understanding of the relevant criteria or standards. She will be able to describe her own performance articulately, having gathered all the data. An introverted or cosy self-assessment would not be accepted. The teacher's job would be to not let the learner rest with an assessment that is inadequate or superficial.

An example

My class of seven-year-olds are working on geometrical shapes. We have gone through the school and on a walk, looking for all the different shapes we could find. Now we are designing solid structures to represent the many possible shapes. Groups of two and three kids have each built a shape . . . there are pyramids, cylinders, spheres, blocks; they are made of paper, clay, wood, and plasticene. Now we have displayed them all on tables and shelves around the room, with a few of the lighter ones hanging from the ceiling. As the facilitator, I ask the students how they want to assess their work: How will we decide if we are satisfied with what we've done? How will we know whether we want to have another go and see if we can improve it.

In our assessment, I might ask them to bring from home some objects which they already have which match our shapes; I'll bring some as well. We can look at balls, wooden toys, packages, and ask ourselves how we could improve what we made. At this point we might test ourselves with a quiz: 'Bring me a pyramid, and tell me how you know it *is* a pyramid.' We are testing the conceptual understanding, and language, along with the practical achievement.

Now that we have made explicit what the standards are, ie now that we know the constant characteristics of a pyramid, we can take some time for everyone to reflect on their individual achievement compared with the newly-understood standards. In a well-established student-centred classroom, this reflection might happen in pairs or small groups, so individuals negotiate their assessment with peers, and then go on to check it out with the teacher. The teacher is probably working with certain individuals herself, because they are just not clear about their work.

At this stage, each child is taking a careful look at that which she has done, and comparing it to the recognisable standard. She is taking some time to record her feelings and opinions about it. She might write: 'I made a ball, it is very lumpy. I painted it red. It is a bit like a football but not as round.'

I ask: 'Now that you've all had time to think about what you could do to make your shapes better, how do you decide whether to do it over again or not?'

After discussion, some students decide that they want to carry on working on shapes. Others feel that they've had enough, or that they've done their best *for now* and are going to get on with recording their work, by drawing or photographing their shape, and writing an assessment of what they learned for their portfolio. The teacher chooses to challenge one or two students. 'Roz, will you stay a minute? What I've noticed is that when you're not happy with what you've done, you get discouraged and decide not to improve it. This time, I'd like to push you to make another shape . . . I'll help you, and we'll see if you can get to a point where you feel really good about what you've done.'

We discuss it at some length, and they choose to have another class come in and listen as they tell about what they have learned about shapes, and point out the features of each one they have built. This may be the culminating activity for this scheme of work. In the preparation for it, a lot of learning will be consolidated, and new learnings will also be encompassed. The students from the other class will be asked to give feedback, thus adding to the assessment. When it is all over, we will do our own final assessment, through some kind of exercise, such as a continuum or a round. We will be asking ourselves: 'Was this a good way to learn about shapes?' 'Did we work well together?' 'Were there any large problems that we need to work on for next time?' The group may choose to record some of these points for their portfolios, too.

All this time, the teacher has been encouraging the kids to look realistically at their work; to come up with their own assessments. There is no hint of a connection between the value of a piece of work and the value of the person. And there is this determined optimism, passed along to the students, that the learner *can learn, can do*. Where there is challenge, it is not a judgement of the person; it's asking the learner to have a second look, and it is not pushed to the point where the student has no choice about it. Where there is comparison with external standards, it is not intended to make a judgement about how good a person is, but is only done to identify the progress that's possible. The purpose of assessment is to support learning.

Student-centred assessment within the national requirements

Now the challenge is for us to keep the student at the heart of the national assessment procedures as they are progressively introduced. The TGAT philosophy, inasmuch as it is going to be upheld, provides us with some encouragement to do this, and Records of Achievement, inasmuch as they will be supported, with an ideal opportunity. The student-centred spirit and practice of the RoA 'movement' give us a rich resource of experience to draw upon. It is easy to see how the suggestions we make below mesh with the central features—student-ownership, negotiation, formative purpose, holistic perspective—of that developmental work.

At the time of writing, the balance between SATs and Teacher Assessment is still unclear and there is little guidance from SEAC on record-keeping and approaches to ongoing classroom assessment. Even though there is much more detail to come, we want to suggest ways in which it is possible to remain student-centred within the requirements as we know them. For example:

1 Whatever is *officially* required, the teacher can still engage the students in various processes of formative assessment and target-setting. This would be a natural part of the teaching style, an unscrutinised partnership between teacher and students, untouched by SEAC. Several practical examples are given later.
2 A teacher can arrive at the officially-required Teacher Assessment with as much student involvement as she chooses. The required data *can* be the result of students' self-assessment, based on feedback from a variety of sources made with an awareness of the official standards. The teacher's facilitation of this will be very much like the example of the 7-year-olds that we gave earlier.
3 The teacher can make Attainment Targets explicit to students, help them to understand them and to recognise them in their work. Students can then become progressively competent in recording their progress against the national requirements and there need be no distinction between these records and the teacher's.
4 The students can take ownership of the Standard Assessment Tasks. We want them, in negotiation with the teacher, to be able to decide when they're ready to take the SATs and which SATs would enable them most appropriately to demonstrate their learning. We are just not sure how much of this freedom there will be for teachers to carry out this degree of negotiation with students, nor how much variety there will be in the tasks anyway . . . . the much-needed crystal ball again!
5 Individual students can be trusted to select evidence of their learning which supports the assessment, and is stored in a personal portfolio. This portfolio, owned by the student, can contain material from the breadth of the student's experience within, and beyond, school. It can include records of formative assessments, the outcomes of SATs, examples of work done, and all the other information that she wants to include. Regularly edited and updated with the support of a teacher, this portfolio is the Record of Achievement.
6 Such a portfolio enables the student to make formative statements of

achievement at any time, including the required reporting times. The student-centred school finds the way to make the student's own statements, both interim and summative, the most valid statements of attainment.

7 No matter how tight the system may eventually become, a student-centred teacher will still consult with the students all the way along, so that the learner not only understands what is being said to the world about him, he also knows that his own opinion of himself is the one that counts most of all. The teacher will continually share his assessment results and observations, and the results of the SATs with the student, presenting them as *feedback*, in a way that says 'Here is some information for you to hear. I want to help you interpret it, and integrate it with what you already know about yourself, so that the final judgement is made by you and I together.'

8 Again, however tight the assessment system may become, the school can support a communication system which includes the students as active participants along with parents and teachers, whenever reporting is to be done. The official assessments need not be 'the last word', they can be part of the evidence, part of the data. In that sense they are like the penultimate part of the process, in which the student constructs a more complete picture of himself, which he presents with the teacher's support and comment.

9 Most importantly, any system can be *Humanised*, and humanisation will be needed more than ever to counteract all the competition and disadvantage that a standardised system is likely to create, however optimistic we want to be about it. There can always be time for unconditional positive regard, for listening, for acceptance, for talking to people in a way which indicates our valuing of them. All of this will add up to students feeling that they are OK, no matter what judgements other people make about them. If we preserve that, we preserve the possibility of their continued learning and growth, and holistic health.

The following fictional account attempts to communicate the flavour of what we're proposing.

I'm a fourth year student, working my way through this assessment model. My next step is a module called The Romantic Poets.

On the first day of the module, the teacher gave us each a copy of the requirements, and we discussed various ways of meeting them. I chose to carry out an independent study of Shelley's life and work, and then to join the teacher's group for two lessons on appreciating romantic poetry. I filled out and signed my contract. I started my research immediately, because I was worried about how much there was to do.

When we come into each day's lesson, or maybe at the end, the whole group meets and we do a 'fishbowl' round, in which one member of each group sits in the inner circle, surrounded by the others, and reports back on how far we've come, and what we think of our work. Other times, we might meet for a few minutes with a partner and talk about how we were getting on; we listen to each other and help with suggestions and feedback.

Yesterday, when I wasn't sure why this certain poem was so highly rated, I talked first to my partner, and then to the teacher about it. The teacher suggested two other poems to read alongside it, and referred me to a chapter I hadn't looked at yet. (So I didn't need telling what my homework was!)

We get on with our work. Other people are using different methods from mine, and have chosen different poets.

Halfway through the module, we take an hour to share with each other our learning so far. We do this partly to keep in contact with the whole group, because we've been working alone, and to give each other a broader perspective on all the poets, and partly to receive the feedback of our peers so that we get an idea of how we might improve the biographies before we record our work and make it ready for assessment. Sometimes Ms. Harper comes and sits by me, and looks at what I'm doing, and we talk it over. Last time she challenged me about the amount of talking I'm doing that has nothing to do with the work . . . I know I talk too much.

I've been working on the word processor; now I'll do my final edit and print out my research.

The teacher has been lecturing us on metre and on critical understanding and appreciation of poetry. I sort of wish we had done this first, but it's too late now. Next time . . . She gave us three examples of romantic poetry, each with a different metre and style.

In small groups, we worked at discovering the rules of metre, and the key elements of each style. In our small group we brainstormed ways in which we could record our understanding of the work. Four out of the five of us chose to find one further example of each of the three types, and to write a poem of our own, in each type. The fifth person decided to write a straightforward comparison and criticism.

When this module is complete, there will be time set aside for each of us to assess our work. To help us with what's still an unfamiliar task—comparing our work to the required standards—the teacher gave us this list of options:

1 She has a test prepared, we can take it and then mark it ourselves, or ask our partner to do it.
2 We can submit our work to one of several people for marking . . . the teacher, or the Head of English, or Mr Robinson at the public library, or my neighbour, who is a published poet.
3 We can submit our work, anonymously or not, to be displayed on the overhead projector and have it systematically criticised by the class.

Having checked out my thoughts and feelings about my work with two of my partners, and then with the teacher, I have now finished my Statement of Learning for this unit:

I know the main events of Shelley's life, and the influences on his work, such as the social climate and the people he cared about. I can write a poem in a similar style, using the correct metre. I understand the differences between Romantic Poetry and other types, and also the differences within the movement. I also know that there are several things I don't like about Romantic Poetry, including the flowery language.

I liked working on my own for just one project, no negotiations, no fights. The part about metre was boring, but not because of the teacher; it was just too technical. I was glad to be working with the others, and found it easier to get lots of ideas going.

I thought Shelley's life was sad and interesting, so I was moved by it, but also critical of it, from a moral point of view. I feel proud of the poem I wrote myself. On the whole, I learned and achieved a lot in this module. My portfolio contains my biographical report, my examples of three types of metre and style, all recorded on audio tape, and my own 'Shelleyan' poem. If I had to choose the piece I liked best, I'd choose my love poem, though I feel like blushing when I write that.

After the teacher has read my Statement of Learning and talked to me about it, I'll file it in my portfolio along with a print-out of the biography and a photocopy of the best of the poems I wrote.

When I've completed the whole set of modules that make up the English course, I'll go through all the records I've kept, look again at the original Attainment Targets, and, with the teacher, compare my evidence with the national statements of achievement. The SAT will help us with this. A final piece of writing will give me another look at my strengths and weaknesses, and then I can write my summary so that it shows my progress, my growth. My teachers will write comments too, after we've talked together.

It's this Negotiated Statement of Achievement that is so important, because my teacher will take it, along with the evidence in my portfolio, when she goes to meet with other teachers and they do their moderating.

Having described an imaginary example of the model in practice, we want to comment on each of the stages in turn. The flow diagram on the next page illustrates the process.

Informal formative assessment

The methods described here are not the official assessment procedures; they are the natural kinds of ongoing evaluations that we would always do with groups of learners.

There are many ways to do formative assessment. Some of them don't involve paper at all, for example:

- Rounds
- Human continua or blackboard continua
- Class discussion
- Classroom meetings
- Interview (teacher to student, student to student, or class to student)
- Role play
- Value voting
- Human statues

The active strategies suggested above are ephemeral; they happen and are quickly over without trace—except that they have done their job. The job was to take a moment to collect the feelings and thoughts about the current state of affairs, *so that progress may be made*. So, they stay in proportion as means to a much more important end.

Formative assessment strategies may also be paper-based and result in some sort of document which can be referred to at a later stage so that the rate of progress can be discerned. Examples of formative assessment activities appear at the end of this section, and in many other publications. But most of all, we encourage you, with your students, to invent your own strategies .... it's fun!

We have found it common for students who are just beginning to take responsibility to shy away from their weaknesses and to want to play to their strengths. Students who are not used to valuing mistakes and who have therefore become skilled at avoiding challenges which might expose 'failure', will often want to carry out tasks which they know they can do. After a while, this can lead to a circular (rather than spiral) curriculum, for the student repeatedly rehearses skills and understanding without moving forward. A student-centred teacher will NOT simply leave him to it. In these circumstances, the task for the teacher would seem to be:

- to continue displaying positive regard for the student, unconditionally, so that the student may come to accept that it will be safe to take risks and 'fail' with this teacher;
- to continue building the safety of the whole-group environment, protected by firm ground rules, so that the student trusts that his peers will accept his mistakes too;
- to continue acknowledging the student's *real* strengths (it's no use exaggerating; that can only lead to suspicion and a lack of trust), so that the student's esteem is high enough for him to see that he will still be OK as a person, even if the next piece of learning is hard to grasp;

Figure 6.6

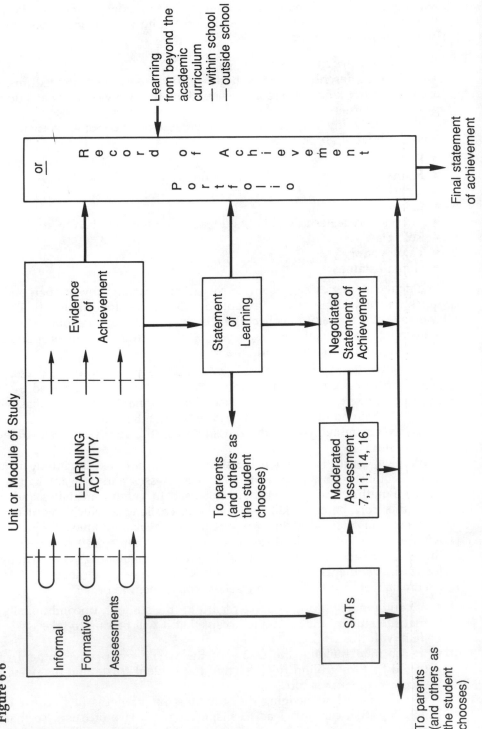

- to help the student to identify, in quite precise terms, current weaknesses in *this* area of learning only, so that the student is not overwhelmed by weakness and can formulate with the teacher a short and clear route to a precise target.

In an English class of 12-year-olds recently, we asked the students to produce posters advertising what they each wanted from the lessons. As we suspected, most students wanted to carry on doing things they were already good at. We held a discussion about how people often avoid difficulty and did a round of examples. Then, each person wrote, anonymously, 'Something I would like to achieve in English that I'm not very good at yet', and the papers were folded, collected in a 'hat' and redistributed randomly. After they had all been read out, there seemed to be a rather more honest and safe atmosphere in the class. Each student then completed a Personal Profile.

In the next lesson, a range of tasks were negotiated with the teacher around a central theme. Students were asked to work on tasks which dealt with their weaknesses rather than their strengths. No-one was forced to concentrate on their weaknesses, and some still chose to play safe. Some worked in groups, others worked on their own. During this activity, the teacher went round and talked with each student in turn about the view of herself portrayed on the profile. This document became the basis of ongoing formative assessment.

Recording the evidence of achievement

Apart from the formative assessments described above, students will need to keep a record of their accomplishments, which can be recalled at any time. Records can be kept in whatever way the students choose, as long as they are accessible:

- in folders
- on walls
- in file boxes
- on computer discs
- audio and video tapes

If a student uses a method of recording which cannot fit into the portfolio, or has contributed to a piece of work shared with other students, he will need a way to represent it in his personal portfolio later; so for instance, the information on the disc can be printed out, a wall chart could be photo-graphed, the video can be copied.

Statements of learning

At any time, it would be possible for students to look back through the records, and write a summary of progress so far. We would envisage this being done regularly, say at the end of each unit of study. These summaries could be copied and taken home to the parents.

Negotiated Statement of Achievement

The statements of learning are stored in the portfolio, along with all the other evidence and are used as the basis for a less regular statement of achievement, negotiated between the student and the teacher. This state-ment takes account of the feedback provided by SATs and relates the student's learning directly to Attainment Targets and levels. It becomes the basis for moderation and the required report at the end of each Key Stage.

Final statement

Using the filed evidence of achievement, along with the accumulated statements, an end-of-school statement can be compiled. This summative statement (which captures the achievement of the *whole* student) and the student's final selection from the portfolio become the Document of Record. This is what that summative statement might read like, written by a student who has come to the end of her time in a student-centred school:

Elena's final Statement of Achievement

If I had to say just one thing I've learned in this school, it would be that I've learned to be myself. I'm still the same Elena I was born to be, but now I have some clearer ideas about who I am, what I want, and who I would like to become.

I completed seven GCSEs last week, and I don't have the results yet, but I've been talking to my friends, and really we aren't very worried. For a long time now, I've been aware of my weaknesses, such as my dreaded algebra. And my teachers have really supported me in working at it until I feel at least adequately prepared. I also knew my strengths, and so there were no surprises in the exams, and I think I have a realistic idea of how well I did.

I've just been re-reading the statements I've written about my academic learning, which I negotiated with teachers along the way. All the details are there in my portfolio, and they've reminded me of just what I've accomplished in terms of knowledge, understanding, and skills. I feel that I have a broad and firm foundation for my further studies.

I feel that my goal of going to a sixth form college to do three A levels and then on to University, is within my reach now. My parents have just about recovered from the shock of hearing that I wanted to do physical science in order to be an engineer. I know they thought I would carry out their intention for me to marry within the next few years. It wasn't easy to convince them that I know this isn't the time for marriage for me. I think it's the first time they saw me as a mature woman.

What I feel now is that even if I were ready to marry, that wouldn't be everything I'd want. I want to use all I've learned in a way which feels valuable to other people as well.

What I got out of being in this school is that I can use my brain for my studies, but I can also use it in my relationships, to communicate my feelings . . . . . and what I managed to convey to my parents was that I'm not rejecting them, or their ideas. After all the talking we've done, they know I understand their points of view. But what I'm doing is building on their view of life.

So, I might choose for myself the experience of marriage and a family and settling into a community, and also a career based on my education and training. At this moment, I intend to have both; it's just that one will have to come before the other for now.

Compared to the shy and nervous person I was when I came to this school, I guess I get on well with people now. I make friends a bit more easily, and the last time we gave each other feedback in our class, quite a few classmates said I was more open and friendly than I used to be. Of course they also said I talk too much. (Will I ever find a middle ground?)

I really feel satisfied about what I've learned, and excited about the future. Just as the last few years have had their ups and downs, difficult patches, and times of rebellion, I suppose the next few years won't be much different. But now I know how to solve problems. I don't keep hammering away at something that isn't working, I look for all sorts of new solutions.

When I go to college, I won't feel I'm in it alone. I expect to work really closely with the others on the course, and will always know how to go to other people for support when I need it . . . . . I can give it as well.

Elena represents to us the fulfilment of a skilful and deliberately implemented student-centred approach. She has achieved traditional academic success, and so much more. Elena has a positive, and balanced self-image. Her self-esteem is high, but not overblown. She is a composite figure; she exemplifies a student who has been enabled to make her own choices from a confident and well-equipped position.

Acknowledgement, appreciation, and approval

Self-assessment is true and natural, as we keep saying. On its own, it is never quite enough for most human beings. A student engaged in the process we have just described would be relating to the teacher and to other students, in a positive manner, and would be giving and receiving lots of verbal and non-verbal messages about self-worth and valuing of others. A healthy, self-actualised adult is able to give and receive acknowledgement and appreciation; in fact, people wilt without these two rare and precious nutrients, and thrive with them.

Acknowledgement and appreciation are *not* to be confused with approval and disapproval; these two over-used and over-rated junk-foods may seem the same, but they do not provide adult interactions. People can get hooked, so that everything they do or produce has approval as its main aim. The other side of that *has to be* fear of disapproval, which provides a negative and child-like motivation.

How to tell the difference?
In our terms, *approval* sounds like this:

'You're a very good girl for colouring inside the lines like that!'
'I'm really pleased with the way you've written this essay, it's just what I meant when I assigned it.'

In the first example, the person is being judged because of the work she's done. In the second, the person has caused the teacher to be pleased. In either case, the reward performance is likely to be repeated for extrinsic reasons. *Disapproval* is the reverse.

Appreciation does have an opinion attached to it, but no strings; there is no attempt to manipulate or control.

'Thanks for showing me your picture. When I look at it, I notice the bright colours, and the time and care you've put into it. It seems to me to be a joyful sort of picture.'

Acknowledgement would sound like this:

'Thanks for your essay. I've glanced at it, and I noticed the way you've woven in all the different points we talked about in class, so that all the comparisons are made. I also noticed that you got it in by your deadline date. I'm looking forward to reading it more carefully tonight.'

Acknowledgement notices, without interpreting, judging or even stating a personal response. We acknowledge that people *need* to be acknowledged, and that both appreciation and acknowledgement have a positive effect on self-concept, while approval has a denigrating one.

5 Resources

Can you imagine . . . ?

We are in a first year, mixed-ability maths class in a large inner-city comprehensive school. The teacher had spent the previous lesson introducing the required concept of ratio. She did this by explaining, inviting questions, organising a few games which illustrate the concept, and also by demonstrating, letting the students 'play with' tangible objects and show each other what ratio means.

Now, in this second lesson, we have just seen the class list real-life situations involving ratio. They have two lessons in which to practice solving real problems, and to demonstrate to each other practical applications of their newly discovered skills. Some of the ideas include:
- increasing and decreasing amounts in recipes—and trying them out!
- playing cards (probability)
- throwing dice
- a role-play about a complicated Will
- making models
- reading and drawing maps
- surveying the school
- dressmaking
- making a machine which involves gears

Some of the students are still not quite clear about the concept. They are going over it again in a small group, with the teacher (or perhaps, sometimes, with one of their peers who does understand, although it is important to make sure that it is not always the same kids doing the helping). Others are watching a video about ratio, or playing a computer game to reinforce the concept.

Those in the class who are confident with the basic idea, and want to get on now with the applications, go to the shelves and boxes and cupboards where they find all that they need. The desks are soon filled with:
- cookbooks
- maps
- counterfeit money
- clipboards
- scissors, cloth, thread, needles, yarn and string
- construction bricks
- weighing machines
- tins filled with countable, tangible, odds and ends, such as plastic discs, buttons, coins
- Leggotechnic

Some people may have chosen to produce something lasting, like a wall chart, a teaching booklet for younger children, a computer programme.

Where did all these resources come from?

Over a period of time, the teacher has consistently gone out of her way to: collect things herself, from jumble sales, second hand stores, house-clear-outs; beg things from shops and factories, local merchants, parents; encourage the students to be on the lookout, always, for useful items. This is how there happens to be a carpet on the floor and a couch in the corner, plus a

mirror and some paintings, not to mention a huge assortment of paperback books. The teacher has gathered a considerable collection of manipulable objects, and also of consumable materials of every imaginable kind, which are kept on the shelves in an orderly manner by the kids, who have direct access to it at all times. She has also been campaigning, long and hard, for extra funding from her Head and Governors, and has sometimes been successful.

All of this has been the result of her personal initiative, time, and expense, and we deplore that it has to be this way. Such 'unofficial' provision is entirely voluntary and beyond the call of duty. The enrichment of learning requires a bounteous supply of varied resources which feed the imagination and which satisfy the appetites of creative students. These ought to be supplied by right, not charity.

So often, we see students get excited about their ideas, and committed to a task that they themselves have thought of and planned, only to be thwarted by the bare cupboards of the stockroom and the meagreness of the school library.

We want students to have *access* to *adequate* and *appropriate* resources despite the criminally poor investment by the State. We suggest nine steps which can be taken by schools and teachers, even now.

1 The teacher who is interested in using student-centred methods will be involved in providing *appropriate* resources. Encouraging students to be responsible for their own learning does *not* mean that the teacher abdicates his own responsibility for obtaining the necessary materials with which to stimulate creativity and achieve the stated goals.

Sometimes a teacher who claims to be student-centred will say to the kids, 'OK, now you go and get the resources you need'. We don't think this is fair, and often it doesn't work. At first, the kids may not have a clue about where to look or how to start. Often, they don't have the confidence, the money or even the parental permission, to do the search. It should be a group effort, closely and practically supported by the teacher. We believe that this is an area in which the facilitator needs to be proactive, and, as a learner with experience, to support the students in practical ways.

2 Waste of precious financial resources can be drastically reduced if those ordering books and materials realise that with student-centred learning there are few times when a class-sized set of textbooks needs to be purchased. Vast quantities of identical worksheets are also not necessary. That same funding could be used for students to reproduce what they need for their own work.

3 The students could be much more involved in the ordering of resources. For example, capitation could be distributed in the form of vouchers, through the Head of Department, to each teacher, who would use them in helping each class to assess its requirements for the year ahead. The vouchers would provide concrete evidence of spending and illustrate the finite nature of the allocation.

4 The idea that students should have open *access* to resources, is understandably difficult for some teachers to accept. Their previous experiences of theft and vandalism have not made them very trusting. In some ways, this is a chicken-and-egg dilemma. How do you create a trusting environment in which students take corporate ownership of the resources and therefore do not steal, destroy, or waste them, unless you first give them the opportunity to show that they can be trusted in this respect? On the one hand, you don't want to give them a real-life opportunity to be trustworthy before you're fairly sure that they can be trusted. On the other hand, they are not likely to become trustworthy unless they are really trusted, throughout the school. Unlocking doors and throwing away keys seems to be a big risk, and this is the price we have to pay for the damage already done. So if some things go missing at first, this becomes a problem-solving venture for staff and students together. In our experience, ownership tends to produce responsibility.

5 Many material resources in school are clearly *inappropriate*. They may be too difficult, too easy, too old, or too biased. We don't want to see kids struggling any more with texts that are linguistically indecipherable or conceptually inaccessible. We would like to see student-centred teachers become more fully aware of the subtle power of written and pictorial images to profoundly influence values and behaviour. We would like the students themselves to understand how they are subject to indoctrination, and how stereotypes are built, and behaviour moulded, for example, to do with race and gender.

So, another way in which the SC teacher can practically support the students is to help them develop the critical thinking which will enable them to review the appropriateness of the resources.

6 Beyond this, a student-centred school is likely to revolve around a communal resource centre which holds all the learning materials and consumable items.

7 *Access* is not just about getting to resources, or being able to understand them. It's about the ability to USE the resources to do a particular job. Carter and Monaco identify five elements of the Information Cycle, based on Marland's (1981) nine steps:

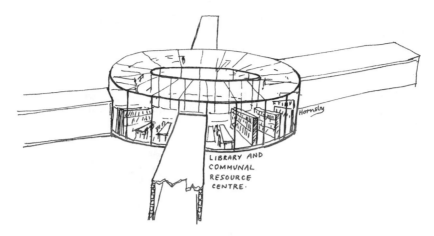

LIBRARY AND
COMMUNAL
RESOURCE
CENTRE.

(1) FORMULATING and ANALYSING the information need (*What have I got to do?*)
(2) RETRIEVING information relevant to that need (*How do I get the information that I need?*)
(3) PROCESSING that information (*What should I record?*)
(4) COMMUNICATING the information (*How should I present the information?*)
(5) EVALUATING the information and the task undertaken (*Have I got all the information I need? What have I achieved from undertaking this task?*) (Carter and Monaco, 1987)

8 What we have said about resources so far has been primarily to do with materials, hardware, software. Now we want to talk about *peopleware*. Human beings from within or outside the school, are the most numerous and the most diversified resource. They bring with them their particular heritage, culture, experience; the school seldom taps into their potential.

9 Places, buildings, events, industries, in every community, provide an inexhaustible supply of resources, if we would only use them.

Resources are learning opportunities. To reduce levels of access, adequacy, or appropriateness is to limit the extent to which the student can reach for potential.

6 Participation ... ?

Kids have to go to school, and kids have to come to lessons. Although we can allow them to express their resentment about it, these are facts of life which we have not (at the moment, anyway) the power to change. But once the students are there with us, we can maximise their choices, and minimise the compulsory elements of school, lessen the amount of coercion in general, and in our lessons in particular. Our experience is that this increases the feeling of ownership, and raises the level of motivation. So we encourage people to participate in classroom activities when they want to, and find alternatives when they don't want to; we endeavour to ensure that when we are working together, everyone who wants to be involved, is, and we have gone beyond the appearance of learning, to real growth.

We try to provide opportunities, where there are genuine choices, for students to experience being able to opt out. We can't say, 'OK, don't come to class', but we *can* say, 'Pass on this round if you want to'. We can say 'You can choose to opt out of this activity; tell me what you want to do instead.'

The concept of optional participation means that people can opt in and out of contributing in class, or joining a group, or making a statement. There is no way to make people learn anyway, we can only make them go through the motions; optional participation just makes the choices explicit instead of covert.

What happens if we pretend to offer an option, when we really can't? And what happens when kids think voluntary participation means they can opt out of the National Curriculum and its assessments as well?

A Fifth Year GCSE Class:

The teacher has recently 'discovered' SCL, and is wanting to implement it across all his classes. He spends the first four periods with 5E using games and exercises and discussions, to create a safe and supportive climate, and to establish the concepts of optional participation and ownership. He remembers to tell the truth, and he lays it out to his class that he himself has changed, and he now realises that he's not responsible for their passing the exam after all.

They look at him as if he's crazy. Of course he's responsible, he's the teacher! He's getting paid for it. He persists, with determined optimism. He passes out a copy of the required work, and goes over it carefully with them, and hands over the ownership of it. But! Some of them don't want it, and triumphantly exercise their new-found right not to take part. About 16 students who divide themselves into groups and start to master various sections of the work, preparing handouts and lesson notes for the others; that leaves eight, who simply don't care. They have stopped working altogether, and spend the lessons reading their motorcycle and sport and fashion magazines. Mr Andrew is really worried now; he thought it might happen at first, but that they would come round. They haven't.

Whoops! What went wrong here?

Mr Andrew dived in at the deep end of our facilitator's continuum, with a class who were accustomed to having all responsibility handled by the teacher, in a system where he is held accountable by parents, colleagues, administrators, and students, for their success or failure. He was at a loss about what to do with the opters-out, and so he left them alone. He got himself into a trap. Mr Andrew is an archetype for many teachers who have challenged us on this issue. So what would we do instead?

1 We wouldn't feel any need to dive in at the deep end. We would take time to weigh up the risks for the students. We'd consider:
   a) what the system requires of them;
   b) how much time they've got in which to achieve it;
   c) their previous experience of handling responsibility;
   d) our own experience in handling what might happen.
2 We would tell the truth, explain about student-centred learning, discuss point *a* (above) say how we would like it to be, and elicit their opinions about it. We would acknowledge for the first, but not the last, time, that there is really a lot of choice about working to pass the exam; in almost all other classes, a lot of people would choose not to bother, and so not to pass. But everyone has to go through the motions. Here, we are bringing the choice out into the open. We're saying that the system doesn't give us a really free choice; there are severe consequences for opting out. The success of the students is measured through assessments and exams, now more than ever, and the more tickets they collect, the more chances they get.
3 We would use communication exercises and games to build a safe climate, and introduce the option of participation or 'passing', *in these activities only*. There would always be alternatives available for those who did not want to join in. It would never be a case of 'You can choose to do nothing if you want to.'
4 We would address the situation very directly. We might use an exercise in which each person said why they were in this class. We would take very seriously the fact that some of them had no intrinsic motivation for being there. We would let them know that we understood their feelings and their reasons, and we would make sure they understood our vested interests in their success, as well as our caring about them.
5 For those who still feel like not bothering? Well, we don't have any easy answers. We would be very persistent: 'I see that you don't want to prepare for this exam, and I am not prepared to have you sitting here doing nothing, so what can we do as a group to help you feel more committed?' Till the last day of class, we would not give up with our opters-out.
6 In the end, there may still be those who choose not to pass the exam. This would be true no matter what teaching style we had used. We accept that student-centred learning is not a panacea which cures all the educational ill-health of the system. But, we do feel that our openness and our determined optimism will get us further, and will have salvaged something for the students in terms of their dignity. They will have faced up to their choices and, at least in that sense, will have taken responsibility for themselves.

We would want to take time to ensure that the activities on offer for the whole group are new and stimulating and rewarding, so that participation is worthwhile, and non-participation is not happening out of disgust, but out of free choice.

In the end, it is about is trust. The teacher may need to adjust her attitude so that she does not start out assuming that kids want to be idle and rebellious. We acknowledge that schools often cause laziness and insurrection, and that they'll carry on being that way, IF that's what the teacher expects.

P.S. We have found that if we give the students the opportunity not to participate, sooner or later they will, because:

- The novelty wears off.
- The kids have made their statement, and that's enough for them.
- There's nothing to kick against, now that compulsion has been removed.
- It's more exciting to be with the group, working, than not to be.

7 Alternatives to punishment

One of the basic changes we would make to the way most schools are run would be to erase the word, the concept, of punishment. Since this is such a radical stance, we want to take time to explain it further, especially since, these days, there is a lot of publicity about discipline in schools. Saying that punishment simply does not work is a controversial statement. We want to put forward some of our arguments against punishment.

1 As teachers, especially headteachers, we would see it as our job to support every person in the school. Punishment is not supportive — yes, it may change some behaviour, it may make a student more acceptable to have around, and it may have comforted and seemed to support an angry or weak teacher. It also creates: resentment; guilt; toughening; motivation for retaliation; and humiliation.

   Punishment may create or reinforce a negative self-image, in which the student sees himself as a 'wrongdoer', a criminal of sorts, an unacceptable person. Hard kids get harder, their shells become impermeable, and then they have an image to maintain. In that sense, punishment has a status value in the alternative culture of the school, and so becomes self-perpetuating. Soft kids get hurt, their self-image gets mushier and mushier, so that they then don't see themselves as capable of behaving responsibly. One way or another, negative behaviour begets more negative behaviour.

   We say, on the one hand, 'hurting people is wrong' yet on the other 'You hurt so-and-so, therefore I'll hurt you back'. We're sending a crossed message which at best results in confusion, but usually results in incredulity.

2 When we send someone somewhere else to be dealt with, we are saying that we can't handle the problem, and that we've given up on this relationship. It's not that we would never ask for support. We might say to a kid: 'Look, I'm just not handling this right now, and you and I aren't

listening to each other. I'd like you to go and sit in the library, I'll call for you there at 12:00, and we'll see if the year head will help us to listen to each other.' We see a difference between that message, and the one that says 'Get out of here, I'm through with you, I'm handing you over to Mr. Y'.

3 When we punish a student, we are taking responsibility for what she has done. On one simple level we are saying, 'You don't have to take charge of yourself. All you have to do is suffer this pain, (or humilation, or exclusion), and then it will all be OK'. As if the wrong has been put right. Dumping extrinsic motivation, from the outside, is so very different from enabling the other person to find intrinsic, logical understanding of her own behaviour; realise what it does to herself and others; and finally, discover behaviour and a way of thinking and feeling that would work better.

Punishment may change outward behaviour, and that is usually all that a school takes time to do. But the point is, the school then has to keep·on doing it, and often escalating it, because it doesn't work. What looks like a reformed student, may be a student who's resigned himself to being good now. And often such reform is at a price. Sometimes the passion, the life, the creativity goes as a side-effect of resignation. Sometimes there is a loss of self-respect. Certainly, there is a loss of self-responsibility.

One of the crazy things about human nature is that if we are doing something, and it doesn't work, we do it more, we do it harder and we do it more intensely.

What we often *don't* do is look for a different way of addressing the problem. We acknowledge that once again, we are being very directive. We are definitely saying, 'We want you to change your behaviour. We hope you will choose behaviour that works better than what's happening at the moment, and we will support you in doing it. We hope you will see yourself differently as a result of this change, and see that you are capable and responsible'. We don't believe that we can change people inwardly, we can only support them while they choose to change themselves. The inward changes are different from the behaviour changes in that they feel good, and they last more permanently.

For all of these reasons, and more, we are totally against excluding students from school, except in the most dire of circumstances. It is their school, they have a right to be there. The very act of exclusion causes enormous damage;

- it rejects and alienates the students,
- it excludes them from the full range of educational opportunities,

- they are removed from the safety and structure of 'normal' school life, so that they often get into more trouble, either at home or on the streets,
- re-entry can become humiliating and difficult.

In most cases, we would say that the student who persistently gets into trouble, is exactly the kind who needs the most support from the school.

What do we put in the place of the well-established sanctions and punishments? First let's look at the evidence submitted by The Children's Legal Centre to the Committee of Enquiry into Discipline in Schools (summarised in *Child Right Magazine*, 1988). Their starting point is that, 'Schools which are tolerant rather than authoritarian reduce disruption'. They go on to say '. . . . . behaviour is better when schools:

- treat pupils fairly and with respect;
- strive to build cooperative rather than antagonistic teacher-pupil relationships;
- do not impose petty and unnecessary rules;
- have a tolerant and positive rather than punitive and authoritarian atmosphere;
- give pupils responsibility and rights to active participation;
- exhibit concern for pupils' welfare, and responsiveness to their needs;
- ensure that teachers themselves provide good models of behaviour.

. . . . We must emphasise that these measures are supported not only because they would make schools more harmonious and productive places, but also because they would provide rights which we believe pupils in principle are entitled to.

The Legal Centre then goes on to outline key points of practice, which we summarise here.

1 Schools should avoid petty and unnecessary rules, including compulsory school uniform.
2 Students should be involved in school decision-making, and the government should lift the ban on under-18 school governors, so that students are represented on the governing body.
3 Schools should have school councils, elected by pupils 'with a real say over important aspects of school life, such as school rules and disciplinary procedures.'
4 Each LEA should establish a student parliament, elected by students, which considers motions relating to LEA policy.
5 The school system should recognise the rights of students to have adequate *choice* of courses of study.

We endorse these ideas and we add some of our own practical suggestions.

Schools are very willing to publicise rules which say what students cannot do; they are not so quick to outline students' rights. We believe that rather than school rules hanging in the entrance hall, there could be a School Charter, which states the rights and responsibilities of everyone in the school.

We should erase punishment from the list of possibilities. Start a school thinking of alternative ways to make things work. *Everyone* needs to be on the thinking team. This takes time and concerted effort, and determined optimism. Few people will believe it at first.

One key to progress here is to have a very good, well-trained, proactive, school counsellor, who sees her job as being available to everyone in the school when they need to talk or work out a problem. No papers, no records, no forms to fill out, no time-consuming busy work. Just availability.

For instance, with the question of truancy, the paper work, record keeping and enforcement should rest with someone else; the counsellor is there to communicate with the kid who doesn't want to be in school. The counsellor needs a quiet, private office, with a waiting room which is comfortable and contains books and magazines and easy chairs. Students who are having temporary problems staying in class could come there, by choice, and if they wanted to, could later talk to the counsellor. But they might just want to be there to cool off.

Cooling off places could be provided for everyone. If a teacher is at his wit's end with a kid, or with a whole class, then he could send for the Deputy or Year Head, and instead of saying 'Deal with this kid!', he could ask, 'Will you take my class for a few minutes while I go and cool off?' Kids could also ask to go, rather than being sent. The room would be a place for calming down and thinking creatively about the problem at hand. 'What am I going to do?' not, 'What are they going to do to me?' It would have a carpet, comfortable chairs or cushions, and *quiet*.

Problem solving and support would be available in class, as well. The peer group can be very positive in helping a student see what he is doing, and working out alternative forms of behaviour. Teachers might get into the habit of doing this when disruptions happen; the time for work would be interrupted anyway, while the war was on, and instead of war, you could have problem solving. Also, as a first step, this sort of assistance could be given during tutorial periods.

If the problem persists, after all of the above, the student could choose to take it to the school council. Or a teacher, or another student, could take the matter there. Another step, which would come to be seen as natural and normal, would be to take the difficulty to the staff meeting, where the staff as a whole could see if they have any ideas or suggestions; *not* punishments.

Contracts are structures which students and teachers can lean on. They are not 'reports' in the punitive sense. A student determines her goals for inner change and resulting behaviour change, and promises *herself* that she will take certain manageable steps. The other person is there to check in with, to see if the contract is working, and if it isn't, to renegotiate.

There may still be incidents that are potentially very violent, or dangerous, for example, the use of drugs or weapons, or using equipment in a dangerous manner. The priority here is to stop the risk of injury, or the violence, or the danger; first by talking, then (in extreme cases) by physical intervention. Afterwards there should be time for cooling off, then going through the non-punitive process.

The key element of the process is the interaction between all the different people. They will be *listening* to each other, purposefully, with good will and the firm intention of sorting things out now, and knowing how to apply the learning next time.

Embarking on this course of action takes time, and requires a very strong leader who is positive, determined, and proactive, and who reminds everyone over and over again; counselling needs to be available for all concerned. At the first sign of slippage, people will be very ready to say, 'Ha ha, I told you so. It isn't working!', so they can return to the much more familiar and comfortable ways they knew before.

8 Clothes

We have had experience of schools where there was no dress code what-ever; the kids wore what they wanted to school, whatever they felt comfort-able in, including shorts or sandals in hot weather, and jeans most of the time. They had no less respect for the teachers, they worked just as hard, they did not compete to see who could outdress whom, and there was no way to spot the 'advantaged' students. Once in a great while, someone might come dressed in a very provocative way, of one description or another, and they would be asked to talk to the school counsellor or Deputy Head about it. Our experience actually made nonsense out of all the stated reasons for enforcing school uniform.

   Our policy would be: there is no dress code. Then any specific instance of what seemed to be inappropriate dress would be handled at the time, by whoever was concerned. We might say something like:

I think your blouse is cut pretty low . . . . I think it's inappropriate, and it's causing a lot of disruption. I care about you, and I care what other people think of you, and also I care what they think of the school. So, I'm not prepared to take the risks involved. I want you to put something on over it; or, if you don't want to do that, you can go and work somewhere in a place that's not public . . . . How do you feel about this, is there anything you want to say?'

(The teacher's and the student's points of view are expressed. If there is still resistance . . . .)

'You'll have to do what I'm telling you right now, and then if you still feel you're right, you can talk to the School Council about it on Friday. Or, if you prefer, we can talk it over with your parents, together.'

Some examples of activities are included on pags 119–150.

Introduction to the activities

On the following pages you will find a selection of formative assessment exercises, along with three contract formats, all of which have been devised and used in the routine of our classroom work. We have included them as concrete examples of the approach we've described in this chapter. There are, of course, many other sources of self- and negotiated assessment materials; we would encourage you to seek them out, but most of all to rely on the ingenuity of yourself and your kids.

If you are looking for problem-solving activities with students, then some of the exercises in the collection at the end of Chapter 8 can readily be put to classroom use. Or, if you turn to our earlier publications you will find much wider selections of group-building, communication and esteem-raising strategies which it seemed pointless to repeat here.

CONTRACT

I, _____ , make this agreement with the rest of the class.

I will carry out the following piece of work _____

_____

_____

I will finish it by _____ , so that it is ready to share with other people in the class.

I will consider the work complete when:

1 _____   3 _____

2 _____   4 _____

To start with, I intend to:

1 _____

2 _____

3 _____

I expect that I will need help from these people:

a) _____   from _____

b) _____   from _____

c) _____   from _____

Signed _____

Signed on behalf of the class by _____

AGREEMENT

List the names of people in your group here:

_____   _____

_____   _____

This is the work we agree to do:

_____

_____

_____

_____

We agree to complete it by: _____

Signed:

Today's date: _____

GROUP CONTRACT

Group members   1 ....

2 ....

3 ....

4 ....

5 ....

Specific task of this group ....

....

Working towards Attainment Targets   ....   levels   ....

....

....

Explanation of how the outcomes of this group's work will be shared
with the other learners

....

....

Details of responsibilities of each member of this group

1 ....

2 ....

3 ....

4 ....

5 ....

Intentions with regard to resources (time, people, places, equipment,
materials, books, IT)

....

....

....

Deadline for completion of task ....

Date by which other learners will have shared in our work ....

Signed by the group:

Signed on behalf of other learners:

Concentric circles

The issue being assessed forms the centre point of an imaginary circle, for example: 'I think we should do a sponsored walk as a fundraising activity' or 'I think we should do more work on Attainment Target 6'.

Concentric circles emanating from this point can be marked out (using chalk, for example) or can be left to the imagination.

Individuals then stand in the place that indicates their opinion ie the nearer to the centre point, the greater the support they feel for the idea.

The resulting pattern gives the group a physical snapshot of opinion.

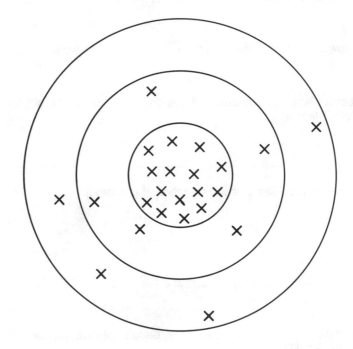

Line assessments

A line (imaginary, string or a line of chairs) represents a continuum for example:

I fully understand all the requirements laid down in this part of the Programme of Study	I don't have a clue about the requirements in this part of the Programme of Study

Group members stand or sit along the continuum to show their position.

Variation
The continuum can be a circle or a semi-circle, making it easier for everyone to 'see' the pattern and talk about the issue together.

Statues

At an agreed signal everyone adopts a statue-like pose to represent how she feels about a particular issue, for example:
Issue: The degree of trust in a group
- An open pose to suggest feeling that there is a lot of trust.
- A closed pose to suggest the reverse.
- Standing upright if she does not want to indicate her opinion.

Variation
Issue: Your sense of achievement now that the work has finished and you've looked at the Attainment Targets again.

Making faces

Simultaneously, everyone 'makes a face' to show how he is feeling about a central issue eg enjoyment of a particular novel, the pace at which we are working.

Variation
Everyone draws a face to show how they are feeling. Display the faces for all to see. Repeat the process to compare.

2-Dimensional value continuum

Similar to line assessments with a specific application to drawing out opinion. It is particularly useful if two aspects of an issue are being considered, eg:

I think we should definitely
invite the first years to share our facilities

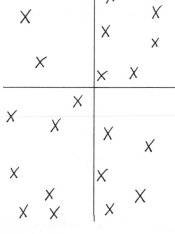

I totally agree with the idea of helping to turn the old gym into a 2nd year clubroom.

I don't agree at all with the idea of helping to turn the gym into a 2nd year clubroom.

I definitely think that we should not invite first years to share our facilities.

Or, at the start of a new topic in the National Curriculum:

I am dead keen to
learn everything I can
about this subject

I already know   I know absolutely
everything about   ————————————|————————————   nothing about this
Electricity and Magnetism   subject

I am not interested at
all in Electricity + Magnetism

Or, mid-way through a topic, to review progress:

I am completely
dissatisfied with the
way we are approaching this subject

I am nowhere near   I have met all the
meeting the   ————————————|————————————   criteria laid down in
required criteria   Attainment Target 6

I am totally satisfied
with the way we
are tackling this subject

Variation

Instead of physically taking up positions, the lines can be represented by string and positions by pieces of card (named or anonymous). Individuals are still free to change their position during any follow-up discussion.

Change places if . . .

The group sits in a circle. In turn, members make statements to complete the phrase:
'Change places if . . . .', for example:
• you are ready to move on to the next topic
• you prefer working on your own.
• you have an idea for our next assembly.
• you have a piece of news you want to tell us.
If the statement applies, then the individuals concerned get up and change places with
each other.

Application
This is also a handy way of mixing everyone up in readiness for random groups or pairs.

Variation
Have one less chair than there are members in the group. The person left in the middle
announces the next 'change places if . . .'

Mountains and hurdles

The following two drawings are recording devices to help students keep track of their
progress towards predetermined goals. The ten steps could be decided through group
negotiation, or they could be an individual student's personal learning plan, or they
could relate directly to the National Curriculum statements of attainment.

The 'encourager' could be another student, a parent or a teacher of the student's
choice.

Label the mountains to show what you can do. Draw yourself at the top of each mountain you conquer.

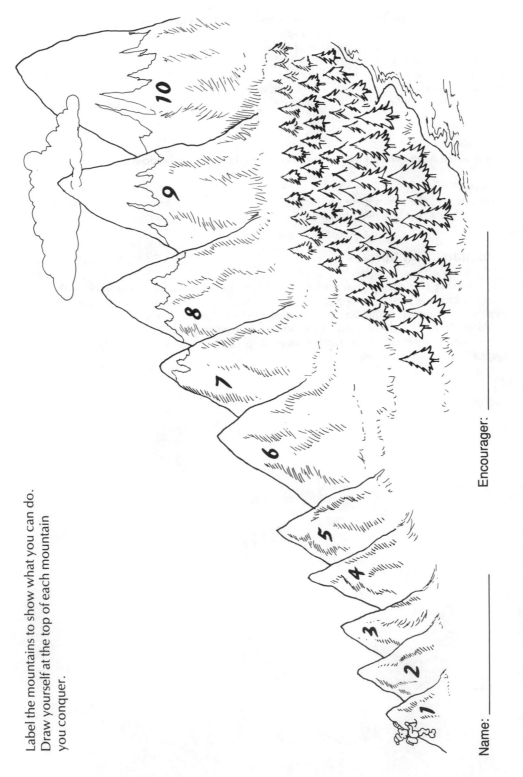

Name: _____

Encourager: _____

The bars can be shaded to show gradual achievement.

FINISH

You can do it

Name: _____

Encourager: _____

Lesson checks

At the end of each lesson, individual students or groups are asked to complete a form which:
- records the achievements of the lesson;
- sets any necessary homework;
- predicts the targets for the next lesson.

It is often helpful to have the form countersigned by a 'shadow', selected by the student or group. The shadow agrees to check, in a supportive way, at the start of the next lesson:
- progress with the homework
- intentions for the new lesson

Variations
1 Have a file box full of index cards or paper cut to size. Students record their feelings, achievements and intentions as they wish without the prompts of a printed proforma.
2 In Science, or other subjects requiring the preparation of apparatus before the lesson, the checks could include a section for students to request their equipment to be passed on to the lab. technician.

Charting your progress

The student keeps a line graph of her progress, with regard to a particular criterion. This criterion could be related directly to an Attainment Target, or some other skill which the student has decided to work on. Time is allocated during lessons for students to reflect on and chart their progress. The 'x' axis records the date and the 'y' axis represents the degree of achievement as perceived by the student herself. If appropriate, a group with similar criteria could discuss the factors which help their achievement, and the factors which hinder it.

Name: _____

In today's lesson this is what I did:

_____

_____

The x shows the progress I'm making
with my assignment:

┼start _____ finish┼

Before next lesson I will _____

_____

In the next lesson I will _____

_____

Signed:

_____

Signed on behalf of the class:

_____

Example Criterion: completion of tasks set in lesson.

Name: _____

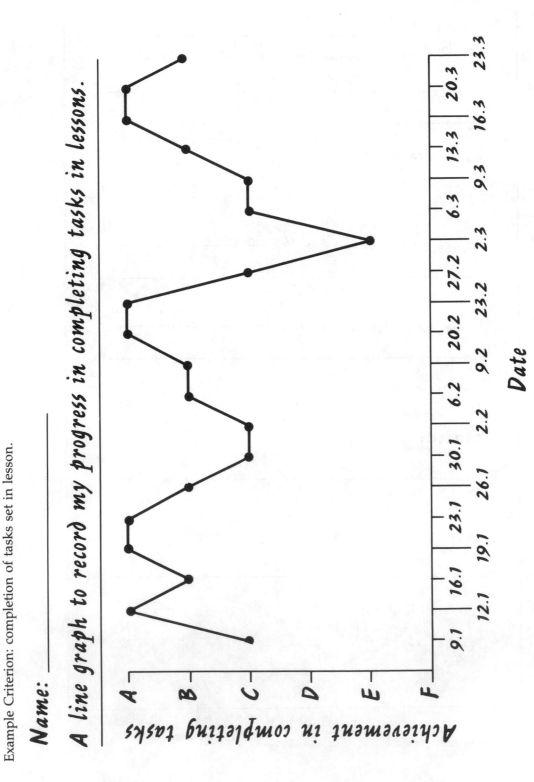

A line graph to record my progress in completing tasks in lessons.

Achievement in completing tasks

A
B
C
D
E
F

Date

9.1 12.1 16.1 19.1 23.1 26.1 30.1 2.2 6.2 9.2 20.2 23.2 27.2 2.3 6.3 9.3 13.3 16.3 20.3 23.3

All squared

This sheet can be used to encourage a *balanced* evaluation of an activity, lesson, course or meeting. If evaluation is going to take place more than once, the same sheet can be used if comments are dated.

<u>*All Squared*</u>

	Good	*Not Good*
M e	*Was a group leader* 21.2.89 *Handed in project on time* 27.2.89	*Didn't make sure everyone had their say* 21.2.89 *Felt bored and didn't finish the notes* 27.2.89
O t h e r s	*Every group got the task done* 21.2.89 *Had a good discussion about the usefulness of this sheet* 27.2.89	*Boys and girls still won't work together* 21.2.89 *Noisy at start of lesson Wasted time* 27.2.89

Name _____

Hitting the target

At the start of a topic or a series of lessons, students are involved in setting learning objectives and personal goals. The targets might refer to:

- *Content*, for example: 'I know all about the Industrial Revolution.'
- *Skill*, for example: 'I can write a simple computer programme.'
- *Personal*, for example: 'I can present my work logically and neatly.'

and can be related to National Curriculum Attainment Targets.

Variation
A large 'flipchart'-size target could be used for the whole group, for example, 'I can listen to and respect other people's points of view'.

Can you hit all the bullseyes in your group work ?

When you have finished working in one of these areas, mark a cross on the dartboard to show how close you are to hitting the target. Put the date next to the cross. This sheet will help you to talk with your teacher about how you are getting on.

Name: _____

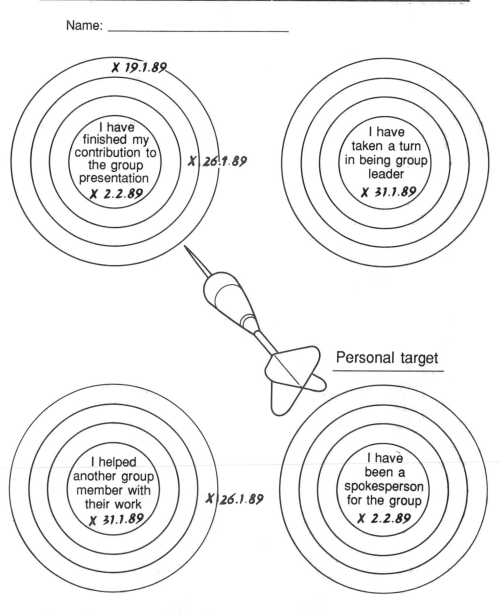

X 19.1.89

I have finished my contribution to the group presentation
X 2.2.89

X 26.1.89

I have taken a turn in being group leader
X 31.1.89

Personal target

I helped another group member with their work
X 31.1.89

X 26.1.89

I have been a spokesperson for the group
X 2.2.89

How did I get on today?

At the end of a lesson, the student considers how he got on in respect of subject and social skills. This sheet can prompt discussion about the conditions needed for effective learning, for example. Also, it is way of keeping skills other than those determined by the National Curriculum, in focus.

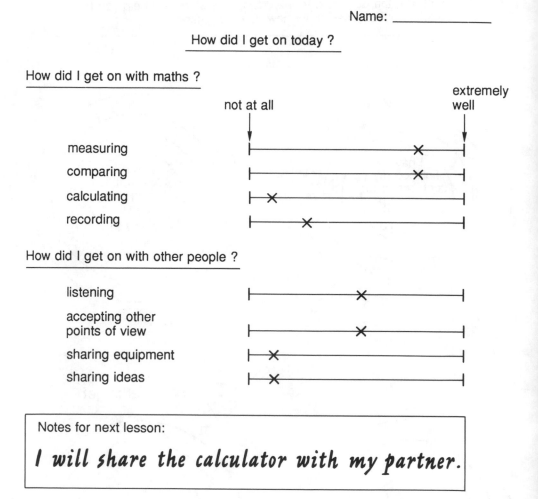

Name: _____

How did I get on today ?

How did I get on with maths ?

How did I get on with other people ?

Notes for next lesson:

I will share the calculator with my partner.

Helping and hindering factors

The basic process in this activity is adapted from Kurt Lewin's concept of Force Field Analysis. A particular situation is highlighted and the evaluation tool is used to record, on one side, those factors which help, and on the other, those which hinder. The length of each arrow indicates the *significance* of each factor.

Application
- *Subject specific*, for example, the helping/hindering factors affecting the growth of a settlement.
- *An initial stage of a problem-solving process*, for example: 'How can we as a group master this part of the Programme of Study?'
- *Self-assessment*, for example, personal strengths and weaknesses with regard to my career decisions.

HELPING /HINDERING FACTORS

NAME: _____

> *Situation:*
> *Designing and making an appliqué wall panel*

Helping	*Hindering*
These things made it easier for me to to do a good job...	These things made it difficult for me to do a good job...
GOOD SELECTION OF FABRICS	NOT ENOUGH TIME
EQUIPMENT WAS OUT ON TABLES AT START OF SESSION	A COMPLICATED DESIGN

KEY LEARNING POINTS

● MORE THOUGHT AT DESIGN STAGE

● PUT IN MORE CONCENTRATION AT THE START SO THAT I DON'T FALL BEHIND

Centralisation

This device could be used to help a group keep track of its progress towards a common goal. It could be drawn as a large wall chart.

At the end of each working session, group members initial and date their positions, or use movable symbols to indicate how far each has got, or feels the group has got.

Variations

1 The process could be made more precise by:
    a) dividing the diagram into segments and allocating a segment to each group member, so that each has her own route to the centre.
    b) placing a National Curriculum 'level of attainment' at the centre eg Maths AT 10, Level 6 — with the diagram divided into quarters for each of the four 'statements of attainment' at that level.
    c) numbering the concentric circles and making each one a specific task which contributes to the overall aim.
2 The device could be used to help a class monitor its progress with a syllabus.

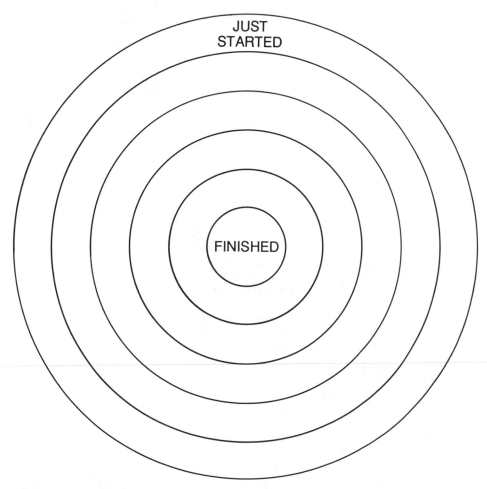

Hanging in the balance

Aims   To support the concept of balanced evaluation.
Materials A pair of pan balances (basic, plastic type will work) and a pile of plastic
             counters.
   OR: A large copy of the pan balance diagram.

Procedure
1 Clarify together the issue which you are going to evaluate, for example, the activities in
   the session just finished or a video the group has made on the dangers of smoking.
2 *Either*
   Using the pan balances, each takes a turn to comment freely on the issue. For each
   statement, put a counter into one of the pans depending on whether it is a positive or a
   negative statement.
   OR:
   Using the large diagram of the balances, each takes a turn to evaluate the issue and a
   scribe records the comments on the appropriate sides.
3 When everyone who wants to speak has done so, the group looks at the balance of the
   evaluation. If appropriate the group can work on ways in which to 'redress' the
   balance.

Variations:
1 Use the diagram as a personal evaluation sheet rather than a group one.
2 Use real weights instead of plastic counters, so that the 'weight' — not just the number
   of statements — can be represented.
3 Insist at the beginning that the two sides must be kept evenly balanced throughout the
   evaluation process.

First steps

This is an example of a profile which has been successfully used with a reception class
(4/5 yrs). The context for this was the Christmas period, which has the potential of
becoming a frenzy of craft, carols and parties. We felt that the use of a negotiated profile
would support the learning opportunities and processes we wanted to provide. We
wanted the profile to be:
- meaningful to the children and visually attractive;
- easy to use 'in situ' so that a student and teacher could talk together amid the activity
  of a reception class;
- supportive of the learning process (sustaining motivation, aiding understanding and
  helping to turn experience into learning);
- of short-term duration and realistically attainable.

We went through the following stages to put it into practice:
1 Identified the specific skills arising out of the 'Christmas' craft.
2 Identified the foundation skills which would support the individual student and sustain
   a harmonious classroom environment.
3 Design the format of the profile and print it onto A3 card.
4 Organised the display and storage of the profiles for ease of access and prominence for
   teachers, students and parents.
5 Introduced the profile to the class in a practical way and thought of a name for it
   together: 'I can do chart'.
6 Referred regularly to the profile as we began each new craft activity, talking about the
   skills we were going to use.
7 Through discussion, during the practical sessions and in the 'profile talk' time, the
   students recognised the skills they had practised and set new personal targets.

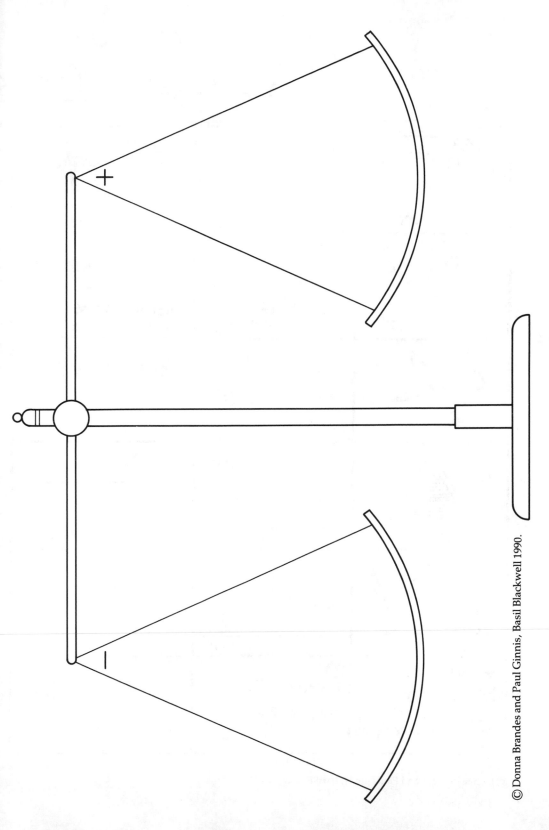

CHIVENOR
What ___ (child

	I can thread.	<u>Mrs. B. Pugh</u>
0 1 2 3 4 5	I know my numbers up to 5. *Pupil colours in triangle.* ✓	<u>Teacher's signature</u> Pupil chooses a picture ink stamp. There was a selection of animals and Christmas symbols.
	I can use scissors.	
	I can draw around a shape.	————
glue	I can use glue.	————
✱ Two blank boxes for child's individual skills. that they recognise or request.	eg I can tie my shoe laces.	

© Donna Brandes and Paul Ginnis, Basil Blackwell 1990.

S C H O O L   1 9 8 8

__name)__ __ __ __ __ can do.

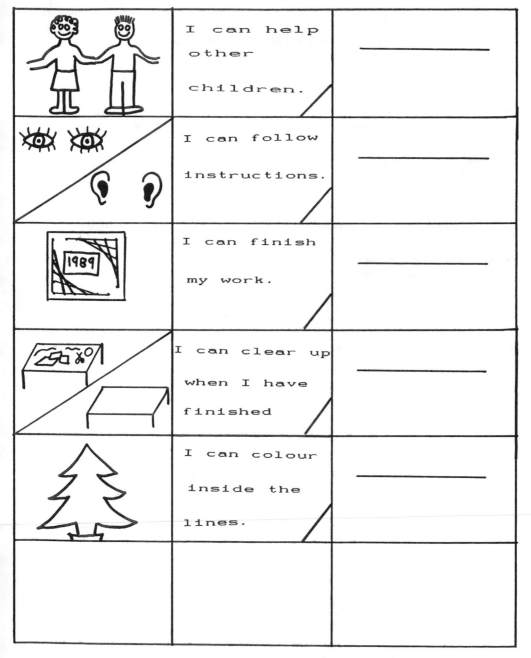

	I can help other children.	_____
	I can follow instructions.	_____
	I can finish my work.	_____
	I can clear up when I have finished	_____
	I can colour inside the lines.	_____

Talk, write and sign

This proforma can be used to record the outcomes of a discussion between teacher and student. The prompts help to support the direction of the discussion and there is room for additional points to be noted.

Peer feedback on projects

These three ideas are designed to support students in doing project work.

- At the start, all students are involved in deciding what makes a good project, as a whole group, in pairs or as individuals. Relevant sections of the National Curriculum are consulted. Everyone fills in Box A and uses this as a checklist.

- Each time a section is ready for peer feedback, the author of the work decides which of the criteria she wants feedback on. She notes this on the second sheet, along with the date.

- When everyone has a piece to be assessed, the work is laid out for ease of access. Students circulate and assess several pieces of work by writing comments in the two columns. They also note down evidence in the work which suggests achievement at relevant National Curriculum levels.

- Students then have the opportunity to follow up the comments in discussion with peers.

- At the end of piece of peer feedback, the student completes the assessment statements on the third sheet.

Variations
This could be used for small-group or individual presentations to the whole class. Each class member has a copy of the second sheet which is used to feed back comments to the presenters at the end of the session.

Talk, write and sign

My teacher, _____, and I have just
looked at my work. We are pleased about

1 _____
_____
_____

2 _____
_____
_____

We think that I could improve _____
_____
_____

In the next piece of work I will_____
_____
_____

To do this I will need _____
_____
_____

Signed _____

Date _____

WHAT MAKES A GOOD PROJECT?

Box A

This is a list of my ideas of what makes a good project. Every time I work on my project I will check that I am sticking to them:

A good project...	1	2	3	4	5	6	7	8

<u>WHAT DO YOU THINK ABOUT MY WORK?</u>

NAME: TODAY'S DATE:

TITLE OF WORK:

CRITERIA I WANT FEEDBACK ON:

NAME	WHAT I THINK IS GOOD ABOUT YOUR WORK	WHAT I THINK COULD BE IMPROVED	EVIDENCE OF A.T.... LEVEL...

© Donna Brandes and Paul Ginnis, Basil Blackwell 1990.

- 3 -

Now that I have seen what other people think of my work, I feel

_____

In this project, I achieved:

1 _____

2 _____

3 _____

Next time I do a project like this, I will:

1 _____

2 _____

3 _____

Signed: _____   Date: _____

7 A WAY OF WORKING . . . WITH TEACHERS

Our way of working with teachers is exactly parallel to student-centred learning with kids. It's about teachers moving towards the realisation of their full potential. This means empowering them to dissolve the constraints, both internal and external, which keep them stuck and de-skilled, and cynical.

Our basic assumptions and principles about learning remain the same for all ages. In this chapter we want to show how we would transfer them to the world of professional development. Teachers, like everyone else, are blessed with a natural desire to learn and grow; the effects of their own upbringing and studenthood leave them with the same varying degrees of readiness to learn as any group of students would have.

Malcolm Knowles makes five assumptions about adult learners:

1 Adults are motivated to learn as they develop needs and interests that learning will satisfy.
2 Adult orientation to learning is life- or work-centred.
3 Experience is the richest source for adult learning.
4 Adults have a deep need to be self-directing.
5 Individual differences among adult learners increase with age and experience.

(Knowles, 1978)

We invite you to compare this list with our own principles and assumptions in Chapter 2.

In the following section we unwrap some negative points about staff development. We don't want you to think we are indulging in *criticism* of our colleagues. We want to describe some of the factors which sabotage staff development, often making it a joyless chore, rather than an exciting challenge.

Everyone has the twin drives to learn and grow on the one hand, and to resist change on the other. But it seems that many teachers have unique and special resistances, arising out of their particular professional culture.

Forced to learn ... difficult to teach

The work people do leaves its mark on them. One effect of this is that teachers become bad learners. They stop listening and exploring, so teachers are difficult to teach ... Every teacher finds his own way of coping within a very circumscribed set of objectives. He sticks to what he can do adequately, and avoids what is new. Innovations are instinctively treated as suspect, especially if they involve any departure from routine, or require close cooperation with colleagues. It's a conservative policy of survival.

(Hargreaves, 1978)

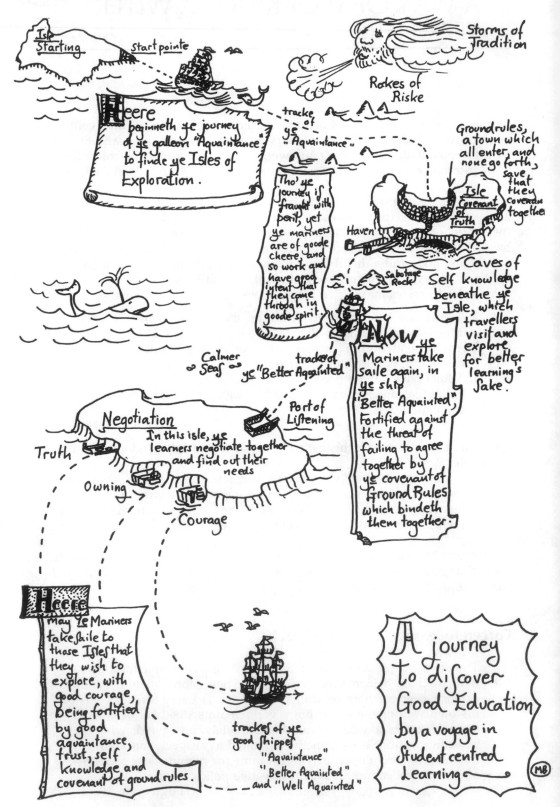

Isle Starting

Start pointe

Storms of Tradition

Rokes of Riske

tracke of ye "Aquaintance"

Heere beginneth ye journey of ye galleon "Aquaintance" to finde ye Isles of Exploration.

Groundrules, a town which all enter, and none go forth, save that they covenant together

Isle Covenant of Truth

Tho' ye journey is fraught with peril, yet ye mariners are of goode cheere, and so work and have good intent that they come through in goode spirit.

Haven

Sabotage Rock

Caves of Self knowledge beneathe ye Isle, which travellers visit and explore for better learnings sake.

Calmer Seas

tracke of ye "Better Aqqainted"

Now ye Mariners take saile again, in ye ship "Better Aquainted", Fortified against the threat of failing to agree together by ye covenant of Ground Rules which bindeth them together.

Port of Listening

Negotiation In this isle, ye learners negotiate together and find out their needs

Truth

Owning

Courage

Heere May ye Mariners take saile to those Isles that they wish to explore, with good courage, being fortified by good aquaintance, trust, self knowledge and covenant of ground rules.

trackes of ye good shippes "Aquaintance" "Better Aquainted" and "Well Aquainted"

A journey to discover Good Education by a voyage in Student centred Learning

MB

Professional trainers, who may actually love their job of working with teachers, often tell us in their own words exactly what Hargreaves says above: that some teachers are difficult to teach, resistant to change, and to anything that will cause them more work (understandably!). We talk about disaffected students who 'don't want to know', but many teachers *know that they already know* and so, in order to know something different, would have to think that they were wrong before. Some even think that they have nothing left to learn. Many teachers find it especially difficult to modify their thinking, when the person encouraging them to do so is younger, less qualified, newer or of lower status than they are.

Through no fault of their own, and due mostly to shifts of policy and reshuffles of the powerful, teachers are constantly being judged, scrutinised, criticised, often in a very public way through unsupportive media. Then *we* come along and ask them to take risks on the understanding that there are no right or wrong answers and that mistakes are 'positive growth points', not failures. No wonder they find this a difficult leap of the imagination!

The climate of a particular school, or even a department within a school, can have a profound effect on teachers' readiness to engage in professional development. In some places, it feels very dangerous to be a keen teacher, never mind a learning teacher. In other schools, of course, the climate stimulates growth; if it's ok to make mistakes, and to turn them into action points, knowing that you can depend on the support of your colleagues, then the natural desires for personal and professional advancement can bubble through.

The system at large does *not* usually work in a way which promotes natural expansion . . . it creates, instead, the energy drain, time pressures, professional paranoia, stress, and isolation. It would be a massive job to overhaul the whole system and eliminate all of those factors, though individual schools can do a lot to reverse the negative trends within themselves.

There is absolutely nothing to stop us from doing with our colleagues exactly what we recommend doing with our students: acknowledging *their* ownership of *their* learning. All too often teachers (like students) have not planned, or chosen, or recognised a need for the learning they are expected to undertake. They have not asked for it and so have a very hard time owning it.

'Compulsion' and 'imposition' are the bitterest complaints we hear from teachers as we go about our work in schools. For example, the deep resentment towards Directed Time (organised in a high-handed way and monitored strictly in some schools) comes across strongly. In one school recently, at the beginning of a participatory management initiative, colleagues unanimously said that they have done much less for the school *since* the introduction of Directed Time than they ever did before. This does not seem to be uncommon; when human nature is told to do something, it tends to do the minimum required. We find that teachers are crying out to be trusted; their self-esteem, and consequently their personal health and professional effectiveness depend on it.

To the mistrust of Directed Time, is added the loss of negotiating rights, the erosion of teachers' pay, the increase of hierarchical distances within schools, the relocation of power to Governors and parents, and a standardised curriculum which makes all the big decisions for teachers and which, by implication, reduces them to minor technicians. Then we ask colleagues to bear the ignominy of compulsory and prescriptive INSET.

We wanted to draw another continuum, but it wouldn't fit on the page. Here is an upside-down ladder instead:

No ownership: INSET is planned, organised, and done to the teachers by someone else.

Increased consultation: the parameters are drawn by someone else, teachers are consulted about details. Their opinions are taken into account.

Real participation: teachers are truly involved in (at least some of the) decision-making.

Almost there (if it's done well!): teachers are asked to identify their needs, so that decisions can be made about provision.

Full ownership: nothing happens until teachers initiate the process.

The bottom (or inverted top) of the ladder may seem like a very risky position to be in as a Head or Trainer. Teachers may choose not to undertake development. We know many senior managers who would say, 'But what am I going to do about the ineffective Mr Slow? He simply would never choose any staff development at all, and he needs it most.' And 'How am I going to ensure that the new policy or the new system is introduced?' And, 'What about all the compulsory initiatives which people are paid to come in and establish? They might not happen!'

We agree. Handing over ownership is risky, and there may well be a stage in which teachers over-exercise their right not to participate. But, in the classroom, this is usually just a phase that learners go through, and we believe that the same principle applies to staff-learners. More importantly, teachers who don't want to learn can't be forced to learn. Even if they are forced to go through the motions, they can become as skilful at sabotaging as the most recalcitrant students. So, other positions on the ladder are just as risky, but less obviously so. If the training has been provided, and the teachers haven't learned, then the organisers can wash their hands and blame the failure on the teachers who were unreceptive. It's definitely *their* fault; we did our best for them.

Often, staff development is approached from a position which is not client-centred. In many cases a Head or Senior Management Team will have a clear idea of the changes they want to see in the school, or the changes expected of the school. It is so easy, with the best interests of the school and their colleagues at heart, to become dogmatic or manipulative in pursuit of these objectives.

Teacher Day behaviour exemplifies these points. We've often experienced being invited as trainers to lead a Teacher Day. The Head or INSET

Coordinator is the only person who has consulted with us beforehand. We arrive, and only a few seem pleased to see us or eager to work with us. Most, it seems, would rather be doing something else; but the only person who is allowed to leave the room (and often does) is the Head who is 'too busy' to attend. So we begin, and the staff sit as far back from us as they can; some even take out their marking or crossword and proceed to chat in the back row. They amuse themselves by challenging us (often quite rudely), telling us '*It can't be done*... Well OK, it could be done in drama but not in English — in English but not in science, — in science but not in mathematics...'

Ironically enough, we can see exactly why they feel this way. We're not criticising our colleagues; it's no wonder that they dislike 'legislated learning'. We're making a universal point about motivation. The missing ingredient in most required training is consultation with the learners. To make matters worse, it seems as though the trend will be to increase this sort of statutory training, in order to ensure that the National Curriculum and its attendant issues are understood and implemented.

At the time of writing, training priorities are, in fact, dominated by the implementation of the National Curriculum. 'Needs' are determined by the Department of Education and Science (National Priority Areas) and local politicians (Locally-Defined Needs). As training grants are attached to these priorities, and delivery is carefully monitored, there seems to be very little room for manoeuvre as LEAs interpret the requirements and turn them into strategies.

So, 'Attainment Targets' for staff development are drawn up and, as with all official prescriptions, there are risks and penalties for not following them. Most teachers will be motivated to train because of the 'exam' in the form of their students' results and school reviews against performance indicators.

On one level, we want to resist this degree of prescription, simply because we think it doesn't work. In many cases the approach to training seems to be constructed on the non-trusting Theory X (McGregor, 1960) assumptions and a transmission model of teaching and dissemination forced by tight timetables and deadlines. It is devaluing and narrow.

A transmission model of staff development may be appropriate for certain types of learning, such as the speedy acquisition of technical information. However, most professional development is highly charged emotionally; it requires shifts of attitude or principle and involves risks and anxieties. In the most successful examples of teachers' learning, the ever-present affective dimension is understood, given space and valued. The whole person of the teacher is involved. Without attention to the emotions of learning, and consequently the quality of the learning climate and support, teachers are more likely to appear apathetic and disaffected.

On another level, we refuse to be defeated or depressed by the situation. Even when ownership is initially in the hands of politicians and officers, we want to find the most teacher-centred way of providing the training which other people require of us. Again we suggest a parallel with the National Curriculum for students and the way in which teachers might support them in taking ownership of it. Advisors, Heads and Professional Trainers can work together to share the training requirements and all related information with teachers, and to involve them in the planning, organisation, implementation and evaluation of their professional development programmes. Also, the processes used in the actual 'delivery' of the agreed training make all the difference. Facilitation skills at the ready!

A staff-centred model

If we were free to apply client-centred principles to staff development, we would adopt the following approach. Our model has three stages; we will unpack each of them in turn:

1 Ask colleagues what they want and need, as a natural part of continuous, formative self-appraisal with peer support.
2 Encourage staff to believe in their individual and collective resource and power; together they could meet many of their own training needs.
3 Provide the desired external resources.

1 Ask them what they want and need

Please don't think that we think this is simple! Sometimes colleagues don't have a full knowledge of what is available, and sometimes they are reluctant to take sufficient time to think about what they really do want. It is not a question to be addressed quickly, or lightly; it needs careful consideration.

Even more fundamentally, many 'needs identification' exercises make an assumption that teachers are open for learning in the first place, that they experience motivation for professional development; in many cases a good deal of groundwork would have to be done before we reached the point of teachers *wanting* to know what they want.

We recommend the same approach that we advocate for students in the classroom, which is: first, build a safe and positive climate.

To do this:

- establish and model open communication, *and act on it*;
- deliberately encourage the giving and receiving of negative and positive feedback, especially in areas which until now have been taboo;
- get people together to solve problems, and maximise creativity by sharing ideas;
- do away with judgements, and find ways of breaking the deeply-rooted game of approval and disapproval. This will mean that people in authority learn the difference between approval and Unconditional Positive Regard;
- make participation optional . . . it's OK *not* to want to learn;
- maintain consistent acceptance of the person (even if not always of their behaviour);
- always make it possible for a person to change her mind, without losing face;
- uphold everyone's right to have access to all information which has relevance to the lives of the teachers;
- *no secrecy and no manipulation!*
- introduce the process of consistent, formative, self-appraisal with peer support.

What we've just done is to describe the conditions in which learners of any age and experience are most likely to want to learn and develop. When these conditions exist, *asking them* is likely to evoke a creative response. Usually, we have found, the question is asked too early, before the conditions have been made safe.

No-one can take away teachers' inherent responsibility for their own learning. We see it as a primary objective in the realm of staff development to maintain a learning climate which encourages openness, mistake-making, risk-taking, exploration, creativity, fun. This message is particularly addressed to those with power in education . . . the climate depends, to a large extent, on your management style. So, we will continue working with those who, with integrity and optimism, are campaigning to change the structures, and the values which underpin them.

If we are in a situation where there is no prescribed training, and priorities can genuinely be determined by the teachers themselves, how do we proceed from the stage where teachers know *that* they want to learn? How do we enable them to sort out *what* and *how* they want to learn?

We would want to establish two ongoing processes:

I Self-appraisal with peer support

We are aware that there will soon be a national framework for teacher appraisal. We want to make any system work in as humanistic a way as possible, and take the principle of self-assessment, supported by peer-feedback, as far as it will go.

In an ideal setting, without an externally-designed system, this is how we would see teacher-centred appraisal working:

First, we would have to agree that time out for self-appraisal for teachers is time well spent, in terms of personal and professional growth. It would have to be given high priority amongst all the other activities that teachers do beyond the teaching day with students.

You could have a mutually accepted partner, with whom you'd meet once a week, preferably when all the other partners meet as well. We would suggest Monday morning, first thing before school; this would give the discussion a very formative feel as it happened at the threshold of a new week.

You could both think back about negative and positive experiences the week before, and what's been on your mind over the weekend, and then begin to look forward and talk about what is worrying and what is exciting about the coming week's teaching. Both teachers would be practising active listening: neither partner is meant to be judging or making assessments about the colleague's performance. You would each be acting as a colleague-counsellor.

Susan Knight, Adult Learning Consultant in Sydney, extols the virtue of this sort of professional co-counselling:

> The attraction of co-counselling was that it offered me the chance of learning to assist other people in personal exploration and to pursue my own in a continuing reciprocal process whereby I could meet as often as I liked with another co-counsellor and spend half the time giving them my attention and half the time using their attention for whatever I wanted to work on...the particular technique which is relevant here is the simplest of all, that of placing all one's attention and awareness at the disposal of another person, listening with interest and appreciation without interupting or engaging in discussion. This is known as giving free attention. It sounds like a very simple process, and it is, but it is also surprisingly powerful...
>
> (Knight, 1985)

The talking could lead to action, so that once a problem was identified, the two could plan together how to solve it; so, the reflecting turns to problem-solving and planning. You and your partner could look for ways of working together, for example collaborative teaching, or any number of creative ways in which you could come to help each other.

As time goes on, perhaps you could bring in videos of yourselves teaching, and share your critique of them. There would be many other ways of providing feedback for each other, for example through structured lesson observation, through swapping places, through role-play... and assisting each other in making sense of it. Naturally, feedback from students will be an important source of data too.

Out of these meetings a list of self-appraisal issues, or personal criteria could emerge, and from them personal targets could be set at regular intervals. We recommend that a journal or some other documentation be kept which could become part of a teacher's personal Record of Achievement.

The keys to these meetings are: they're regular, informal, and formative. All sorts of outcomes could arise from them...

Some suggestions for keeping staff development journals
(These are for when you can't think what to write in your journal, but, we want to point out that these ideas can also be used with students.)

1 If you had a giant pair of scissors, what would you want to cut out of today?
2 Write feeling paragraphs, starting with: *I feel excited about* ....
    I feel happy about ....
    I feel angry about ....
    and all the rest
3 Draw a picture using stick figures, showing you and your students in relation to each other.
4 Draw stick figures showing the staffroom with some colleagues in it, and show where you belong in that picture. Write about how you feel about that picture.
5 Visualise the National Curriculum as an animal, and draw a picture of it.

A Case Study
This is Paul telling a true story from his days as a Staff Development Tutor. We see this as a client-centred attempt at supporting a colleague's self-assessment, which is just one example of the various ways in which teacher-partners could help each other:

A head of an art department asked one of the art teachers if she would like to work with me, and she agreed, not knowing what would come out of it. It was the first time she had ever had a fellow professional in her classroom. She was nervous about that, afraid that I would turn out to be judgemental, and that I would be telling her how things ought to be done. In particular, I think she was concerned that I would try to change her teaching style.

So the first job was to relax, and spend time establishing a trusting relationship, which in practical terms meant not intefering with her lesson planning and style. I simply worked alongside her, rolling up my sleeves and joining in the teaching that she was leading. Also, we spent time just chatting about everyday things. After a few lessons, we began to talk about the lesson, in a completely non-technical, and certainly non-judgemental way. We allowed the informal de-brief to take its own course, and while we were feeding back some rough comments to each other, we began to see some kind of shape. Together, we began to see a series of balances in her work, for example, between challenging students and supporting them, between instructing in technique and leaving students free to make their own decisions. I kept checking out that the teacher felt OK about what was being said. We established a kind of framework within which the teacher was beginning to see a pattern to her own teaching behaviour.

She wanted to look more closely at her own style, to identify her strengths, and points for improvement more accurately. Now there was no pressure, and she knew that she could call a halt at any time, and she could do whatever she wished with any material or ideas that came out of our work.

We decided that a video camera was the obvious tool to use. She said that she would supply the tape, so that it would really be hers. We filmed a lesson, and she knew that she could erase the tape as soon as she looked at it at home. She watched it, and was keen, the next day, to tell me about what she had discovered: 'Now I know what I'm doing wrong!'

I had two jobs to do: listen actively while she told me her weak points, and then ask her what she had noticed herself doing *well* in the lesson. She was just as clear in understanding her strengths, just more reluctant to talk about them . . .

We now know that we're going to preserve what she is doing well, but the 'What I'm doing wrong' has turned into 'Let's take a closer look'. Increased confidence, and a belief in teacher-partnerships has led this teacher to launch out and work with another colleague on a weekly basis in the same way that I have worked with her.'

If a pair of teachers could work together to create a non-threatening, mutual, self-appraising relationship, then the discoveries could feed into the wider school. A department, or a year group, or some other sub-grouping of the staff, could then meet, say, half-termly and colleagues could be invited to share their single most important growing point over the past month.

Since part of the function of a client-centred senior manager is to know the staff well, and keep in touch with their learning, there would be some way for him to meet with individuals and be brought up to date with their achievements and plans; the journal could contribute to this process, if there were no threat attached. Managers might make appointments to see each teacher.

These appraisal methods would build a very client-centred source of identified needs for staff development, which would come from the hearts and minds of the teachers themselves. All individual needs could be collected, and could then be offered back to the staff so that decisions could be made about corporate needs.

Our model is not entirely dissimilar from the original DES guidelines; it includes many of the same elements. However, in consulting with teachers who are struggling to deal with many new initiatives, the overwhelming opinion seems to be that schools *must* establish appraisal systems which involve full ownership and designing by staff, which will work effectively to promote professional and personal development, and which will continue to function as they assimilate new government directives. Educators seem to agree wholeheartedly with us, that the key issue is *how* to take the first steps in building an atmosphere of trust and consultation throughout the entire staff, so that appraisal is non-threatening and beneficial.

2 Widening horizons

We also have a job to do in opening new doors for teachers, so that they can see fresh and creative ways of meeting those identified training needs. Initially, this may mean providing teachers with new visions of what is possible, so that they don't remain limited by their previous experience. Some ways of doing this might be . . .

1 Teachers team up in pairs or small groups to create a new sort of lesson, which is then filmed or videoed. For instance, the advisory teacher for Drama and the biology teacher might plan a module and teach it together.
2 Primary teachers swap places with colleagues in a secondary school for a day.
3 The timetable is suspended for a day, and colleagues are asked to work in· small teams to create an integrated experience for a cross-age group of students.
4 Any colleague could do a series of book or resource reviews in staff meetings. The materials, suggesting fresh ideas and describing divergent practice, could then be left on display for a while.
5 Use a mandatory training day to go on a 'classroom crawl'. Teachers in groups move round to each other's classrooms, pausing in each one while an example of recent work is explained and discussed.
6 Hold semi-social events where the staff members from two or more schools get together to share experiences and ideas informally.
7 Have a party at the teachers' centre . . . invite a few schools to show films, share ideas, ask questions, solve problems.
8 Have teachers choose someone to swap with (a colleague from another discipline), so that they have a new experience of teaching an unfamiliar subject.
9 Ask the students to say what they think their teachers could learn about.
10 An advisory teacher team could go into a school, or to a staff meeting, and do a show (rather than the usual talk) about all they can offer.
11 The team could set up and leave an exhibition, with a slide show and videos and books and display boards . . . showing what they could offer to teachers.

The two processes which we have just described and which are closely intertwined (self-appraisal and widening horizons)—combine to bring about the desired result. If a person is enabled to take a clear look in the mirror, and a good look at what's possible, then we can trust that personal priorities for professional development will emerge, naturally.

2 Encourage colleagues to believe in their individual and collective resource and power

Once (at long last) the collective personal priorities have been established, it often turns out that the required resources are right there within the staff. What's needed is a safe environment where people feel free to offer their expertise, and are empowered and encouraged to do so. (If staff members believed in themselves, and in their colleagues, this could mean that we staff development people would be out of a job, so please don't take the above paragraph too seriously!)

Empowerment for self-development, we argue, has two main components: raising teachers' self-esteem, and putting colleagues in closer touch with each other.

These could be achieved, for example, by . . .

- everyone getting into the habit of noticing and commenting on good practice;
- ensuring that any negative feedback is accompanied by practical suggestions for improvement;
- senior colleagues in the school keeping in close touch with classroom practice, and therefore valuing it;
- participatory management; consultation in all decisions that affect them.

Staff may come together through voluntary support groups focusing on particular interests, or through task groups in Directed Time (and, naturally, we suggest that teachers are trusted to use and account for their time without being directed) which teachers select from a menu. Particular experience and expertise within the school can be shared on mandatory training days. Reading, writing, even teaching for each other are again ways of sharing expertise in the DIY INSET programme.

3 Call on external expertise

This happens with the teachers still in control of the programme, after definite needs are identified. If the first two steps have already been done properly, then this stage is worth much more in terms of eagerness and cooperative learning, than if the unfortunate external agents are brought in too early.

Holistic staff development

Whatever specific needs and wants they express, we believe that all teachers benefit from an holistic experience of 'development'. For schools to be healthy places for children to grow in, teachers have to be healthy people to enable that growth. Likewise, managers have to be healthy, so do staff development providers . . . and so on through all the levels of the system. In other words, we need *pastoral care for everyone*.

Here is our colleague with his teaching practice notes again:

Before the teaching practice started, I had expected to do a little work each evening . . . in the event I did none. I was simply, no, not simply, rather strangely, exhausted. Within two or three days I was quite self-consciously spending my evenings in my own recreation . . . I came to think quite clearly that the best preparation I could make for the next day was to make sure that I was at my best as a person. So, preparation became not so much the wrapping up of the next parcel to hand out, but rather something more akin to the preening of a large bird after a storm — but even that may be misunderstood, because popularly, and wrongly, preening is understood in terms of appearance and narcissism, rather than of pre-flight maintenance.   (David Lambourn)

Our thesis is that:

Pastoral care for $\implies$ Natural personal growth $\implies$ Natural professional
teachers   development

Teachers are faced, daily, with the complexities of personality and potential
in dozens of students from diverse backgrounds and at widely differing
stages of emotional and mental growth. If they are not at peace with
themselves, in a state of self-awareness and high self-esteem, they can have
very little to give to others. All of us, at times, are impatient, sarcastic,
upset, dismissive, unsympathetic, accusing, blaming, angry, cynical.

So, all of us *need* to be

- aware of our own negativity when it is there;
- able to deal with it effectively;
- on the receiving end of positive attention and caring, so that we ourselves
  can thrive, and in turn enable those around us to grow.

We are trying to be positive here, but our experience is that very little of this
kind of nurturing attention is given to teachers in schools. Teachers on our
courses repeatedly tell us, 'But we can't keep giving out that kind of
unconditional regard to students in our classes, when we don't receive it
ourselves'.

Some teachers are able to be replenished and nourished in their personal
lives outside of school, and so can exist in a barren school climate. Others
believe that they can keep their personal lives, outside, separate from their
professional existence. But this takes its toll... it is very demanding and
draining to keep up, all day, the pretence that everything is OK; but deep
down, the personal issues subtly creep into behaviour and well-being at
school. Still others have life circumstances outside school, which do not
support or sustain them, and so are not being cared for on any level. We
strongly believe that the heart of staff development is to provide some of
this sustenance for teachers.

The table on the next page shows the conditions in school which either
dehumanise or enhance teachers.

We would be happy to see schools providing counselling for anyone in
the school who wanted it, not just for the most disturbed of the students. In
some other places and professions, the concept of personal counselling for
staff is already acceptable. In Western Australia, for example:

> The creation of the new employee assistance program follows
> complaints from the State School Teachers' Union about the lack
> of a counselling service for teachers. In announcing the plans, the
> Minister for Education, Dr Lawrence, said they would assist
> employees who sought help voluntarily.
>
> 'They are assured of confidential and compassionate assistance
> from a team of skilled professionals', she said. The government

Unhealthy (dehumanising)	Healthy (enhancing)
lack of consultation	participatory management
paper communication	close interpersonal communication
'professional' norms which inhibit personal disclosure	human interest and contact
hurry and worry	spacious timetable and relaxed atmosphere
demand to enforce petty rules and regulations	strong school-wide commitment to minimum ground rules
degrading and neglected surroundings	care for people's comfort and well-being
mean amenities, like hard and non-absorbent toilet paper	generous provision (this does not mean extravagance . . . it is a sound investment)
rigid hierarchies	open access
appraisal which features superior judgement	self- and negotiated appraisal
low value placed on interpersonal skills	pre- and in-service training which emphasises positive human interaction
constraining and stifling predetermined curriculum	creative and open curriculum

recognises that teaching is a demanding, often stressful, job. The Ministry relies on teachers working at full capacity, yet they have no specialised support.'

Dr Lawrence said the extra support would also benefit students by improving teacher effectiveness, which could be hampered by personal problems.   (*The Western Australian*, December 27, 1988)

And in this country, we were surprised by the advertisement in the *Guardian* shown opposite.

Whether staff development is school-based or provided through central courses, it is incomplete if it does not pay attention to the whole person of the teacher, and contribute to the enhancement of the whole school climate. Often, those who provide 'training', or who encourage it in the school, are either unable or unwilling to be aware of this omission, or are resisting the personal or institutional changes which would be necessary. They may have major investments in status or tradition, in the structures which they have always known, which are cherished and very hard to move away from; thus

Specialist Personal Counselling

c£18,000
Investing in people–
a major Post Office initiative

A revolutionary new approach to caring for people at work is taking shape at the Post Office which we believe could set the scene of occupational health in the 21st Century.

We are about to embark on a 3-year pilot project to assess the value of in-house psychological counselling for staff at all levels, with a view to future expansion.

We are looking for two highly experienced and qualified behavioural scientists to initiate the project, with the professional confidence to define parameters and establish the importance of the service throughout the business.

A significant amount of your time will be spent in practical counselling — on the personal and work-related problems of staff. You will be expected to build a network of influential contacts both within the Post Office and with specialist "caring" organisations outside.

Naturally, we would expect you to be fully professionally qualified and preferably with at least 3 to 5 years experience including a good background in personal counselling and an understanding of behaviour in organisations. Your academic background will include a qualification in the behavioural sciences.

One Counsellor will be based in Leeds, the other in Manchester and both appointments will be for an initial period of 3 years. Salary will be in the range £16,100–£19,800.

An application form and further details are available from Jim Waterhouse, Personnel Controller, Royal Mail House, 29 Wellington Street, Leeds LS1 1DA — tel Leeds (0532) 447201. Please quote ref TG. If there is some aspect of this project which you would like to explore before applying, please telephone Professor Cary L Cooper of UMIST on 061-236 3311 ext. 2272, who is advising us on the project and on these appointments. Interviews will be held in June.

The Post Office is an Equal Opportunities employer.

Our business is your future

the Achilles' heel in the school, caused at least partially by teacher impoverishment, is made weaker still.

A golden rule for us is that

Pastoral care and personal growth must be included in any programme of staff development.

A communal aspect to the programme would so greatly enhance development, that we regard it as essential. A group experience, well facilitated, allows people to experience what is possible when the conditions are right. And it can go a long way to make up for the often-missing nourishment.

From a harrassed teacher in Birmingham:

> 'If the system which is now being introduced within the classroom (SCL) were also applied to teaching staff within our schools, then this country would have an education system second to none throughout the rest of the world.'
>
> (Joy Smith, 1988)

School-based support

We are firmly convinced of the benefit of combining training which takes place away from the school with support in the school — at the colleague's personal chalk face, where the risks are real and the stakes are high. Here are some suggestions, based on our experiences, for how a client-centred trainer or support teacher might work with classroom teachers in a school.

1 It might be possible for trainers or advisory teachers to become attached to a school, as members of staff, and have their own classes. They would be timetabled in, as additions to the regular, established teachers. They would work in their own rooms, and anyone could be free to come and visit, observe, or participate. If we were doing this, our classes would be conducted in a student-centred manner throughout, and we would be modelling the new ideas. If the trainer were extra to staffing establishment, there would be some room to experiment, for teachers to meet together, to plan and de-brief.

This approach makes a resource available, and leaves responsibility for training and development with the teachers. No-one is being forced by the Head or anyone else to engage in any training he doesn't feel is appropriate for him, but the provision is there for anyone who wants it. This is a come-and-get-it rather than a go-and-give-it approach.

Management would have the responsibility for enabling staff to visit our classes. So, this means that they would have to give the project high status in the school's overall priorities.

As the classes would be our own, we wouldn't have to worry (as much as when we work in other people's classrooms) about treading on colleagues' toes, or offending other teachers by working with their classes in a way they're not used to. It's non-threatening, and teachers who want some benefit from our work can watch or participate in whatever way they prefer and take away with them whatever they experience.

2 A second approach would be to work alongside colleagues in their own classrooms with their regular classes. Initially, the trainer and the colleague would need to establish their relationship, so that a degree of trust and openness are quickly achieved. Of course, to many colleagues, the idea of having someone in the classroom with them is new. Some may have had negative experiences of classroom visitation, and in any case the vast majority of teachers were brought up through an education system which valued individualism and competition, rather than group work and co-operation. So the trainer must be sure to communicate a non-judgemental, non-interfering, utterly supportive intention. Even so, it may take a leap of faith on the part of the teacher, and an early experience of the partnership as productive and non-threatening, before the relationship feels secure.

Once underway, such collaborative teaching requires regular time for planning and debriefing. Frequent talking keeps the partnership healthy, ensures that both partners know what's going on in the classroom, and provides an opportunity to reflect on matters beyond the scope of the target lesson.

Co-operation is practised (and, incidentally, modelled to the students) with the teacher contributing ideas on an equal footing with the trainer. Naturally, the classroom load is shared, as is the evaluation. Through the processes of planning and reflecting together, themes, underlying principles and all kinds of other lessons for the teacher (and the trainer) begin to emerge. All the time the client-centred trainer is helping the colleague to:

- make sense of the experience;
- articulate feelings and ideas;
- recognise her own practical theory;
- think laterally and creatively;
- identify alternatives;
- take risks;

- evaluate herself, taking account of feedback from various sources including students, colleagues and the trainer;
- view mistakes and weaknesses in a positive light, as learning points;
- make use of resources available to her... including herself!
- periodically review her learning to date, and if appropriate set a new direction for the future.

Professor Jean Rudduck stresses the value of classroom support in helping teachers to see through the familiar and analyse what's behind it. When teachers look at their classrooms on their own they tend to 'reconstruct them in their own image', and the classroom supporter brings the 'eyes of the stranger' (Lecture, December 11, 1987).

By the way, we have found that laying on demonstration lessons, led by the support teacher and observed by the classroom colleague, can be very tricky. If the lesson is a success, especially with a 'difficult' class, it can leave their teacher feeling failed, resentful and definitely unsupported, and the advisory teacher can have a hard time living up to the reputation. So, demos have to be approached with a good deal of understanding and preparation. When done appropriately, they provide an opportunity to model behaviours and can be an effective short-cut to understanding an idea. In the past we've often found them to be most productive as training instruments when they've not worked too well! Then it's time to show how mistakes can be treated as positive learning points.

There is as much to learn from the trainer's client-centred behaviour with the teacher, as from her behaviour with the class. There needs to be enough time, regularly, to debrief both.

As you might have guessed, we assume that this relationship would be founded on open self-nomination: strictly volunteers only. Forced or manipulated involvement in a development programme does not work. Imagine this conversation with a Head Teacher:

Head   So, as a Head, what am I supposed to do with teachers that desperately need training but won't admit it.
Trainer Don't give them any.
Head   WHAT??!! Just let them go on ruining my school, damaging my kids, upsetting my parents?
Trainer How successful have you been in changing their ways up to now?
Head   (After long pause for thought, several Harummpphs and a growl): Hardly at all.
Trainer (Sweetly smiling) Well then, neither will we be ... (Pause for reflection). However, we can keep talking to your staff, working and sharing with them, and hope that after a while, when they come to trust us and see the good results of what we're doing, they might just change their minds and want to give it a try.

We suggest that the trainer works with a group of teachers in each school, so that a mini-Core Group can be formed which enables support to be given and received, and, through reflection together, the experiences of the classroom to be turned into learning. Encouraging links with other schools —exchanging classes, releasing colleagues to go and work alongside their opposite number for a day, joint training and social events—are all valuable. The Core Group could then continue as a resource after the trainer has left.

The Group could work out a plan of open door classrooms, after school training sessions, lunchtime discussion groups, offers to go into other people's lessons, or just the informal exchange of ideas in the staffroom. But we would want the responsibility to make use of these available resources to lie with the other staff members.

We recommend that networks be allowed to grow naturally and organically, and that they are based on motivation and interest, rather than the pre-planning of other people's learning in the name of efficiency and good management. What managers do need to prepare is a framework of opportunity, in addition to the provision of adequate resources, flexibility, and status—and above all their own involvement in the changes along with everyone else.

The training partnership

The nature of an effective relationship between the professional trainer and the teacher (or teachers) is akin to that of a client-centred counsellor with his client. All the facilitation skills and qualities described in Chapter 5 are required ... so, you'll be relieved to hear, we're not going to repeat ourselves and go into detail here. The relationship is characterised by warm personal regard, acceptance, listening, and the very subtle skill of following in the client's footsteps, rather than charging ahead and choosing the direction. All of this has the goal of enhancing the self-esteem of the learner, so that learning continues to be possible.

Gunnar Handal and Per Lauvas recognise the essence of the approach we're describing:

> ... counselling is a form of training in which the learner is placed in focus. The counsellor cannot limit his task to the transmission of his own understanding but must take the skills, knowledge and values of the learner as the point of departure.
>
> Counselling is also characterised by close and direct contact between supervisor and learner. In this respect, it provides a favourable environment for learning.
>
> (Handal and Lauvas, 1987)

We recommend that the partnership be based on a negotiated contract with the colleague(s), which might include:

- shared, explicit objectives
- confidentiality
- clear understanding of roles, responsibilities, and expectations
- firm agreements as to time and structure
- commitment to safeguarding the time for planning and evaluating together
- an agreement to review periodically
- joint contributions to reports

The contract is intended to build trust. We suggest that other features of the trusting relationship include:

- keeping agreements
- communicating honestly, even about mistakes and problems (Otherwise, positive feedback is devalued.)
- getting stuck in, in the classroom
- humour
- the trainer's fallibility
- being able to make mistakes (all of you)
- sharing in dilemmas, rather than having the right answers
- credibility achieved through displayed competence

There is, of course, always the possibility of creating a dependent relationship, so that the teacher wants to cling on at the end of the contracted time. But if we are being truly student-centred, we are enabling independence and responsibility, and not colluding in the dependence. This is not to say that neither one might be sad when the relationship of working together comes to an end; there is a difference between dependence, and sadness at parting.

One piece of feedback that often comes back to us is that teachers, trying a new style or method, often go through a phase where they feel de-skilled. They have an initial experience with the new style, but are not yet fully competent in it; yet they are already dissatisfied with their old ways ... so, for a while, they feel they have nothing.

In the graph on the following page we've adapted an idea from Pfeiffer and Jones:

Figure 7.4

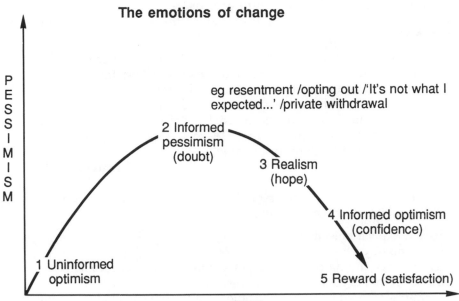

The graph is self-explanatory — we hope — and the phase of informed pessimism, when the teacher has discovered all the things than can go wrong, is where the trainer has to provide the most support, and where she will need to call on her interpersonal skills. The trainer can't afford to be pessimistic herself; she will have the job of enabling Humpty Dumpty to put himself back together again. When the stage of informed optimism has begun, it is also the time to move towards independence, building in what some call 'planned termination'.

A client-centred approach considers colleagues to be responsible for their own learning; they can really learn to take ownership and responsibility only by having the experience of taking it. The learning may be richer, more permanent, more relevant, as people discover it *for themselves*, and do it *for themselves*. It makes all learning *first hand*. Sometimes the skill of the facilitator is about knowing when to step in and help, when to intervene or not. Sometimes people need to experience discomfort, frustration, longing to be rescued, wanting the theory explained, dying to be told what to do, experiencing impatience, anger, even some fear, before they finally take on responsibility for themselves.

Whole-school change

We have just been talking about the development of individual teachers and small groups. If the culture or practice of a *whole* institution is to change, new methods must be introduced at all levels. Top-down innovation doesn't work because it isn't owned by those below; bottom-up innovation doesn't work because it is not owned by those above. Change cannot be forced in either direction, even though both groups often go around believing they can make it happen. Both managers and workers feel that they can force change on the other, and then what happens is blocks, blaming, resentment; this can then turn into confrontation, disillusionment, and cynicism. An irresistible force meets an immoveable object.

Let's describe two examples of the kinds of situations which we encounter regularly.

Example A

Several teachers in a department have been on a course, and have come back feeling very enthusiastic. They work in their own classrooms, trying things out, making mistakes, learning, coming on follow-up days, back to school, try a few more ideas... Other staff have begun to notice and take interest, perhaps go on some courses themselves. Now we arrive at a time when, unless something happens in the upper echelons, we run into a stone wall.

At this point, we suggest, managers of all ranks must become involved, and by that we mean personally committed, or nothing much will change in the rest of the school.

Example B

In this case, the Head, for whatever reason, has decided, in his wisdom, that the school must change, throughout, in some way. Increasingly, one of the ways this might happen is through reviews of effectiveness measured against performance indicators, or through inspections of one sort or another. Motivation for whole-school change might come from Governors and parents, exercising their new powers, and thus creating a new set of pressure points.

The Head's Leap

Now we come upon a phenomenon which causes great resentment: the case of some senior managers who say that the school must change and the teachers must change, but have no intention of changing themselves, nor even the idea that the problem might be anything to do with their management styles or their own limitations.

Trainers or support teachers may then be commissioned to 'Get The Job Done'. The change shall be done unto the teachers, and thence unto the students, none of whom have taken ownership of this initiative. The Head wants to have the staff motivated for this. He blesses the initiative and supports the project to the hilt. *But*, he withdraws himself, being unwilling, unaware, or unconvinced of a requirement for change on his part, and on the part of other senior colleagues. In this case the poor trainer, dangling perilously between the Head and the rest of the staff, ends up being the only one with an investment in the change.

In both cases what is required is true support from the top, which is about senior managers owning that 'I am part of this problem, and its solution'. Without this commitment, and the visible evidence of the process of personal change, the innovation loses status: 'Oh, it's good enough for us, but not for them, so it isn't good enough.' The most effective support that senior colleagues can give is not to praise, to publicly agree with, or even fund the innovation: it is to *do it to themselves*.

When the whole school is being asked to move along the continuum towards student-centred learning, there is a double irony: we have one person autocratically telling other people to be democratic.

Somehow, a process of personal and structural change at all levels has to begin, if the whole school is to change. This usually does not happen unless the very top level sets the example. So, it's a case of saying, 'EVERYONE, let's begin to think about this together... EVERYONE, are we ready to commit to this? .... EVERYONE, hold hands and we'll all put our toes in the water at the same time, one two three...'

A good ideal of preparatory work—thinking, and talking, and achieving common ownership—has to go on before the originally-intended changes begin. Many schools (also LEAs, government bodies, parents and governors), seem to want the final performance without any of the rehearsals. 'It is important to realise that major changes can take 3–5 years from initiation to institutionalisation.' (Weindling, 1988).

In this environment, the carrier of an innovative idea could be enthusiastic teachers, the Head, a Head of Department, a trainer or a parent. And then, as we have already said, comes a very demanding process of explaining, demonstrating (we hate to say it, but 'selling') even arguing, convincing ... until there is commitment from everyone in the school to begin to start to embark on some changes.

People are not usually convinced by talk (nor, unfortunately, by reading books) alone, but by experiencing successful practice, and by understanding the benefit to themselves if they should change. Ideas which could be explored at this stage might include:

1 Getting people to go and see good practice elsewhere in similar circumstances;
2 Experiencing a simulation or role-play of what the change would involve;
3 Asking people to suspend judgement and try the change for a short period of time only, and then assess it;
4 Talking with colleagues who have themselves made the same changes;

5 Encouraging Heads to talk to people whom THEY would consider to be credible authorities on the proposed kinds of changes.

Whatever whole-school change we might consider, whether it is new teaching styles; implementation of a new government initiative; endorsement and ownership by everyone in the school will make the changes more easily begun, and more successfully sustained.

Ours sincerely . . .

We're still holding on to our dream of a school which is entirely populated by learners, and is person-centred to the core. Here, staff development begins the day that staff are appointed, and we appoint only people who see themselves as learners. The question we would ask is, 'What is it that you want to learn for yourself that will enhance you as a person, and, therefore, help you to be a better teacher?' It may take time and reassurance to convince people that we mean this question to be as global as it sounds. We are not just talking about getting better at academic subjects or managing assessments. We mean that we are concerned about the emotional, social, and intellectual fulfilment of our teachers.

So, for instance, if a teacher wishes that she knew how to repair and maintain an automobile, we would encourage her to find some other people with the same interest, call in a good mechanic/teacher, and set up a course in which she and her students could participate.

At our first staff meeting, we would say to all of our staff members, 'We are totally behind you in whatever you need to learn and develop as a person. This school will be much more effective if everyone in it is happy and healthy. We regard this school to be a learning environment for us all; if we're taking care of our own holistic needs, then we're looking after our students at the same time.'

Introduction to the activities

Many of the activities offered in this short collection can be seen as starting points for teacher self-appraisal. They have been devised and trialled to fit with the model of self-assessment-with-peer-support which we've outlined in this chapter. Others have been designed to introduce or deepen teachers' thinking about student-centred learning and its relationship to their values, their practice and the National Curriculum. Some of the exercises can be done in pairs or small groups, although most of them are suitable for whole-staff participation, in staff meetings or on Teacher Days; they have the underlying aim of bringing colleagues together in a positive, constructive and open way.

Moving house

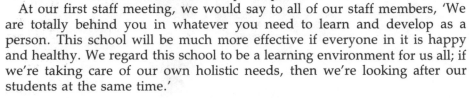

Aims   Raising self-awareness
           Active listening
Materials Plain paper
           Felt pens

Procedure

1 Reflect for two minutes, with eyes closed, on yourself as a teacher using a 'house' analogy:
   - If I were a house, I would:
     Look like....
     Be built of....
     Contain....
2 Pair up and each take turns to be a) the vendor and b) the estate agent. The vendor describes his house whilst the estate agent makes a note in words or sketches of details. The estate agent feeds back, interpreting her notes with particular emphasis given to the 'selling' features. Swap over.
3 Remaining in pairs, take turns to be a) a potential buyer and b) the estate agent. The buyer describes the house he is looking for, in other words the teacher he wants to be. The estate agent makes notes (words or sketches). When both roles have been taken, each partner takes a few minutes to turn her notes into a prospective house.

Keeping the energy flowing

Aims   Self-awareness
             Stress management
Materials Large sheets of paper
             Felt pens

Procedure

1 Each person draws a circuit diagram or picture showing several personal and professional appliances plugged into her energy supply.
2 Pairs take turns to describe their diagrams and talk about how they each feel about the 'current' range of demands.
3 Partners think up an unexpected demand for each other, for example:
   - daughter announces that she is getting married in three months and you have to plan the wedding;
   - your car is out of action for a fortnight.

   Add this new demand to the diagram and imagine what would happen to the circuit when it gets plugged in.
4 The whole group rejoins and suggests ways of coping with the usual demands and handling the unexpected. These could be listed, eg
   - switching off one or two appliances;
   - lowering the wattage;
   - adding more sockets.
5 In pairs, partners work out a personal plan of how they are going to cope with demand at peak times.

Variations

Group members act out one person's range of appliances as a human circuit board with the 'energy source' (the client) in the centre. The client chooses how she wants to the group to proceed, eg
- group verbalises the energy demand simultaneously building up to a loud discord. Client expresses how she feels until she is ready to take charge.
- positioning them as she wishes going through a day, or a week, switching on and off at her command.

Role diffusion

Aims   Raising self-awareness of the different roles which we each take.
Materials Paper and felt pens

Procedure
1 As a group brainstorm all the roles we might occupy in relation to others.
2 Working on your own, map out your own role pattern by:
   • drawing yourself at the centre of a large sheet of paper;
   • representing each role with an arrow pointing outwards. Show by the length of the arrow the significance of this role to you.
3 Exchange and discuss role patterns with a partner. Decide any readjustments which you intend to make. Turn this into a personal contract with the support of your partner.

Payoffs on parade

Aims   Raising awareness of personal change
Materials A pile of plastic bricks or similar

Procedure
1 List three things you would like to change about yourself.
2 Working with a partner, tell one another your fantasy of what you would be like if you changed these aspects of you.
3 Take it in turns to pick the one that's most important to you.
4 Now tell your partner all the payoffs you get for *not* changing, starting each sentence with 'If I don't change, I don't have to . . . .'
5 Use a plastic brick to represent each payoff and another set to represent the rewards you would get for changing.
6 Now arrange the objects by putting the most important ones closest to you.
7 Discuss with your partner what you've learned from the exercise.

Labelling game

Aims   Raising awareness of the effect of labels which schools give students.
Materials Large sticky labels

Procedure
1 Brainstorm 'labels' given to students by the school system, or by teachers.
2 Write these terms separately on sticky labels, and distribute them randomly to the group so that each member has one. Labels are worn on the front in a visible position.
3 Interact a role-play situation, for example, at breaktime, reacting to each person in the group according to his label and the role you are taking.
4 Debrief:
   • How did you feel about your role?
   • What didn't you like about school, when you were in role?
   • What if you couldn't take your label off now?

Variations
1 After stage 3, exchange labels and proceed as before.
2 Labels are stuck on the back and as the roleplay proceeds, individuals guess what their label is.

Humpty Dumpty

Aims   Self-awareness
             Exploring what personal and professional changes might result from taking a
             more student-centred approach.
Materials One copy of *Humpty Dumpty* for each person.
             A set of instructions for each person.

Procedure
1 Introduce the notion that a teacher's 'style' is a complex ensemble of skills, experience, qualities, values and methods. Teaching styles are as varied and unique as
   individuals. This activity is designed to help teachers think about their current
   professional persona and to consider which of these characteristics are likely to change
   if they choose to become more student-centred.
2 Pairs read through and follow the instructions.

Extension
Whole group comes together to annotate an enlarged version of Humpty Dumpty and to
discuss the relationship between the suggested characteristics and principles of student-
centred learning. *OR* partners support each other in identifying personal targets for
change.

1 The picture of Humpty Dumpty represents the teacher you have been up to NOW. Label parts appropriately to indicate the components which make up your style eg your skills, your experience, your qualities, your likes, your values.... For example, you might label your heart with the word 'MARKING' to show that's your greatest love! Your memory may be full of things which you used to do and believe... and so on. Please write the words directly onto the appropriate bits of the drawing.

2 Now take a pair of scissors and cut out or cross out the bits which you feel you've lost, are losing or will lose as you become more student-centred. Save the bits you cut out and put them on one side. On the parts which remain, indicate how comfortable you feel with them. One way might be to draw nerves!

3 What does the result look like? What does it feel like? At this point join with a partner and talk it over. Discuss what you could put in place of the missing pieces to make you whole again.

4 On the bits you cut out cross out the original labels and write on the new ones you've identified.

5 Now fit yourself back together again—all the king's horses and all the king's men couldn't do it—but YOU can!

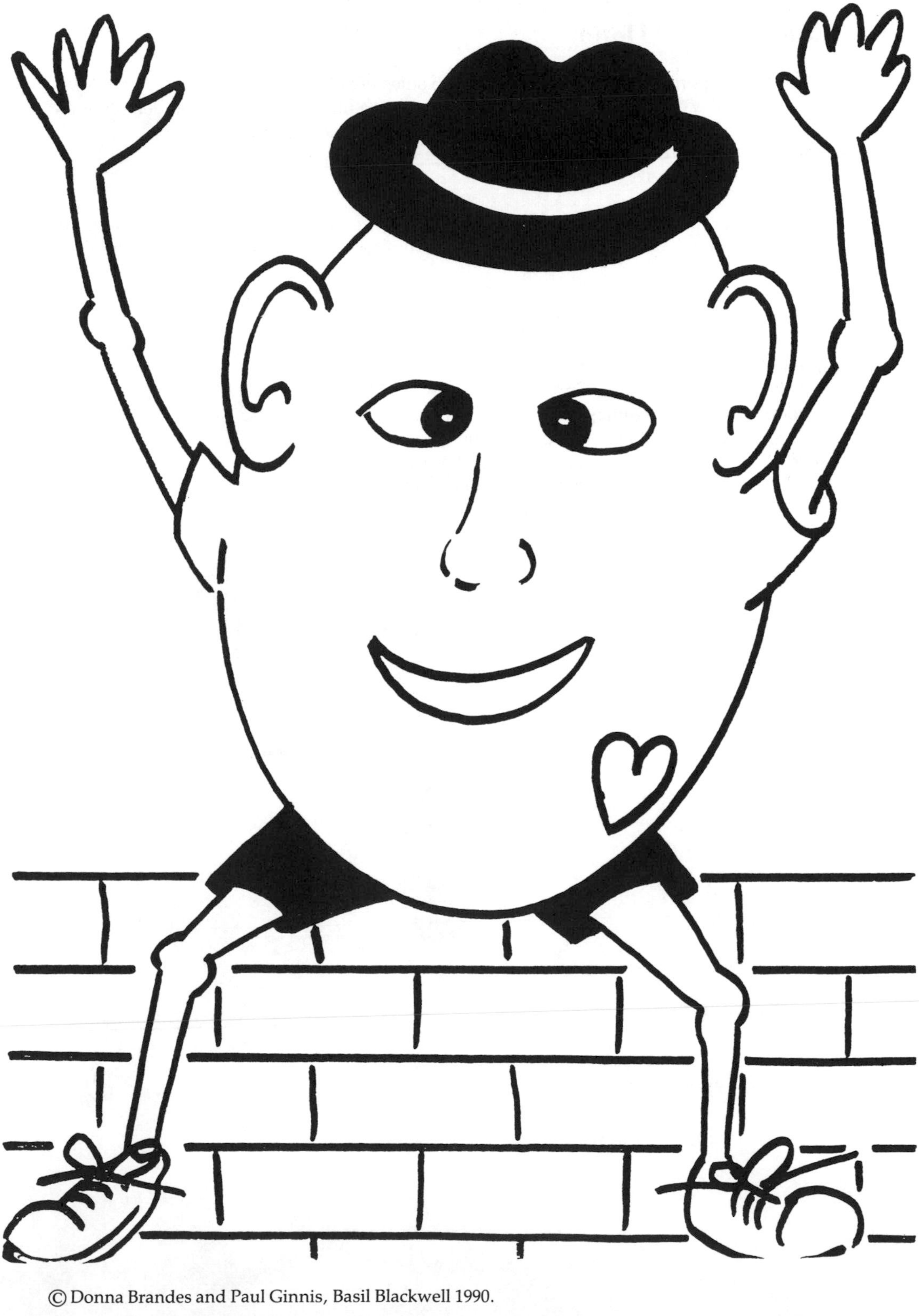

Student-centred lotto

Aims   Opportunity to reflect on personal values regarding keys to effective learning. To consider some of the particular characteristics of student-centred approaches and to compare these with personal values.

Materials A copy of a lotto sheet for everyone (see opposite)

Procedure
1 Distribute lotto sheets and ask individuals to read the given statements and if appropriate to add one or two of their own in respect of what they believe to be keys to effective learning.
2 Each person identifies their three top priorities and labels them on the sheet.
3 The group mingles and colleagues compare their choices in the search for a partner with similar priorities.
4 Pairs exchange views on their choices.
5 Each pair then sets off to find another pair with different priorities, so a group of four is formed. Group members discuss their reasons for their choice.
6 Debrief. Some of these prompts may be helpful:
   • What were the dominant themes of the discussion in fours?
   • With regard to the prepared statements, what are the underlying values/attitudes?
   • How could this activity be adapted for classroom use?

. . . asking students for feedback so that I can improve my teaching and their learning.	. . . encouraging pupils to talk to each other in pursuit of a learning task.	. . . putting a lot of time into building high quality relationships in the classroom, between teacher and students and between students and themselves.
	. . . negotiating with students the content to be learned.	
. . . having lots of pupils' work on display, with a high turn-over.	. . . seeing pupils' assessment of their work as being more important than the teacher's assessment.	. . . treating matters of discipline as problems for the class to solve.

A student-centred classroom

Aims   Raising awareness of personal values with regard to classroom practice.
Exploring together what a student-centred approach might be like in practice.
Materials Copies of '*A student-centred classroom*', reprinted from *A Guide to Student-Centred Learning* (p. 30–31).
Sugar paper and felt pens

Procedure
1 Read description individually.
2 Form groups to discuss and note down:
   • What I warm to in this description.
   • What I react negatively to in this description.
   • The key elements of 'the best possible learning climate'.

Variation
Debrief the description as a value continuum. Group members stand on an imaginary line to represent their position:

This is the most   This is the
perfect learning   worst learning
climate possible!   climate ever!
        ↓   ↓
    ├───────────────────────────────────┤

Volunteers comment on their position on the continuum.

A
STUDENT-CENTRED
CLASSROOM

Imagine that you have been invited to visit a well-established student-centred classroom. This is what you *might* see and feel—a collage of your impressions. Of course, by the very definition of student-centred learning, *every classroom will be different*. This is just one example.

The first thing you notice is that you do not immediately see the teacher. You then realise that she is seated in the circle with the rest of the group. You are welcomed by one of the students and invited to join the circle; a chair is brought for you.

One of the other students tells you that they are preparing to work on a project in small, self-selected groups, and shows you the brainstorm of ideas which has just been completed on the blackboard. The teacher asks the students what deadlines they want to set for themselves and a spokesperson from each group responds with a different date and plan. One group shows the rest a board game which they designed and produced themselves as their last project. Everyone applauds and then the teacher asks for feedback in the form of two questions: 'What things do you like about it?' and 'If it were to be done again, what improvements would you make?' Various answers are given to the two questions, but none of the comments is derogatory.

What you are feeling is a sense of warmth and an all-pervading air of positive cooperation and trust. (This is on a good day!) You also notice that not all comments are directed through the teacher, but that people tend to look at, and listen to, the person who is speaking. People are speaking spontaneously without raising their hands and without interrupting. Some people are participating more than others.

One of the students says 'There are only 35 minutes left; can we get started?' The teacher asks if there is anything else that anyone would like to say first. There being no response, she nods and everyone leaves the circle.

There is a sense of purpose as students get out the materials and start to work together. Everyone seems to know where they are going and what they are intending to do. You notice that people seem to be doing a lot of different things, and that students seem to go to each other for help and to the teacher mainly for advice on materials and sources of information: they have access to the cupboards, shelves and the stockroom. A student walks up to the teacher and says 'I'm just going to the Woodwork room to turn this piece of wood on the lathe'.

There is a good deal of talk and laughter and general buzz; all of it seems to contribute to an atmosphere of getting things done. A girls walks into the classroom. It is quite late, the period is half over, and she says 'Sorry Miss, I was late back from Community Service'. She sits down—in her group with her coat on—and starts work.

Occasionally, students go to a large chart on the wall to tick tasks that they've completed and to add assessment comments. One lad seems to be daydreaming. No-one says anything to him for a long time. Then, one of the other boys says 'Come on, we said we'd get this finished today'.

A girl by the window says 'The bell's gone'. People begin packing up at their own pace. One lad dashes out of the door, saying 'I've got to see Miss Roberts. 'Bye'. Another says to the teacher 'Can I come back to your office with you to get my Duke of Edinburgh's Award book?' Others put things back in the stockroom. People say to you 'Goodbye. Thanks for coming.'

Field Trip

Aims   To discuss some practical strategies involved in applying a Student-centred approach in the classroom.
Materials Copies of the 3-phase dialogue from chapter 2

Procedure
1 Read each of the dialogues and with a partner note down the strategies the teacher employs in each, and the features of the relationship between the teacher and the students.
2 In small groups discuss the changes that the teacher is likely to have gone through in moving from the first to the second situation, and from the second to the third.

Variations
● Role-play the bits in between represented by the asterisks.
● Role-play a continuation of the third dialogue.

The Field Trip

1 Customary proceedings

Teacher: The exam syllabus requires us to do a field trip. I've decided that the best place is the Peak District—we've been there for the past few years—so I've got all the necessary information and the worksheets for you to do. The coach will leave school at 9 o'clock next Tuesday and we will be back by 4.30pm. Here's a letter for your parents. I would like the reply slip and a £1 deposit by Friday.

Student: What do you want us to bring? Are we allowed to......

2 Teacher beginning to share responsibility

Teacher: I want to remind you that in order for you to pass the exam, we need to do a field study.

Students: Where are we going?

Teacher: Well, I was going to find out what you thought.... see what ideas you had.

Students: (blank looks)

Teacher: Can you think of any place we could go to study settlements, for example?

Students: (silence, looking down, up, at each other, not at her)

Teacher: (waits briefly) Well, last year we went to the Peak District...

Students: (brightening up) OK, that sounds like a good idea... My brother went there and said it was all right.

3 A student-centred approach, once it's already established.

Students: We've been looking at the syllabus, because we were checking to see how far we still had to go... it talks about a field trip, and it's getting late in the year to plan it.

Teacher: What are you suggesting?

Students: Could we spend some time talking about it... the whole group?

Teacher: Well, go ahead and organise that, whenever you're ready.

Students: Sitting down together, the students use the syllabus to check on the requirements, and ask the teacher to explain any constraints that they might not know about. Then they use a problem-solving process to generate a plan.

Get off my back

Aims   To consolidate understanding of student-centred learning, mixing, fun, communication.
Materials Sticky labels and pens.

Procedure
1 Everyone writes out a label, describing something that a student-centred teacher might be doing in the classroom.
2 Each person takes his label and sticks it on someone else's back.
3 Each person moves around, talks to other people, and asks 'yes-or-no' questions to find out what he is supposed to be doing, according to his label.
4 When he finds out, he sticks his label on the front, and goes to help other people find out about their own labels.

Variations and extensions
Take turns setting up scenes or tableaux using the labels to start them off.

Freeze frame

Aims   Demonstrating and discussing good student-centred classroom practice; creativity, improvisation, fun.
Materials None

Procedure
1 Small groups prepare tableaux of classroom incidents. For example, students are working in small groups, and it is hard to see where the teacher is. This is set up as if it is just one frame in a moving picture.
2 The audience can ask the 'actors' to go back three frames, or forward six; in fact, as many as they want.
3 The actors must move in slow motion in whatever direction the audience asks, miming and not talking.
4 Each time the movement stops, the audience discusses what has happened, and how the actors got there.
5 The actors can be questioned by the audience.

Variations
Anyone in the audience can join in after the first three moves.

So that's how you do it

Aims   Reviewing student-centred methods.
Materials None

Procedure
1 Find groups of three, and decide who is A, B, and C.
2 In the first round, A is a student, B a teacher, and C an observer. The student brings problem to the teacher, the teacher responds in a student-centred manner, and the observer writes what she would have said if she were the teacher.
3 Everyone switches round, so that each one has a turn in each role.
4 Still in the small groups, discuss, argue, debate, and de-brief.
5 Come back to the large group and do a Round of 'I noticed . . . .'

Variations
The teacher, in each round, could try various kinds of responses, such as didactic, critical, or directive; she could then ask the student and the observer how they felt about her responses, and what they would have liked to say back to her.

Student-centred learning meets the National Curriculum

Aim   To practice ways of introducing and handling the National Curriculum in a student-centred way.
            To empathise with students beginning a new course.
Materials Enough copies of a chosen section of the National Curriculum to go round the group.

Procedure
This activity is carried out in role. It is a simulation of the classroom. One colleague is the 'teacher'.
  1 *Getting started*:
    Explain which Attainment Target is to be tackled. Then explore students motivation by:
    either by ● a round of why we are here and what we expect to get out of the course.
    Or   ● using a 2D value continuum:

I know everything about this subject.

I really want to do
this course and I want
to devote the rest of my
life to the study of X.

The last thing I want to
do is this course.

I know absolutely nothing about this subject.

  2 *Introduce the corporate task*: to understand and organise the way we work so that we deal with the requirements in an effective and enjoyable way.
  3 *Guess what's in the programme of study related to this Attainment Target*
    either through brainstorming
    or   do a round with each person in turn, stating a concept or a piece of content or a form of assessment it might contain. Note all ideas on a flipchart keeping the round going until it naturally finishes . . . . or it gets boring!
  4 *Read through* the section in small groups recording what is noticed.
  5 *Debrief* by collecting the differences between the guess list and what was noticed. Any feelings or comments now that the section has been seen?
  6 *Introduce any additional information*, eg time available, assessments, resources.
  7 *Ways of working*
    a) Each group of four makes a deck of cards; individuals suggest:
       ● ways of working, for example, whole group together, small groups, pairs, individual.

- specific activities and approaches which have helped her to learn in the past or that she feels would be helpful in the future, for example: a timeplan of targets for a specific period; groups/pairs take responsibility to research a topic on behalf of class and prepare a presentation including a set of notes; a visual 'memory lane' of topics covered, annotated with key points; lecture style input at the start of a unit.

NB There needs to be at least 24 different cards.

b) Each group of four plays a version of 'Rummy':
  - Shuffle cards and deal out four each.
  - Place the remaining cards face down with one upturned card beside them.
  - In turn, pick up and discard with the aim of getting a set of ideas which you would recommend.
  - Let the game run until each player is satisfied with her hand.
  - Group looks at the recommendations and presents them in an understandable way for everyone else.

8 *Time to look at other ideas.*

9 *An agreement is made* as to how these ideas can be taken into account. For example, the teacher draws up a proposal for the course ahead with the help of a small working party. This proposal is then discussed, modified and reviewed together as appropriate.

10 *Debrief the process* out of role:

10 Debrief the process out of role:

  As teachers, what did you feel and notice?

  What are the benefits and the possible pitfalls for teachers and students of this approach?

  How would you respond to colleagues and parents who have different expectations?

  What other ways of sharing the syllabus can you identify?

Jargonometer

Aims   Clarification of specialist terms (for example, if we use the term 'Unconditional Positive Regard', an uninitiated person will not know what it means, and might, wrongly, call it jargon.)

Materials 3 × 5 cards, with jargon terms on them, one to a card; rattles, drums, tooters, noisemakers of some kind, for everyone.

Procedure

1 The group writes jargon terms, to do with their subject or concern, on cards.

2 Someone picks one, at random.

3 He reads the card, and then explains the term in non-jargon terms, that is, in ordinary non-specialist words.

4 If he uses a jargon word in his explanation, all the noisemakers go off, and he has to hand the card to someone else.

Variations

Make up consequences (not punishments!) that happen when the noises go off. For example, the talker then has to continue by speaking Gibberish.

  Use the technical terms needed to revise for any subject.

In other words . . .

Aims   Encouraging individuals to think about personal definitions
Demystifying current educational terminology
Finding common terms of reference
Increasing confidence to talk about current themes and issues

NB This activity can be useful in the initial stages of a course looking at student-centred learning in order to find a common language.

Materials Large sheets of paper
Several sticky labels for each person

Procedure

1 Introduce the purpose of the activity and ask pairs to identify some current educational terms as a warm up.
2 Working as a whole group or in groups of 6–8, a volunteer calls out an educational term which is written in the centre of a large piece of paper. Each person notes down, on a sticky label, a word or phrase which sums up the meaning of the term for them. The labels are attached to the paper surrounding the term.
3 Repeat stage 2 for as many terms as is appropriate.
4 Allow time for the separate collections to be looked at.
5 Debrief:
   • Any observations about the range of terms called out?
   • How much consensus emerges from the collections of definitions?
   • Was the activity useful? Could it be used in class?
   • Which of the terms does the group want to discuss further?

Prompts for reflection

You may find the following questions helpful when reflecting on your own lessons or observing someone else's. They could be used as 'prompts' for a reflective diary, which is a recommended way of recording your professional growth. Perhaps you could select just one or two questions per week, rather than try to keep an eye on the whole daunting list!

The students

1 How much choice is there in the work the students are doing?
2 Can they keep on task, be deeply involved and not distracted?
3 Do they seem to be on top of their work? ... Are they self-propelled as they move from one task to the next? ... Is motivation internal or external?
4 Can the students argue a point with each other in discussion, without the teacher's intervention?
5 Is every student looking after herself in using resources and moving from one task to the next without needing the teacher?
6 Do the students understand where they're going and how their present work fits in with the purposes of the whole programme or syllabus?
7 Are students helping and supporting each other?
8 To what extent are people making fun of each other, putting each other down and vying for position?
9 When something goes wrong, do students blame each other, or do they own their own behaviour?
10 Can they enter the room, sit down together, talk quietly and wait for the class to begin, without help from the teacher?
11 Are the leaders who emerge leading the group in achieving positive ends, or in creating mischief?
12 Do the leaders, in their turn, share responsibility with other students, or do they 'hog' the limelight?
13 Are the students capable of assertive behaviour, ie expressing their feelings without being aggressive.
14 Do they naturally, as a matter of course, practice active listening with each other and the teacher?
15 Can they use independent study skills, alone or in small groups, such as taking notes, making outlines, finding references in books, asking for help from outside sources, inviting visitors, carrying out research, writing a summary?
16 Do the students look bored, restless, scornful, angry ... or relaxed, satisfied, busy, involved?
17 Is there a big difference between their manner and behaviour toward the teacher and other adults, on the one hand, and their interaction with their peers on the other?

18 Are there a lot of 'trivial pursuits' going on in corners and between neighbours?

19 To what extent is their learning being given and to what extent is it being discovered?

20 Dewey argued that 'children don't do what they learn, they learn what they do'. What are the students not doing that they could usefully learn?

21 Do the students seem shy and fearful, or confident and outgoing?

The overall impression of a person's self-esteem is very difficult to quantify, yet we do it all the time. We notice things like: a firm voice, direct eye contact, a strong stance rather than a retiring one, smiles, head up, moving among groups of people without looking fearful. Noticing these sorts of behaviour will give the observer some clues about the students' self-confidence.

The teacher

1 Am I having to 'Shout and Shhh' in order to be heard?

2 How much am I asking the students and how much am I telling them?

3 How do I set objectives and how do I know if they are being achieved?

4 How lonely, exposed and isolated, OR secure, energetic and fulfilled do I feel during the lesson?

5 How do I feel at the end of the lesson?

8 A WAY OF WORKING . . . WITH EVERYONE

A very special school

Once upon a time, in 1989, there was a large inner city school, for students with a wide range of special educational needs and learning difficulties. Two Advisory Teachers were invited to support the school through a period of curricular reorganisation.

Colleagues were concerned to get to grips with the National Curriculum and TVE. There seemed to be a sense of urgency about producing a curriculum document which pulled together all the current practice in the school, and developed it in accordance with the new initiatives.

When we arrived for the first meeting, we were informed that the Head was leaving, so we were naturally disappointed and confused about how our work would go. We met with the three Deputies instead, and as the discussion got under way it became clear that there were lots of issues in the life of the school that would need sorting out before the curriculum objectives could be fulfilled.

We booked in a couple of days to spend in the school, simply walking around and talking to as many people as we could, starting to build relationships with colleagues, getting a feel for the place, listening to opinion. We combined these impressions with what we had learned from senior colleagues.

There seemed to be a lot of resentment around, about communication and decision making, for example; there were huge gulfs in knowledge and understanding of what each other did, especially between the three departments, (Primary, Secondary, and Continuing Education). Togetherness was blocked by secrecy, suspicion, and a range of professional and personal barriers.

We returned to the second meeting with a plan of action. We proposed that three underlying issues needed to be addressed before there was any hope of succeeding in the curriculum tasks:

1 Ownership   2 Self-esteem   3 Open communication

If we were to achieve common ownership of the school's direction, and raise everyone's self-esteem, the staff would need a degree of open communication that was far from the current norm. Everyone understood that this would involve a *big change* of management style, along with all the risks involved. Without hesitation, the deputies (by this time one of them had been appointed Acting Head) understood the sense of what we were saying; they felt instinctively that it was right, and the only way to move forward creatively. So they committed themselves to the implications!

At the same time, we suggested that we could work not only with the senior team, in supporting a participatory management style, but also in classrooms, collaboratively teaching with colleagues; thirdly, we would find ways to support teachers in the school in collaborating with each other in their everyday work. We were offering support at three levels to achieve the same objectives.

We were surprised at the degree of trust that almost all of the senior colleagues placed in us so quickly. We presented all of our points as observations, not as judgements, and committed ourselves to support the school, and not to abandon them to carry out the tasks without us. It seemed that our suggestions made good sense: the senior colleagues recognised the need for positive action in order to establish trust and teamwork which would ensure stability at a time of changing roles and curriculum development.

So we met in the Christmas holiday, to plan the Baker Day at the beginning of term; the big moment when the new intentions would be spelled out. The Acting Head saw that she would need to start the day with an honest statement of what was being planned, and of her own personal programme of change and development during the time she would be leading the staff. The whole staff was together for this.

Throughout the session we used a series of activities to explain the underlying thinking, to ask colleagues to assess their level of support for this new direction, and to express their most deeply felt concerns about any aspect of life at the school, and to prioritise them. The issue that was of strongest concern to everyone was the use of Directed Time after school. (All of the other items were held over, and anyone could raise them again; they were not lost.) We then carried out a problem-solving process on this issue, and came up with a plan of action which completely transformed the previous practice:

On Monday nights, every week, the staff would commit themselves to each other and would be available for meetings of one sort or another. The meetings would be flexible and respond to stated needs. The equivalent of a second night would be used by staff as they wished, but suggestions included:

- *voluntary curriculum working groups (to take forward the originally intended development);*
- *a range of workshops provided by staff for staff;*
- *a self-help group;*
- *any other business that colleagues wanted to get on with.*

We agreed that the staff's second-priority issue would be placed as an item on the agenda for the first Monday meeting. The agenda would be posted in the staffroom, and anyone could add items to it at any time up to two hours before the meeting. We turned up early to set up the tables and get the coffee ready, only to find that it had all been done. The staff were already taking ownership!

The senior managers realised that for participatory management to be genuine, their own meetings must be opened up. So they offered an invitation to colleagues to attend and participate equally in their Tuesday meetings. The end of secrecy!

A 'second night' meeting was called for the Wednesday night. Because it was voluntary, more than 90% of the staff turned up. They formed themselves into four separate working groups, with a commitment to report back to each other at a later date.

Beyond the willingness and the underlying attitudes, the senior management team are just realising that certain skills are needed to run effective meetings. They include:

- agenda setting
- chairing
- skills of participation for group members
- strategies for group work
- problem solving
- effective feedback from staff
- processes for converting proposals and theories into action

We can hardly believe that it's only been a week since that first Baker Day. One teacher commented to us in the car park that she was seeing people change before her very eyes.

Three weeks further on...
It has been important for us to keep building our communication with as many staff as possible—there is no short cut for this—and to keep on supporting the managers, especially the Acting Head. Her feelings are based on a strong conviction, but at times are overlain with anxiety about other things not getting done, and 'What have I let myself in for?' and positively, a recognition that there are many skills to be learned.

The Acting Head said: 'I feel this was the best INSET I have ever experienced at the school because it involved all the teaching staff in tackling *real* problems together. There were *real* outcomes which provided an incentive for actively continuing with a process during a *real* term in order to achieve some *real* goals, which have implications for two vital elements of a living school: its ethos and its curriculum.

The extent to which this initiative will actually be sustained depends on a number of factors. The most significant of these is the managers' determination to continue and their eagerness for training. External circumstances also play a part; many senior colleagues tell us that the pressures created by recent legislation tie their hands, demanding a more hierarchical, less democratic style of management. We want to suggest that the reforms can provide us, in fact, with the opportunity and motivation for a radical rethink of the sort we've just described.

All change

Through Local Management, almost every school in the country is able to take hold of its individual destiny in an unprecedented way. LMS involves either a radical change *for* school management, or a radical change *of* school management. Coopers and Lybrand, in their key report to the DES, recognised the shifts required:

> In short, the change at school level is from administration (of centrally-determined programmes) to management (of local resources). What is required is a fundamental change in the philosophy of the organisation of education. Thus, the changes required in the culture and in the management processes are much wider than purely financial and should be recognised as such.   (1988, p 8)

Again, Coopers and Lybrand acknowledged that

> the success of the change will in large part depend on the clarity with which management structures and processes are established... Heads and governors will need to decide what consultations there should be with teaching and non-teaching staff and with pupils.   (p 34)

The need for a new management vision is clear, as is the need for effective consultative structures. We want to encourage Heads to seize this opportunity and move along the continuum of management styles towards the full, rather than limited, participation of everyone in the processes of management.

We are already seeing managers dazzled by the immediate concerns of LMS and the power of the market forces which it unleashes. In the glare, some of them seem blind to fundamental issues concerning the management of *people*. Ignoring the human pressures on management is a costly business.

> Humans today want more than to survive: they want to flourish. They want their institutions, their governments, and their work places to be responsive to this need, to assist them in their flourishing, to assist them in becoming whole.... How management deals with this need for self-actualization, is, as I see it, THE central management issue of the 1980s. (and, we add, of the 90s).
>   (Blumberg, 1983)

Leaping heads

We salute the skills and courage of Heads, who, in an unpredictable and perilous environment, are constantly required to stop the buck. Held accountable by everyone for everything, the expectations and demands placed upon them must at times seem crushing.

We are not, and never have been, Headteachers ourselves, so we made it our task to talk with Heads in Birmingham, Chicago, London, and the North East of England. Although some of them described the stimulation and satisfaction of their work, many more spoke to us of living constantly 'close to the edge' of crisis; expertise; legality and constraint. They seem to feel as if they are on a high ledge, dangerously close to a sheer drop in front of them, and restrained by a cliff face behind. It's a risky business, yet some find it exhilarating. Almost all of them felt far less powerful than other people assumed they were.

The Head's Ledge
(v. diff.)

One Birmingham Headteacher, Max Johnson, wrote to us:

> We are continually being told that 'better management' is required in schools. I'm not entirely sure what this means, but it seems that it has something to do with planning ahead, better communications, value for money, identifying objectives, measurable outcomes, assessment of performance, and so on.
>
> To find out just how this is to be achieved we are often told to look to industry and learn from them. There is, I think, an implied criticism of Heads here. Now while recognising that we can always learn from others, my contention is that we haven't done too badly, whereas industrial managers haven't got all that much 'to write home about' if we look at the vast numbers of skilled people doing nothing, record number of bankruptcies and the balance of payments, to mention but three performance indicators.
>
> In schools we can't hire the people we want nor get rid of those who are no good; we have totally inadequate resources, badly-maintained, inadequate equipment, little control over the clientele, a lack of data and information for planning, an ever-increasing number of conflicting and ever-changing instructions, a level of administrative and clerical assistance which is quite hopeless, a lack of training and re-training opportunities, not to mention a perpetual barrage of criticism from a variety of sources. Incidentally, I don't see why we should be held accountable for things over which we have little or no control, or for all the ills of society.

If a manager in industry were to be told that his factory was not going to be maintained, there was to be no investment in new machinery, that he was not to know how many workers there were going to be, what skills they would have, or what salaries he could offer; there was to be no clerical help, and furthermore no one could say for certain what the product was, but that neverthless he was to improve efficiency, motivation, productivity and profit, it is not difficult to guess what his response would be . . . 'Thank you very much and good morning'.

Heads can't do this. They have families and mortgages, and yet schools run remarkably well, there's a lot of good practice and initiative, and academic standards are rising. As for Local Management, the National Curriculum, Opting out, Open Enrolment and the rest, Heads once again will 'fix it' despite everything, so how about a little credit there it's due?'

In these conditions, it's no wonder that one Headteacher remarked: 'one of the key qualities of headship is stamina; there's a need to be in top mental and physical health. It's resilience, rather than brilliance, that's needed.' The manifold role of Heads is more complex than ever; it's not the job that many existing Heads applied for, or were trained for, or even want! Constraint, risk, and crazy conditions are stressful enough in themselves. They are aggravated by the fact that the pivotal position of the Head seems to leave her no resting place. She is continuously and everywhere *accountable*, a sort of 'junction' for incoming and outgoing traffic.

As a sort of bottleneck, if you'll excuse the term, the Head is bound to experience pressure, especially as the volume of traffic seems to be increasing in both directions. The two-way funnel easily gets jammed; even when it is operating with efficiency, it can, by its very nature, allow only a limited amount of business and development through at a time. The positive effect of this is that the Head can keep out potentially dangerous interferences with the school, and keep in matters of confidentiality. So, in this protective sense, the Head makes school life less risky for everyone else. Some Heads work *more than* 24 hours a day, in order to let as much come through as possible. On the negative side, it's easy for other Heads to find blocking strategies to gum up the works, and to divert attention.

This system is unhealthy, as we see it, for the Heads themselves, and for the rest of the school community. In a recent report about stress among Headteachers, Mike Kelly of Manchester Polytechnic obtained 2638 returns from primary, secondary and FHE managers. These led Kelly to conclude

that negative stress is a significant factor in the occupational quality of school and college management in Britain; that the consequent combination of dissatisfaction with the job, and low levels of mental well-being makes it a potentially unrewarding occupation; and that the personality and behaviours of those attracted to the job could involve an unacceptable level of danger, unless effective and comprehensive stress management strategies are developed at the system, organisational, and personal levels of British education.

(Kelly 1988)

Kelly's report revealed six leading stress factors for Heads. In order of importance these were:

1 Work overload (in the returns to the questionnaire this was particularly associated with managing continuous change, managing time, effects upon lifestyle and quality of life, and meeting deadlines).
2 Handling staff relationships, and those with other colleagues.
3 Resources, and the market approach.
4 The demands and constraints of LEA's.
5 Handling inadequate staff.
6 Feeling undervalued.

The participatory style of management which we're advocating in this chapter will, we believe, relieve management stress. The funnel effect can be reduced through sharing output and input functions with other colleagues. The relief of corporate responsibility and the nourishing effect of closer relationships will counteract isolation, both personal and professional. Heads will be released and everyone else enhanced through new opportunities to be responsible and valued, as they participate in the life of the school much more fully.

Reaching for potential . . . that remains our central theme, for Heads and the whole school community. Stress constrains and debilitates; it is defined by Kelly '. . . in terms of a *gap* between the subject's conscious or unconscious *awareness of threat*, and their *coping resources*, which leads to *stressed behaviour*'.

Participation *in* management of all those affected *by* management is a very effective 'coping resource'. We hear teachers saying that they want to be empowered, not at the expense of the Head and Governors, but *along with* them and everyone else.

When contemplating this leap into participation, Heads we have talked to have expressed a belief that there would be comfort in sharing responsibility; a lot of weight, a lot of loneliness would be removed. Feeling like part of a team, more security, corporate responsibility, and the end of Us/Them suspicion, were factors that they mentioned. But the other side of the coin, they told us, would be: first, worries about their own lack of skill, experience, and training for handling this new approach; and second, the tension between sharing responsibility within the school, while at the same time being held accountable externally. Confidentiality is another primary issue; there are many things a Head knows that no-one else is supposed to know.

The leap involves the Head saying, 'I'm going to be open myself, and that means being open in my management style, increasing participation, telling the truth. I'm going to see what I can learn and develop in myself, so that I support the changing of the school climate.'

The Head will be looking for ways to increase trust and create closer relationships with all colleagues. Some small steps which she could immediately take, include the following:

1 Have Senior Management meetings open to the rest of the staff to observe, in a 'goldfish bowl', without participation.
2 Practise 'management by walking around' . . . that is, spending plenty of time in the staff room, classrooms, corridors, and playground.
3 Do some team teaching, or ask to teach a lesson which the regular teacher observes and gives feedback on.
4 Take an active and equal part in all systems of self-appraisal within the school.
5 Delegate some more of the usual Headly functions; eg representing the school to the media or parents.
6 Consider holding a 'listening clinic' for staff, students, parents . . . for anyone who wanted to come in and talk, with the guarantee that they would be heard, and not challenged.
7 Have elected teacher representatives on the Senior Management Committee who have equal decision-making powers with the other members.
8 Have elected sub-committees of the main Senior Management decision-making group, which inform, in a direct way, decision making on specific issues.

Staff meetings . . . the next step

It is the whole-staff business meeting which, perhaps more than any other aspect of school life, betrays the management values of the Head. Participatory management, in our terms, means the full involvement of the whole staff in running school. So, sooner or later, the staff meeting will need to change. For a Head wanting to move in the direction of increased participation, this could be the next step.

Introducing the change would require the self-disclosure of the Head, what we call 'telling the truth'. She would need to explain her reasons for wanting staff meetings to change, along with any doubts or worries that she may have about them. She would also need to explain the official and legal parameters of the proposed changes, as well as her own bottom lines (all of which would have been worked out clearly beforehand).

While the Head is beginning to lay a new foundation of trust, there may be resistance and suspicion among the staff. She would need to accept their resistance, and allow plenty of time and encouragement for the expression of negative feelings. Above all, she can show that she is listening to, and understanding, all points of view. She may have just learned about these methods herself, and be trying them out for the first time, therefore she could not have consulted her colleagues in advance. So she want to say something like:

'I know that these ideas may be new to most of you, and that I am now consulting you about them for the first time. I realise that there is no way I can initiate participatory management without your commitment, and from now on I will be consulting with you in advance, much more than ever before . . . '

The conversation might go something like this:

Teacher 1   Where did you get these ideas?
Head   I've felt for some time that I was not properly sharing responsibility with you, and yet couldn't see how to begin changing. It also seemed to me that it would be a big risk, which I haven't really been prepared to take before. Through recent reading, and conversations with Headteacher colleagues, and also going on a course which was run in a participatory manner, I now have some ideas about how we could do it if I could elicit your support.

Teacher 2   It sounds like a clever way of getting us to do what *you* want by letting us have our say so that we'll be more committed to the decisions. Everyone knows that you're in charge; it's just a con. It feels like manipulation to me.

Head   You feel that I might be manipulating you, by just giving you the illusion of consultation. I can understand that, in the past, you may have experienced consultation as something of a con. I know that it can be used to block development, or buy time, or to let issues disappear altogether. And especially commonly, it can be used to keep everyone happy by consulting over trivialities only, and keeping important matters for more important people.

I'm asking you to trust that things are changing now. If my intentions were to manipulate you, I wouldn't be telling you about it. I'm consulting you now so that you can be in on the planning from the beginning. Also, basically I'm asking you to develop more trust for me, and to believe that I have no other intentions than the ones I've stated.

Teacher 3   Even so, you're the one who's paid to take this responsibility and make these decisions. Being Head means being accountable, and if things go wrong, you're paid to take the blame. This is a neat way of getting out of carrying the can.

Head   You feel that sharing responsibility means sharing accountability, and sharing the consequences of our joint decisions. I'm very aware that, no matter what we decide between us, I will be held accountable by those outside, including the LEA, the DES, parents, and the community. Of course, I am directly accountable to the Governors. Also, I think that if things don't go very well right away, you and the rest of the staff may blame me for it. In this sense, it is my job to represent the whole school. However, I'm willing to take that risk because I deeply believe that things will work so much better for all of us this way.

Teacher 4   Our job is to teach the kids, not to make policy decisions. You're asking us to take on extra work, and to shoulder a larger burden. My union won't let me do that.

Head   I hear you saying that you can't take on any more responsibility. In fact, if you begin to share responsibility in the classroom with your students, and we all do the same throughout the school, we are not talking about increasing, simply rebalancing the responsibilities.

If resistance persists, it may be tempting to show irritation and impatience, which is only human . . . just remember that resistance is not a barrier, but a necessary stage in innovation.

Some of the ways to behave, at this stage, could be to:

- ask colleagues who feel strongly to come and talk further;
- spend more time in the staff room; make it a priority to be in the midst of the discussions without dominating them;
- if colleagues don't come forward, seek them out to talk and ask their views;
- include in the next decision process all those who are ready to be involved, and acknowledge their participation without implicitly criticising those who are choosing not to take part;
- when a decision is actually being taken, ask people if they would feel better if they were voting anonymously;
- keep the door of participation open at all times so that people can move in and out freely;
- above all, don't give up easily. Inner strength and assertiveness (not domination) may be the key. The Head may need to ask many times for staff members to try small steps in this direction.

It is our experience that the stage of resistance will pass, or at least the level of resistance will reduce so that the *balance* tips and there is sufficient will to go ahead. Let us imagine that this point has now been reached, and the staff have decided that they're willing to try some new ways of working together.

The next move might be to introduce a new brand of agenda setting. Nothing more is being asked of people at this stage than to contribute ideas, and to have their say. The person who is in charge of an agenda has a great deal of power; he can choose what the priorities for discussion will be, which needs are to be met, and whose items will be omitted when time runs out. In a subtle way, agendas reflect, or even create, the values of the school. So, the agenda can be seen as a function of the institution's culture.

This is why adopting a new agenda-setting procedure is an important instrument of change, as it involves a relocation of power. We believe that this power can be shared rather than monopolised.

Here is one example of how this might be done:

The Head asks each staff member to take a piece of paper and (anonymously) complete a sentence:

'The thing I'd most like to improve about this school is . . . '

or

'My top three priorities for this year's school expenditure are . . . '

or

(regarding a particular decision) *'The solution I favour most is . . . '*

These papers are put into a 'hat' and one staff member is asked to list them on a large chart or board. Of course, there may be repetition — in which case tally marks are used, and so priorities naturally emerge. Our reason for doing it this way (initially) is that teachers may feel more free to be honest if their responses are anyonymous. Both the formal and informal hierarchies temporarily disappear, and this can be a stepping stone to a later stage where people find it safe to be openly honest, and where the question of position in the school ceases to be so important.

While the bits of paper are being written up, quietly in a corner, the Head can proceed to explore with the staff how person-centred meetings could be run in the future.

There is a likelihood that the staff will wish to model their meetings on parliamentary procedures, as this is so common and is likely to seem logical. For example, they may wish to elect long-term officers. Yet this structure is not in keeping with the principles of fully-shared responsibility.

The responsibility of being in the Chair could belong to a different person at each meeting. The principle of voluntary participation would operate, so the Head could work out with the staff how they wanted a rota to be established. It would seem a good idea at this point for the staff to agree upon the role of the chairperson.

In fact, it may be necessary to provide some training for the whole staff in carrying out this role, as it is so different from the traditional model. A client-centred chairperson would:

- make sure someone is recording the procedures;
- ensure that meetings begin and end on time;
- establish and stick to set times for each agenda item (we will explain how these are obtained);
- remind people about the ground rules when necessary;
- help the group to focus on an issue;
- remind people to listen to each other;
- assist people in moving forward when they seem stuck on one point;
- help people to resolve conflicts (the Chair may have to remind people that there are often many ways of looking at a situation, and that more than one person can be 'Right') use active listening himself, and occasionally summarise where the debate has got to at the moment;
- provide brief exercises for re-entry (at the beginning of a meeting), and closure.

These are simply the skills and responsibilities of a facilitator, applied to the specific job of chairing meetings. As in the classroom, the facilitator here is hoping to create, with the group's help, a safe environment where it is OK to say what you think and feel, and where mistakes are consistently regarded as learning points and not failures. No matter who the chairperson is, he must be allowed to make mistakes too, without condemnation, so that he can learn from them. As time goes on, and the group sees that it is 'safe' to be in the Chair, the principle of voluntary participation may not remain a problem.

We might recommend that the Head speak to the staff about holding meetings regularly, say, every week; perhaps for one and a half, or two hours. The Head could seek the agreement of the staff and their Associations for a trial period of two terms, at which time the issue would be reviewed. Attendance would, of course, be optional. Ideally, the Governors, or at least representatives of the Governing Body, would also attend, so that decisions could be made there and then without reference to some other occasion.

While acknowledging that attendance after school is voluntary, it would also be clear that real policy decisions would be taken in the meeting, so that anyone not present would be missing their opportunity to influence the outcomes. The staff might then address this as their first problem to solve communally, and might decide an alternative structure. All the time, the Head would be reiterating her intention to achieve a sense of community and mutual support, to remove the distance, and even hostility, which can arise in a hierarchical school when people do not regularly meet together.

The Head may go through a period of feeling de-skilled, and may even wish she had never embarked on this change; in this time of doubt she may need increased support from colleagues.

> The proof of the pudding will be in the eating, over the course of the term, and hopefully beyond that. Let me say that in week three of the term I am still optimistic, but physically and mentally very tired. Let no one say that the open, participative style of management is a cop-out, or in any way easy. It is extremely demanding. It requires structure . . . . but I see and feel examples all the time of stimulating and constructive ideas being put forward by staff who, I believe, are prepared to back up their ideas with action. There are many good signs. . .
>
> (Jenny Taylor, an Acting Head who has just 'dived in')

Participatory policy making

Once participatory staff meetings are established, the agenda belongs to everyone, and could be organised in a number of ways, for example, as follows:

The chairperson for the coming meeting is given agenda items and will have announced a deadline for submission at the previous meeting. Each contributor is asked to indicate the length of time they think their item will require. The Head and senior staff use the same methods as everyone else. The chairperson is responsible for organising the agenda; that is, he arranges the items in order of priority and allocates a block of time to each. In fact, the staff may have previously agreed that items are allocated on a first-come-first-served basis, or that staff should indicate the urgency of their items by marking them with one, two, or three stars.

Other ways of collecting agenda items include:

1 Have an agenda box, into which people can drop items, any time up to 24 hours before the meeting.
2 Have a flipchart, or a BIG place on the notice board.
3 If the group comes to a point where agenda items are becoming trivial or dull, you could 'pep' up the business by inviting everyone to write 'I've had an idea for running this school, which I've never told anyone yet...' This could be done anonymously on paper in the agenda box, or in a round, or you could have a day when everyone in the school writes that sentence. These items could then be prioritised in Home Rooms or in School Council.
4 Have two boxes by the notice board, one with blank cards in it, and some bright coloured felt pens. People write agenda items on the cards, and pin them up. Other people come along and tick the ones they think are most important, and write their rationale in a sentence on a piece of paper underneath. 24 hours before the meeting, the most-ticked ones are taken and made into the agenda. The others are put into the other box, where they stay for one week, and can be resurrected and pinned up again while the author campaigns for support. After that, the un-ticked ones are removed, and the authors of those ideas have to find another way to deal with them. Someone will need to be responsible for handling this procedure. And remember, if people don't care enough to tick the cards they want, then the ones who do will have their way! This whole process depends on good will and trust.

Back to the participatory process: Let's imagine that a Modern Languages teacher has just returned with a group of students from an exchange week in France. He feels that changing to a Continental day (meaning an earlier start and finish to the day) would be a refreshing and effective change for his school, so puts it on the agenda for the next meeting and asks for half an hour to discuss it. This amounts to a major policy decision.

At the meeting, when this item comes up, the chairperson invites the language teacher to present his case in five minutes. (He has been given advance warning.) Ten minutes are then given to an open discussion of the pros and cons of the Continental day, and then the chairperson firmly moves the meeting on to deciding whether or not to pursue the issue. If the group chooses to carry the idea forward, then the chairperson helps them list points for action; for example, finding out the views of the LEA, the unions, the non-teaching staff, the parents, and asking the Student Council to consider it. Volunteers will be invited to take on each of these responsibilities. Deadlines are set, and agreements made to report back at the next meeting; the chairperson asks that these reports should be no more than brief summaries of the balance of each group's opinion. The item is then automatically placed on the agenda for the next meeting.

Perhaps you may be wondering *how* they decided to pursue this issue. It seemed very slick. We see the following possibilities and you may know of others:

Consensus—the rare occasions when everyone can agree on an item. We see this as the most satisfactory choice; if everyone is seeking consensus, the tone of the discussion will be different, and dedication to achieving the agreed outcome will be increased. This may seem idealistic, and does depend on more 'give' than 'take'; people are asked to give up their vested interests, to replace them with the interests of the community as a whole. We don't want you to think that we're being cosy, that we expect everyone to agree all the time. In this way of working, what consensus means is: 'Ok, we'll give it a try for now and if we don't like it we can change it'. We're trying to do away with the win-lose, success-failure syndrome; we are asking people to drop, temporarily, their opposition, rather than to be converted.

Compromise—changing a plan slightly, so that, if possible, everyone gets something of what they want. This is OK for the people involved; it may preserve something in the life of the group. However, it may sometimes mean that the plan is either changed out of all recognition, or diluted to the point of ineffectiveness. This can produce dissatisfaction for everyone, if the compromise does not contain enough of each person's interests. We have the notion of 'positive compromise', where people say, 'I'm willing to accept this; it's not my first choice, but I'm not dead set against the idea, so I'll give it my support, knowing that the situation can be reviewed at any time'.

Voting—the good old democratic system. It is quick, clear-cut, and final... *for now*. It is, however, a win-lose method, and can produce people who are distinctly undedicated, angry, and potential saboteurs. You can also get into lobbying, fragmentation, sub-grouping, and other Voting Nasties. A good chairperson can handle this in such a way that the negotiations happen *before* the voting... staff members may need to gain some experience of conflict management first.

None of these methods is ideal; we feel that all of them are improvements on autocratic or consultative (rather than fully participatory) decision-making.

Now for the second meeting in this policy-making process. The various volunteers report on their findings. If all of the parties who were consulted agree that a Continental day is worth trying, then the staff may find the decision easy to make. If, however, there is diverse opinion, a problem-solving session, to a strict time limit, could be useful. The outcome of the problem-solving will cue the chairperson as to which of the above methods (consensus, compromise, voting) could be used to reach a final policy decision.

This may sound like a long-winded way to make policies; we think it's worth it. Not only do staff members feel more valued and more committed to carrying out their own policies if they are playing a real part, time will be *saved* in the long run, as people become more skilled at these meetings and tasks are efficiently shared.

It is not only chairing meetings that requires a set of skills and self-discipline:

> Group members have rarely had training in how to be responsible
> members of a problem-solving group. Since most teachers and

principles spend so much of their professional lives working in groups, it is astounding that they have had, at best, only minimal training in this crucial skill.   (Gordon, 1974)

Here are some ways in which you could put these skills into practice:

1 Come to the meeting prepared, having read the minutes from the last meeting; know what you have to say about items, and how you want to say it.
2 Say what you think and feel about it all *at the meeting*, don't gossip or moan about it outside the group.
3 Don't expect other people to keep asking you for your opinion; it's your responsibility to participate.
4 Support the chairperson in time-keeping and in promoting active listening.
5 Realise that you own the corporate decisions as much as anybody else. Keeping silent at the time does not give you the right to undermine the decisions later.
6 If there are any delegated assignments or agreements, keep your own, and support your colleagues in keeping theirs.

> People who make a difference in the world, have found a way to take responsibility for the circumstances. They have found a way to master the circumstances. People who haven't yet made any difference in the world have good solid circumstances that explain why they are ineffective.
>
>   (Werner Erhard)

The role of senior management in a participatory school

Any Head comes to her job with a set of values developed from personal beliefs and professional experience. Furthermore, she is (at the time of writing) appointed by the Local Authority to administer its service to the community, and in this sense is accountable to the Governors, the LEA and elected members, or directly to the DES if the school is grant maintained. There are legal requirements of Headship, along with pressures from groups of varying influence, including professional associations, parents, and employers. Synsthesising all of this, the Head creates a personal style.

Once the Head has moved on to the idea of participatory management, he may find that he is overcome by worries and anxieties. He may feel he is losing control, or that other people will *think* he is. He may actually be accused of laziness, of not wanting to do his job properly or carry out his responsibilities. He may feel that he is handing over decisions for which he could later be held accountable. There is a big question about where to draw the line ... which things can he legally let go, and which things may contradict his personal beliefs and intentions?

What about all the emergency decisions that need to be made? Don't experience and expertise count for anything any more? Will the unions interpret it all as manipulation? Besides, all this takes so much longer. Is it really efficient?

Sceptics may point out that shared decision-making requires considerable time. Time, they add, is expensive. There can be no disputing these assertions. On the other hand, few people advocate replacing our democratic form of government with a dictatorship, even though the latter may be more efficient. The point that many citizens — educators and non-educators alike — sometimes overlook is that there are other worthy values besides economy and efficiency. It is time to think seriously about the merits of organising schools on the basis of values other than this pair borrowed from private industry.

(Duke, 1984)

Even in industry, the power structures are changing.

The weak power structures of the 'new times'... tend to be decentralised without a single point of leadership; communication is horizontal; structures are cellular rather than pyramid-like. ... The units and cells tend to regulate themselves, rather than being governed by rules and commands that flow in more than one direction at once. Though pyramidal bureaucracies are very good at implementing a given set of rules, they are strikingly ill-suited to creation and innovation.

(Mulgan, the *Guardian*, 28 Nov. 1988).

Before entering into the uncharted territories of participation, the Head may need to think through very carefully where his bottom lines are drawn, where his boundaries lie. This is exactly parallel to the process we ask staff to go through in approaching student-centred work in the classroom. Right at the outset, when presenting to the staff a new way of working, it might be best if the Head said exactly what he means: that there are certain issues which are not negotiable, that there are fixed points, and that when these are reached he will make his feelings known.

There is a delicate balance here, between enabling the staff to take responsibility and maintaining his own integrity; between the staff perceiving this sharing of ownership as genuine, or watering it down so much that they see it as a farce, or, at worst, a con. The balance can only be achieved, we think, by absolute honesty over a long period of time. This will require considerable openness on the part of the Head so that the staff get used to the idea that he means what he says and says what he means. It may take some time to undo the tangle of suspicion that often exists in schools.

Once the bottom lines have been clearly drawn and the area of negotiation is understood by all, the Head may want to do an exercise with the staff by which she elicits from them which functions they see her retaining of necessity, and which ones they could receive from her. As a member of the group, she can add or subtract, agree or disagree, according to the parameters that she has decided. The staff may need to take into account the Head's daily diet of letters, visits, phone calls, emergencies, discipline problems, meetings and assorted crises. How practical will it be for her to consult staff over every one of these? What about matters of confidentiality? And what can be left to the Head's discretion? Such negotiation may need to take place before participatory staff meetings and joint policy making can proceed smoothly.

When a division of labour has been agreed upon, which is satisfactory to all concerned (including all the professional associations), it could be formalised into a written contract, circulated for last-minute amendments, and then displayed, like Ground Rules, for all to see. After this point, the Head really has only two choices if he is to maintain trust: one is to stick scrupulously to what he has agreed; the other is to renegotiate the contract. The same choices are open to the staff. Schools can sometimes be riddled with the secret planning of strategies and manipulations; these would be counter-productive in the system we've described.

Incoming staff would, of course, be informed about these systems when they were interviewed. Then, presumably, people who did not like the idea of working that way would not want to accept a position in that school.

When emergencies do arise, and rapid decisions are needed, and it isn't possible to bring the issue to a full staff meeting, one way to communicate with colleagues would be to place a large notice board in the staff room marked 'urgent items', on which the Head can list these matters and their deadlines as they arise. There can be an agreement that any member of staff can have their say in person or in writing, but the Head is left to act as necessary, having taken all received views into account. Again, if the Head abuses this agreement, trust may well begin to disappear.

The idea of a negotiated role, which we've described above, would in some way need to be applied to the rest of the senior staff. It would be undermining to have deputies making more unilateral decisions than the Head. This system would work best if senior managers made it a priority to be in the staffroom at breaks, so that they were approachable and available for discussion.

The school council

Actually, we would take an even more radical stance than the one we've already described. We would *really* like to see a joint staff/student council running the school. This is the second leap. The first one was when the Head and (to a greater or lesser degree) the Governors, decided to involve all teachers. This one is the decision—by the Head, the Governors and all teachers—to involve all students.

Here we want to suggest a run-up to the jump: some practical guidelines for those who wish to move along the continuum from traditional practice to a situation in which students are as much involved as staff in managing the school's affairs.

For a first step, we would envisage a school council with elected representatives from each class, and from the staff, which functions as a consultative body only. The council, which would meet in between each staff meeting, would be informed of the staff's business, and its opinion and reactions would be sought. Likewise, the council could ask questions of the staff meeting.

Little by little, as trust and skills develop, the staff may become willing for the powers of the council to be increased; for example, it could present issues for the staff agenda. It could respond to issues on the 'urgent items' board. Our experience of other school councils suggests that often the kids' concerns are about the needs for refreshment and entertainment and school uniform, in short the things that are most immediate in their lives. In this sense, their perspective may initially be different from that of the staff. Again, a period of introduction to deeper concerns of school management will need to be handled with delicacy and sensitivity. Linking council meetings with staff meetings seems to be a natural way to achieve this over time.

Most times, when student councils are mentioned, people say things like, 'Oh, yes, that's all been done before.' 'Everyone knows that they'll only want to get rid of school uniform, and that they can't.' 'It's only a game like Playing House. We *pretend* that they can make a difference. We pat them on the head and act as if we're listening, then condescendingly ignore them.' We want to emphasise that what we're trying to do is to end all that. Where one of these puppet councils exists, we want to begin by talking to the students about how it *could* change. A selling job will probably be needed, and a learning period required. But nothing really *will* change unless the council is trusted with more responsibility regarding real issues.

It may be much later before a full-blown school council can be accepted. By this we mean equal representation from staff and students, on a body which replaces the staff meeting as the policy-making forum.

In our dream student-centred school, the school council will be the real, true, and only decision-making body. It will be composed of representatives from student support groups, and from the staff. Apart from these representatives, anyone who has an investment in the school can attend and take a full part in the debate and in the decision-making. At first, it may be hard to let it sink in that there will be no staff meeting, no Senior Management Team meeting, and no other secret society. It may be very hard for new staff members to accept that they will be supported, will still have their personal power . . . and will still have the chance to talk among themselves or to the Head privately.

We envisage the council meeting for one full afternoon per week.

Representation will be by rotation, rather than voting, with an opportunity to 'pass' when your turn comes around.

Initially the meetings will be chaired by some experienced person, because of the time needed for everyone to adjust to this way of working and

meeting; later, this position too would be rotated. In the beginning, it will be very important for us, as chairpeople, to model true consultation, and to be training everyone in negotiation and collaboration.

Distribution of responsibilities

With the Head in a negotiated role, a number of functions that traditionally belonged to the Head will now be shared by the staff. How could this work?

Helen Hadley, in her dissertation 'Extending the Principles of Student-Centred Learning into Staff Organisation' (1988), suggests a concentric organisational model:

> A non-hierarchical model for staff organisation might be composed of two rings or tiers of staff. The inner ring would comprise staff who were willing to take on some kind of responsibility beyond their classroom teaching. All posts of responsibility within the school would be available for a finite period of time—say one or two years; any staff interested in holding that post would put themselves forward for consideration by the whole staff. Over the course of several years it would be possible for an individual to have had the experience of holding a number of different posts of responsibility.
>
> Once the responsibilities had been shared in a way which everyone agreed to, then they could be written up as a contract and made clear to prospective applicants from outside the school who could then decide whether or not they wished to work in this way before pursuing their application.
>
> The outer ring would be made up of staff who, for any of a number of reasons, felt themselves to be unable or unwilling to take on responsibility beyond their basic teaching load; possible reasons could be—they were probationary teachers who wanted some time to find their feet, they were teachers new to the school who wanted to acclimatise, they had recently been ill and needed to recuperate or were experiencing personal problems, they were coming up to retirement and wanted to take things more easily or they wanted a period of less involvement in order to concentrate

on classroom responsibilities—choosing to spend some part of one's career on the outer ring would not be viewed negatively, nor would it debar one from moving into the inner ring as one wished.

All staff would draw the same basic salary, with allowances being pooled and those on the inner ring receiving an agreed amount for their extra responsibilities. Both inner and outer ring staff would have the same access to information and the same voice in decision making.

(pp. 42 and 43)

We would imagine the 'price tags' on each of the duties being negotiated with the teacher associations. Decisions about who does what would be linked to the model of regular self-appraisal suggested in Chapter 7.

We feel that such an organisation would be releasing for everyone. It would overcome many of the blocking constraints that teachers experience by redistributing opportunity and access, and by relieving colleagues from the stresses of overload on the one hand and exclusion on the other. We want the same for teachers as for students, which is holistic growth in a very positive environment. It is a potential-orientated model, rather than a product-orientated one, and in this sense goes against the grain of the current trend for schools to imitate commercial businesses ever more closely. Yet it is not unprecedented:

> In what may be an unprecedented move, to give teachers increased responsibility in school management, the Taylors Falls School District has received state approval to replace its principal with an elected group of teachers.
>
> (*Education Week*, June 17, 1987)

Assertiveness and conflict management

As the routine of participatory management is being established, and even when it is fully functioning, the Head is likely to remain a key facilitator, and any facilitator will at times find himself managing conflict: within himself; between himself and another person; and between two parties within a group. The aim is to preserve self-esteem all round, by setting up a win-win situation, and this requires assertiveness. We find it easiest to define the term in opposition to aggressiveness, on one extreme, and meekness on the other.

People who are assertive know how to ask for what they want without creating a win-lose outcome. They can negotiate without playing games or manipulating. They feel OK about themselves, and behave confidently. Their manner and body language portray neither fear nor dominance. When they say what they want or need, it comes across as a statement, not as pleading, nor as a demand, or an order.

We would want the whole school to be a Win-Win environment, where everyone is able to behave assertively. In the student-centred classroom, assertive behaviour will be beneficial and appropriate for students, as they negotiate with the teachers and with each other. It will be essential for everyone in the school if participatory management is to be effective.

1 Awareness of personal rights

On a recent assertiveness training course, we asked some teachers to do a round in which they each completed the sentence 'I have a right to...', Some of their statements follow:

I have a right to say what I think.
I have a right to be heard.
I have a right to influence any decision which affects me.
I have a right to say 'no' to any unreasonable demand.
I have a right to say 'no' to *any* demand if I feel like it.
I have a right to choose not to take part in voluntary activity.
I have a right to make mistakes, so I can learn from them.
I have the right to change my mind.
I have the right to say 'I don't know', and 'I don't understand'.
I have a right to be myself.

You can find similar lists in popular psychology books on success and self-esteem; courses and weekends and seminars on assertiveness are very fashionable. This seems very healthy to us, because it means that an increasing number of people are feeling free to live by these principles, to overcome internal constraints and start tackling external ones from a position of personal strength. To our way of thinking, these are basic rights which extend not only to teachers, but to students, to non-teaching staff and out of the school gate to every home and workplace. Raising awareness and acceptance of such rights is a first step; identifying specific rights in specific situations can come later.

2 Recognising what we want and need... and saying it

Part of assertiveness is knowing and stating what you want. We recognise that for many people this takes some getting used to. First of all, most people have been so conditioned to politeness, stepping back and letting everyone else have their way, that by contrast, assertiveness may seem selfish and inconsiderate. Second, in schools the hierarchical structure is so entrenched that teachers tend to be muzzled by suspicions and fears about possible consequences if they were to speak their true opinions. In most decision-making procedures, this step is not given time.

With regard to the Continental day we mentioned earlier, each teacher is likely to have a personal investment, based on her own lifestyle. Encouraging individuals to recognise and express personal *wants* is a step that is often missed out. The decision making often goes ahead with everyone pretending that they are only thinking about the good of the students. Of course they will have this factor at heart, as well, but what we're saying is that if the personal wants are expressed first, then the foundation for the next stages of negotation can be much more honest and healthy. If this initial step is overlooked, the door is wide open for games and manipulation, as personal needs compete with consideration for others, but not openly, and this can lead to secret dissatisfaction.

We are not suggesting that decisions are to be made on the basis of these personal wants; airing these is only the first step, intended to make the rest of the process more open and productive.

3 Listening and accepting

Win-win negotiation depends, on the one hand, on learning to clarify and say what I want and, on the other hand, displaying a willingness to listen to and accept another person's point of view. In aiming for a no-lose transaction, a willingness to hear, genuinely, what's being said from the other position(s) is essential.

Some people think that if they really listen, and are willing to compromise, they are giving away some of their personal power. Ironically, the balance of power doesn't work that way. We can retain our power if we give up the need to be *right*, to have the last word, and instead work together for a compromise. In fact, people who always need to be right often lack a healthy and strong self-concept; often, underneath their behaviour, there is an unarticulated feeling of: 'I *need* to be right, because otherwise I would be *wrong*, and I couldn't bear that. I don't have a sufficient supply of self-esteem not to be right; that's how I maintain my status, and my fundamental belief in myself.'

On the other extreme is the person who listens and readily agrees, saying to himself: 'If I stand out for what I want, I'll lose their approval'. So, this person gives in, rather than seeking a mutually-satisfying compromise. Wanting approval overrides the other wants, they feel that perhaps they will be praised for their 'cooperation'. Self-sacrifice carries certain rueful rewards.

The *skills* of assertiveness can be learned, but they only provide a fragile base. The fundamental purpose of assertiveness training is to strengthen self-esteem. We want our negotiators to be able to speak out, and to hear other people speaking out, and to do both of these comfortably, without feeling at risk. Active listening is the crucial ingredient here, and often... amazingly... prevents the conflict entirely. Active listening, in which the other party *knows* she is being heard, can be a primary peacemaking agent.

When we're feeling threatened, it may seem very hard to accept that there is more than one pont of view. Thinking that there is only one possible way to look at an issue or an event is a pretty sure way to be catapulted into conflict. But what if you *know* you're right? How can you pretend that you aren't? It's not about being false, it's about a deep understanding that the other person feels right as well, and just as sure.

If you really do listen carefully you may be astonished to find that the other person is not intractable, and that all she wanted was for you to understand her point of view. If you can accept that her view is right *for her*, but just isn't the one that you want, then the way is open for discussion and, maybe, compromise.

4 Negotiating

If you use your listening skills and remember that the other person has an equally valid point of view, you go into the discussion with an open mind and heart, ready to hear and to negotiate. The aim of negotiation is to find a solution which leaves both sides feeling OK about themselves, and about each other . . . a no-lose outcome.

Even if you are not feeling in a compromising sort of mood, even if you are feeling stubborn, entrenched, or rattled when you start talking, to miss out the listening stage would be taking a big risk. Not being heard tends to cause people to dig their heels in even harder. If this happens you are on your way to a serious confrontation, even perhaps to an irretrievable loss on one side or the other.

We recommend going in with an attitude of determined optimism, aiming to get what you want, and feeling hopeful that you and the other person can work things out in an adult sort of way. Of course it may happen that the other person is not in such a positive frame of mind. You don't have to let that influence you. You can be true to your own position and remain firm, in your attitude and your behaviour, about what you are intending to do.

Most experts in assertiveness training recommend moving from an inflexible position in an encounter by using a combination of active listening and reiteration of your own point. The dialogue might be something like this:

Diane (a history teacher whose 'classroom' is in a prefabricated hut);
It's freezing in my room this morning. I've taken a temperature reading and it's . . . degrees. (*Giving information*)

Ruth (the Head):
Yes, it must be terrible at this time of year. That's the problem with these huts. (*Sympathy, and no action*)

Diane It's too cold for us to work in there today. I'd like you to find us another room. (*Stating what she wants*)

Ruth I really wish I could. But there just isn't any space available in the main building. When the kids come in, it will warm up. Take another reading at lunchtime, and let me know what it's like then. (*Dodging the issue*)

Diane   I understand that the school is crowded, and it's too cold for us to work in there today. (*Listening and reiteration*)

Ruth   Well, there just isn't anywhere. You don't expect me to kick someone else out, do you? Anyway, it's almost time for the bell, so it's too late to organise room changes today. (*Still no action*)

Diane   I can see that there are problems with giving me another room. I don't feel we'll be able to work in the hut. Perhaps we can find another alternative, if we think for a minute. (*Listening and determined optimism*)

Ruth   Well, there definitely isn't a classroom, but I suppose you could use the hall . . . if I cancel assembly, and you can get some desks sorted out. Then I'll only have the second year music class to move . . . (*Compromise*)

No-one lost, nor was there a bitter taste left behind; the ending feels 'OK'. Perhaps an understanding has been established which will help these two to work together in the future. There's still the long-term question of getting better heating in the classroom, but that can wait until another day, and the door to that negotiation is now open.

This sort of routine could apply no matter how many people were involved on either side.

Another way out of a deadlock can be to use a problem-solving process, so that everyone has a stake in the negotiated solution.

5 Taking risks

Looking back at the dialogue above, we can see that Diane may have taken a considerable risk in standing up to the Head. Perhaps that is not her customary behaviour, but in this case the need was urgent enough for her to postpone feelings of 'What will the Head think of me. I don't want to cause any trouble . . .' The bottom line of assertiveness is self-esteem. In this case Diane may have been thinking more of the kids than of herself, which provided sufficient motivation and courage.

Perhaps you can think of situations in which you are afraid to ask for something just for yourself. Other ideas about yourself get in the way: 'I'm not worthy', 'I'm not experienced enough' 'They'll think I'm daft/stupid/pushy/awkward/Left-wing/selfish'. Add your own top ten self-put-downs. In this sense, assertiveness is a risky business.

Perhaps it's time to be your own 'best friend'.

Dealing with strong feelings

The sorts of conflicts discussed so far have been mild enough for people to resolve them rationally. What happens when stronger feelings are involved?

Sometimes our customary ways of dealing with feelings can actually escalate them so much that people say and do things which are unproductive, to say the least. This can be avoided. We do not want to control people's feelings in a manipulative sort of way. On the contrary, we want to maintain an atmosphere of trust in which feelings can be freely expressed. Strong emotions do not have to mean a breakdown of communication to the point where work cannot continue. It's all too easy to slide down this slope and end up with a slanging match, a banging of the table, a flourishing of fists, and a slamming of the door.

Ten ways to arrive at a conflict:
1 Exaggerate, use words like 'You never', and 'You always'.
2 Interrupt.
3 Don't believe what the other person says.
4 Interpret and analyse what the other person is saying, putting in your own meanings and ignoring theirs.
5 Use as many put-downs and labels as possible.
6 Accuse the other person of manipulation and other such deadly sins.
7 Take on a 'critical parent' role, and treat the other like a child, ensuring crossed transactions.
8 Be insincerely sympathetic or kind.
9 Be generally disrespectful; sneer at their comments.
10 Start every sentence with *you*.

Now, let's turn these around and look at ways of behaving which may tend to clear up disagreements and allow emotions to be expressed in safety.

It is usually helpful to start by owning your own feelings, starting your statements with 'I feel...'. This provides little basis for argument. As we've already said, validating the other person's point of view, acknowledging their feelings, gives a sense of acceptance, and builds trust. Listening while someone tells you just how he feels is the most peaceful action you can take. If you yourself are feeling angry, sad, threatened, or upset, you can say so. It doesn't have to be shouted, if it isn't heard the first time, you can say it again; this way, you are more likely to have it received than if you scream it.

Once you start screaming and accusing, you have lost. What you say will probably not be heard, and the chances of getting what you want are very slim, unless what you want is a drama or a fight. It's possible that that is what you want, though maybe not on a conscious level. There are pay-offs for fighting, such as having a target for further blame and griping. If you stage a dramatic walkout so that everyone knows how mad you are, you save yourself the effort of working for compromises in the future. The personality clash can become a permanent excuse for remaining uninvolved; this means you never have to change your position, or take on board a new idea. If your drama stars the Head in the antagonist's role, you could perhaps become a hero and win some medals for bravery from your colleagues.

As teacher in the classroom, or chairperson in the staff meeting, here are some things you might offer when trouble is brewing:

1 Ask people to listen actively to each other and persist in reminding them about it.
2 Enable people to see each others' point of view by, for example, asking them to swap places and roles for a while and continue the discussion from these changed positions. Physically changing seats can often cause a change of viewpoint as well; when ranks have been formed, getting people to move about seems to weaken the corporate position, and open up new interactions.

3 Remind people of the Ground Rules (this is exactly why they were needed in the first place).
4 Curtail the time by sticking to agreed limits.
5 Encourage people to express their angry or upset feelings by stating them out loud, as loudly as they like.
6 Provide an outlet for excess anger in the form of cushions to pound or something soft to throw, such as pillows.
7 Widen the debate by doing a Value Continuum or Concentric Circles exercise in which the spread of opinion in the whole group can be perceived.
8 Use problem-solving processes.
9 Ask people to state again what they want, and add how they might be willing to compromise.

After all the listening, after all the expressions of opinion, the crucial step, which many people seem to forget, is that there are usually options to consider. There are many ways to view a problem. Often, the simple question: 'What options do we have?' is enough to shift the discussion to a positive note, and to make it evident that the problem is shared. Making options explicit means that choices can then be made.

The role of the chairperson here is obviously a vital one. If it is you, you can learn about managing your own feelings, while enabling others to handle theirs. We believe that these are necessary skills for students, teachers, and managers alike, and they are well worth an investment of time and funds for staff development; the end product may well be participatory management that works.

Building a positive climate

In establishing the everyone-centred school, the two issues to be worked at are those of *ownership* and *climate*.

The solid belief which underlies all the thinking and practice in this book, is that every person is naturally motivated to be in charge of their own life and achieve self-actualisation, and, in the right conditions, will move in this direction. Creating the 'right conditions' is a vital part of the equation; so far in this chapter we have dealt with the question of ownership by explaining

how responsibility can be shared throughout the school community. But without the 'right conditions', little progress is likely to be made.

What do we mean when we say that a certain locale has a wonderful climate? Allowing for the fact that 'some like it hot, some like it cold', what we usually mean is that the environment is comfortable to live in. We mean that living things grow well; life flourishes. It's easy and comfortable to be within its boundaries; people feel free and unencumbered—somewhere between swaddled and stripped.

When we transfer that metaphor into school, we're referring to the total personality of the school. It is that almost indefinable something that we call the 'Gestalt' of the school; meaning that the whole is greater than the sum of all its parts.

The climate of a school is neither inevitable, nor unchangeable; it is recreated day by day as we continue to behave in the same ways. With determination and optimism the norms can be shifted.

Getting closer

Let us begin building our person-centred Gestalt, by admitting that very little can happen until people are willing to move closer to each other, not just collaborating professionally, but also opening up personally. Without instituting major reforms (those may come later) the contagion of collegiality and closeness can begin to spread in an ordinary school. To reach a real feeling of community, we could embark on a purposeful bringing together of people, across all ages and from all groupings, both within and beyond the school. Ways in which this could be achieved include:

1 Staff training in the fundamental skills of active listening and negotiating.
2 Colleagues (especially senior colleagues) using some non-contact time to release others to teach lessons together.
3 Directed time set aside for whatever the people involved may regard as fun.

4 Including interactions that are not just business, so that individual feelings and ideas are out in the open. (Here we could use structures like Rounds, Wishes in a Hat, Brainstorming.)

5 Staff, or whole-school, breakfast or tea once a week.

6 Cross-age tutoring.

7 Parental assistance in the classroom.

8 Parents being invited to join courses and learn with the kids.

9 Job-swaps among the staff for short or longer periods of time.

10 School clubs and societies being open for parents and other family members.

11 Providing crêche facilities (staffed by qualified personnel, courtesy of locally managed funds) so that no-one is denied the chance to take part in events.

12 Arranging for the school canteen to serve meals to whole families.

13 Classes inviting other forms to events in their classrooms. For example, seminars, exhibitions, 'art galleries', poetry readings.

14 Once a week, instead of assembly, volunteer groups put on events in different rooms, and the rest of the school (and parents and other visitors) choose which they want to go to.

15 Time set aside, perhaps on the penultimate afternoon of term, to play 'wide games' (outdoor adventure games such as are often played at camps), making sure that everyone can play regardless of age or ability.

16 Anything that will enable people to do things together, on an equal and positive basis.

17 A trip for the ancillary staff and the teachers to go on together (one school invited all the adults who worked in their school, on a Christmas shopping day-trip to France.)

18 Sleeping overnight in bivouacs in the school grounds . . . students, teachers, and parents could all join together in organising the event and building the makeshift shelters.

As our participatory Head will find himself delegating a lot of previously administrative tasks, paper work can be reduced and shared out. He will have to come out from behind his desk, and to work on eliminating physical or emotional blocks between people. Personal communication will begin to replace paper communication.

Important visitors can be greeted by students and staff, while the Head can be seen to be 'managing by walking around', (Peters, 1985). Guests, whether they be parents or inspectors, premiers or local political figures can be taken to look for the Head somewhere about the school, and learn a lot on the way. Again it will take a shift of attitude for many people to understand that the smallest student is just as important as the biggest bigwig. Reverence is for everyone, not just for the high and the mighty. The Head may still need his office, but not the badges that go with it.

Respectful informality can also replace meaningless ettiquette and rigid codes of conduct. First names can be used for everyone who is comfortable with that mode of address; everyone in the school can feel free to make a choice about what they want to be called. Planning for approaching festivals and holidays which belong to the various cultures in the school is a joy which can be shared by staff and students.

Birthdays can continue to be celebrated throughout the school year. The computer could keep track of birth dates, and a birthday party could happen every month, for everyone born during that period, no matter who they are or how old.

Here are some further suggestions for building on environment where people can feel safe and close to each other; a few procedures, policies or mini-activities that we have tried and tested, and that we think could help . . . . .

1 Appreciation Visits

All staff member's names are in a hat.
Each person picks a name, and visits that person's classroom.
She writes down ten positive behaviours or ideas that she notices during her visit, and later feeds them back to that teacher.

(P.S., we can hear some cynics shouting, 'But what if we don't find *anything* positive?' To them we would say, 'It's hard for us to believe there is nothing positive in that whole classroom. How about sorting out your own attitude, and then paying another visit? Look a little harder next time, with the determination to find out what's working well in there.')

2 I've never said this to you before . . . . .

Sit down quietly with a colleague, and tell them something that you have often thought about them, but never told them. Check out how the other person feels after that.

To begin with, it may be best to make only positive comments. Later, as trust develops, this exercise could be used to introduce negative as well as positive feedback. In any case, enough time should be left for a thorough debriefing.

3 Creative jobs

The aim here is to break down hierarchical assumptions. In pairs, invent new job titles for existing jobs, or for new jobs that need doing, and write creative job descriptions for them. Compare notes with other colleagues and see if these new jobs and titles would help your staff to work together more effectively.

4 If I had your job

Write your own job title and job description on a card. Swap cards with a partner.
Sit by yourself and write down the first three things you would do if you had this job.
Now meet with your partner and ask each other. 'Are you already doing these three things?' 'If not, what's stopping you?' 'If you are, is it working well?'
Then decide if you are going to make a contract with yourself to implement any of your partner's ideas.

5 Getting to know WHO?

Divide the staff into two groups, Interviewers and Famous Persons. All Interviewers choose the person on the other team whom you think you know the LEAST about. (Especially how they see themselves in their job.) Then conduct an interview, as if for the public media. Write these up with photographs, and either collate them in a book, or hang them in the halls of the school. (Students could do the same exercise with each other, or with staff members.)

Trust building

Trust building is a slow, but not necessarily painful process. It starts with telling the truth. So, at some point, the Head will have to say to everyone concerned, 'My primary goal is to win and keep your trust. I'm going to begin to do this by changing my own ways first and by enabling you to change yours'.

Here follows a list of small, but mighty, intrinsic methods which will help the Head to sow a climate of growing trust:

1 At all costs avoid manipulation. This means being open about plans, decisions, policies, and intentions.
2 Secret decision-making must be reduced gradually until it disappears altogether because it breeds suspicion, resentment, and us/them atmosphere.
3 Give out information, freely, and request input on all topics related to school life. Share news about the school community with everyone.
4 Use self- and peer-assessment methods for staff (as well as student) appraisal at *every* level, so that no judgements are being passed from above.
5 For all tasks of responsibility, selection-from-the-top is out; self nomination and appointment-by-common-consent are in.
6 School rules can be negotiated through the School Council and upheld by consistent reminders and open communication.
7 Remove physical barriers when communicating with others, and do without the symbols of authority and status.
8 The school building and all components thereof should be locked only at night, so that they are protected from exterior forces — guarding it from outside invasions rather than from the people who own it and live in it. (After all, the non-believers out there have not yet had the benefit of our trust-building efforts!)
9 Publicly acknowledge the contributions and accomplishments of students, teachers, non-teaching staff, Governors . . .
10 Create a situation in which everybody wins. Some examples would be:

- non-competitive sports and games
- plays that everyone can choose to participate in
- art, music, and drama exhibitions (*not* contests)
- recognition of individual differences combined with confidence in everybody's ability to achieve

11 Use trust-building exercises in student support groups, in staff meetings and, where it would be beneficial, in lessons.
12 Keep agreements, no matter who you have made them with, so that rank-pulling, hi-jacking time and agendas, and other status-ridden reasons for breaking commitments do not give the message: 'you are not as important as . . .'

Above all, no matter how traditional and regimented this school may have been before, and no matter how slowly some of the changes may come about, the one factor which can have major impact is that good old four-letter word L-O-V-E. If you, as the Head, can dare to love, laugh, touch, be yourself, call on your sense of humour to rescue you from tense situations. Respect, honour, and appreciate your co-learners... if you can dare all this, then you will see how much influence you do have, whether you presently believe it or not, over the ethos of the school.

Encouraging humour

Like bread without yeast, a school without humour has no buoyancy. It often seems that everyone in a school behaves as if the consequences of every act are global and disastrous, that without extreme seriousness we will not achieve academic success, let alone discipline and responsible behaviour. Yet in other contexts, most people would agree that life without humour is unbearable.

Without switching from humourlessness to legislated laughter, we want to suggest a few ways to inject some yeast into the dough of everyday school life.

1 Put up cartoons and (appropriate) comic strips, and encourage everyone else to join in.
2 Show funny films at lunchtime and break.
3 Have funny assemblies designed by kids, invite humourous speakers, encourage staff/student entertainments.
4 Make a point of educating the school community about the difference between ridicule and irony, between sarcasm and the ability to laugh at oneself.
5 Consider jokes academically as literature; study them in their national, cultural, and historical contexts.
6 Teach the art of the pun, Spoonerisms, metaphors.

7 Encourage people to collect and share items from the media which tickle their funnybones.
8 Get into the habit of asking, even in meetings, 'Can we look for the funny side of this?' This could provide some non-sarcastic exercise of the wits.

A humane environment

You know what kind of a feeling you get when you come in to work in the morning. Most people understand the impact of their surroundings on their feelings of creativity, worth and motivation. Yet, in many schools it seems as though the fabric and decor of the place is designed with only a functional purpose in mind.

With their LMS cheque books, schools are in a position to do something about the physical environment; it's only a matter of priorities. We are suggesting that investing in a humane and positive environment would pay handsome dividends in terms of holistic learning.

This exercise gives you an opportunity to assess your present state of physical comfort, identify potential improvements, and so determine priorities for change—and expenditure!

Please look at the chart on the opposite page. Consider each aim in turn, decide to what extent the present environment fulfils this objective, and spell out the developments needed. Even in our list of school priorities, many other considerations would appear above environmental needs (for example: salaries which attract and retain high-quality staff, assistants for teachers, counsellors, resources). Even managing their own finances, schools probably won't have enough cash to make sweeping improvements. We continue to campaign for more substantial resourcing.

Student support groups

Much has been written about tutorial period in recent years, a good deal of it stemming from the classic developmental group work of Leslie Button. The concept of 'home base' is central to this way of thinking. We share the same aims, which include:

> fostering support, care, and concern for one another . . . . the tutor period is to provide a regular time for a group to develop an identity and a sense of belonging for each individual; a familiar group of people, who know each other as individuals, warts and all, taking stock each week of how they're progressing
> (Jill Baldwin, 1986)

Rather than one or two short periods for tutorial, PSE, or guidance, during the week, we would like to see one-to-two hours set aside, so that each time the students meet together there is time for re-entry, agenda setting, group work, and evaluation. The focus would be on personal growth, human

AIMS	ENVIRONMENTAL NEEDS
Increase dignity and self-esteem	_____
Sensory stimulation	_____
Intellectual stimulation	_____
Various sizes and shapes of groups	_____
Comfort	_____
Cheerful and positive feelings	_____
Opportunities to be alone and quiet (staff and students)	_____
Quiet movement	_____
Adequate and accessible storage	_____
Access to resources	_____
Encouraging creativity	_____
Welcoming visitors	_____
_____	_____
_____	_____

development, and other areas of students' interest. Adolescent students need to understand and be able to deal with all the changes that they face; Support Groups can provide the opportunity to explore these changes in some depth, through discussion and activities.

> In their lives they (young people) experience dramatic patterns of change. The physical, physiological and emotional upheavals of adolescence are among the most powerful forms of change we all have to cope with... For the adolescent, life is changing: new friendships, new skills and interests, new concerns—all form the richness of personal experience that is the basis for pupil talk.
> (David Settle and Charles Wise, 1986)

Students want to talk about the excitement of the current changes in their lives. More and more attention is being paid to tutorial work in schools; we need to allow enough time for meaningful interaction.

School Council representatives can use this time to report back to their groups, new agenda items can be discussed, so that there is a two-way communication between Council and support groups.

Re-entry

Re-entry time is designed to enable everyone to prepare for the day ahead. This has been one reason for the early morning assembly, although in most cases it is used for inspirational exhortations or announcements, rather than interactive communication.

Two teachers in a Birmingham comprehensive school contributed this next account, to share with us their achievement in changing assemblies:

> 'We believe that lack of active participation by the pupils often indicates a lack of any learning taking place. As our pupils stood quietly in straight rows, fiddling with buttons and bits of cotton, longing for the holidays, the need for change seemed obvious. Could assembly with 270 children be 'Active and stimulating'? Could we design a pattern for a 'safe' active assembly and would this evolve into a situation where the participants themselves became responsible for the leadership of future activities?
>
> Problems encountered included convincing pupils and colleagues of the validity of this different approach, and relating numbers to available space. The former was overcome by a great deal of experimentation and practice, and then pressure from the participants who began to enjoy it. The latter was alleviated by the exclusion of chairs (by pupil choice), and the use of outdoor playgrounds when the weather was suitable.
>
> We began by using group building and trust exercises modified to suit our situation, such as 'Blind Forest Leading' and a giant 'Circle Sit'. We have now progressed to constructive staged conversations in twos and fours, with positive feedback from all participants. From this experimentation and feedback, many new activities have been developed, and a few have been discarded.

Initial scepticism has subsided with the recognition that this approach has real positive value and is good fun for all sharing in the process. Amongst the many benefits that have been identified so far are concluding and introducing the week's active pastoral work, and strengthening the identities of the Year and Tutorial Groups, thus developing and increasing the size of the available support groups.

(John P. Clark and Michael H. Brown)

What about re-entry for staff?

Many schools have an early morning briefing for staff, which succeeds in bringing teachers together to experience for a short time their corporate identity and purpose. We feel that these moments could be used more excitingly and productively.

Can you imagine, at the start of each day, the staff being eager to greet each other warmly, perhaps gathering in the staffroom for a ten-minute warm-up: handshakes, smiles, taking turns to bring music, a poem, a sample of favourite breakfast food to share, maybe a round of 'news' and what stops this happening?

After this in the staffroom, each teacher could go to her classroom and do a similar exercise with the students during a ten-minute re-entry period.

A re-entry period is useful because people come into the room with baggage. Think of what teachers may go through before they get to school:

- family quarrels
- heavy traffic
- housework
- hangover
- preparing breakfast
- getting the kids off to school
- taking care of ailing family members
- last-minute lesson preparation or marking
- bad news in the post or the media

add some of your own

We suggest that all this excess baggage can be dumped, either by talking about it, or by doing something relaxing so that it drains away. Once people have left their previous experiences behind, they can feel more prepared to get involved in the present learning environment and activities.

Re-entry exercises can provide students and teachers alike with a feeling of leaving the world behind and coming into the group which we have previously established as a safe and comfortable place. Teachers are often ready to interpret the side conversations between kids in a classroom as deliberately disruptive, sinister sabotage—which, of course, they some-times are. We would suggest that often people need to tell their friends about something that has just happened, or is of urgent concern to them. Do you find it easy to turn your mind to written work when you are worrying about paying the bills this month, or to settle to lesson preparation straight after a difficult phone call?

We are not suggesting that such conversations should never be stopped, rather that the teacher takes a slight shift in attitude and sees the possibility of their being necessary communication between human beings. A brief reentry period, far from being a waste of time, can be an eliminator of later interuptions.

What we want at the beginning of a lesson (meeting or INSET session), when we haven't seen the group for a day or so, or a week or two, or maybe ever before, is:

- to relax, to laugh or just rest a minute;
- to leave outside concerns behind;
- to remind ourselves that this group has a safe and trusting climate.

To accomplish this we often use short re-entry exercises, no more than 3–5 minutes long, and thus become ready to start on tasks.

Milling exercises:

Walk around the room . . . . . stop in front of someone, shake hands (or hug) and say:
  'Hello, I'm _____, you may learn to trust me because . . . '
  or
  'Hello, I'm _____, and if you knew me, you'd know that I . . . . '
  or

'Hello, I'm _____, and one thing I want you to know about me is . . .'
Any of these could be done as 'Rounds.'
If the group already know each other, milling exercises can still be fun:
'Hello, Bill . . . . what I'm going to do in this lesson is . .'
'Hello, Sheila, have you got any ideas about what we're going to do today?'
'Hi, Kim, I've got some news for you . . .'

Getting rid of baggage:

('Baggage' is concerns from the outside world, which might get in the way of working)
1 Facilitator, or a chosen person, walks around with a rubbish bin, plastic bag, or old box. People throw in a 'piece of baggage', by saying it out loud and going through the motions of throwing it into the container.
2 In a round, send a telegram to someone you've been thinking about, with the most urgent message that's on your mind, like:
'Dear Sharon, I'm sorry I shouted at you last night. I was really angry about something else entirely.'
3 In a round, pass around a 'Magic Box'. The Magic Box can contain cuddles, holidays, or anything of any size. Each person says 'If I could have whatever I wanted right now, I'd wish for . . .'
Afterwards the group could mill around, just for a minute and grant as many wishes as they can, or talk about them with the people who made the requests.
4 Keep an old suitcase in the room. Sometimes, when starting the lesson in a circle, put it in the middle. A person might then say 'I need the suitcase today because it's full of sadness because my goldfish died'. Someone else could say, 'No, I need it most because . . .'. Then, whoever needs it most can keep it until they feel ready to let it go by throwing it into the corner.

Closure

What often happens at the end of a lesson or a meeting is that a bell rings, or a time period ends, and people either dash out or drift away. We like to have a sense of completion, of wrapping things up tidily, so we often do an exercise for the last few minutes (which takes a bit of time-watching). Here are some short and simple ones:

1 Ten minutes before the end, get together and take turns saying: 'We accomplished heaps today because . . .'
2 For three minutes at the end, mill around and whisper messages to be delivered to other people, as in: 'Tell Amy she's got a lovely jumper on . . .'
3 Stand at the door and offer people a hug or a handshake (they can take their choice). Or let someone else be the Goodbye Greeter. Or walk round, shake hands or hug, and say 'Congratulations on . . .'
4 Play 'Teacher Taps', that is, have an agreement with the class that, in the last few minutes, any student can tap the teacher on the shoulder, and thus become the person who asks everyone to wrap up what they're doing, get ready to leave, and come together for a closing exercise that the Tapper chooses.
5 Let everyone make a verbal resolution or contract about what they're going to do next time, and walk around and tell it to people.

6 Play 'Shaboom': when it's time to leave, anyone can shout 'Shaboom', and then an adverb, like 'sneakily', and everyone leaves the room that way.

Have a session with your class, where you all brainstorm for ideas for openers and closers.

How are we doing? . . . monitoring and evaluation

When we think of evaluation, we imagine a series of concentric circles. At the heart is the experience, event or process under evaluation, along with the people who are experiencing it. Other kinds of assessment ripple out from that centre. The further away you are from the experience, the more possibility there is of dilution or distortion and of inaccurate interpretation because other critera (either conscious or unconscious) may influence the judgement. The most valid and productive assessment, in our view, is carried out *at the centre*.

The model we have presented in this book is of self-assessment informed by feedback from various sources. If it is valid, then there are implications for school evaluation: self-assessment by the whole school of the whole school. The whole school community would be asking: 'Are we as effective as we could be? What do we want to retain and what improvements do we want to make?'

At the time of writing, the debate about performance indicators, criteria against which a school can be evaluated, is going strong. David St. John Jesson describes the basic theme:

> 'The simplest model of performance takes the following form:
>
> Input   →   Process   →   Output
>
> where 'Output' is the visible measure of what the individual, school or local authority produces. 'Input' is what the pupils, teachers, schools, the community and other sources supply to the agency doing the 'processing'. 'Process' here includes organisational arrangements as well as 'style', 'ethos' etc . . '

> (Jesson, 1988)

We are keen for schools to review their effectiveness, but are distressed by the commercial language, and the commercial concepts of product and profit underlying the attempt to measure performance in this way. For the sake of the statistical operations involved in such measurement, all the evidence has to be quantifiable. For example:

> *Examination Objective 2*: On reaching the end of the fifth year of secondary education [65] per cent of pupils should have achieved 5 or more passes at grade F or better in the GCSE, including passes in mathematics and English.
> *Non-timetabled Objective*: Provision of non-timetabled activities during the past term should have been such that [90] per cent of pupils had participated in at least [3] separate voluntary activities.
> *Disciplinary Objective 2*: To keep the proportion of pupils found

guilty of indictable offences below the average level for the age group within the locality.

Demeanour Objective: Pupils' behaviour and appearance to the public on arrival to and departure from school should be classified as other than objectionable and selfish by at least [90] per cent of those approached in a sample survey.

(Wakefield, Director of Statistics, DES, 1988)

These examples, all from Wakefield (1988), indicate the thinking within the DES at the time of writing. Quite blatantly, one of the main reasons for this information is to assess a school's cost-effectiveness: 'Performance indicators will among other benefits give guidance on value for money' (Wakefield, 1988)

Evaluation carried out against indicators such as these is, to us, hopelessly incomplete. Quantitative information of this sort can never describe the quality of the educational process; the need for it comes from a belief in the sanctity of market forces, rather than in the holistic potential of each individual child. The student-centred school will want to know about:

- the extent to which each person feels empowered
- personal and social values, skills and behaviours
- the extent to which self-confidence is being built for individuals and the school community at large
- the learning climate
- self-awareness, openness to continued learning and knowing how to learn
- creativity, aesthetic awareness
- the value of the surprising, the unexpected, rather than the intended

Such concerns can only be assessed qualitatively, by asking those who share in the experience of them. So, we suggest that one of the first tasks of the student-centred School Council would be to develop a set of its own internal performance indicators for the school. Assessments by teachers and students could provide evidence to the Council on a systematic basis, enabling it to describe (not measure) the school community's accomplishments, weaknesses and future targets.

Love

We'd like it to be OK to be loving towards our schoolmates of all ages. The love of knowledge is respectable in school, and so it should be. So is the love of books, language, art, music, drama, dance, science, mathematical order — all the richness that we inherit. But we must also love originality, creativity, the freshness of our daily interaction with our students and colleagues. This means love *of* learning, and love *for* people.

> Love is patient, love is kind. It does not envy, it does not boast, it is not proud. It is not rude, it is not self-seeking, it is not easily angered, it keeps no record of wrongs. Love does not delight in evil, but rejoices with the truth. It always protects, always hopes, always perseveres. Love never fails.   I Corinthians 13. 4–7

In other words, the perfectly safe climate.

Introduction to the Activities

When we made the following selection of activities, we had this overall aim in mind: to bring the school community together to work through issues affecting the school's life. The first three exercises, for example, are intended to share thinking on potentially controversial subjects, and could be especially profitable if carried out in unusual groupings eg Governors with students, ancillary staff with parents, teachers with.... They are a useful way of identifying common concerns and the issues raised could feed into the business agendas of the school.

The next two exercises work at the school's intentions and progress with regard to student-centred principles, and are designed to help a school keep on course in the choppy seas of change.

The rest of the activities support participatory management and arise out of the experience of schools we've worked with. Most of these strategies are written with the whole staff group in mind, although, with minor modification, they could be scaled down to suit the management of a department or working party, for example, or scaled up to fit that visionary full School Council.

Butterfly

Aims   To raise awareness of how a school might damage, or support, students' learning.

Materials Copies of the passage from *Zorba the Greek* by Kazantzakis

Procedure

Read the passage, then:

1 ● Think of a time when you have inadvertantly damaged someone or something.
   ● Share this with a partner.
   ● What would you do if you had your time again?
2 Translate and substitute what belongs in there in place of a butterfly, for example, a child beginning school.
3 Think of the times when your teachers interfered, and hindered you in your learning. How could they have supported you?
4 Think of times when you may have interfered in and hindered the learning of your students. What could you have done and, in the future, what could you do to support them instead?
5 Draw a butterfly
   ● any size, shapes, colour you want
   ● imagine it to be alive, what would you have to do to ensure its survival?
   ● think of yourself as this butterfly. Write on the wings how you are going to look after the butterfly (ie yourself).
   ● hang it up, enjoy its beauty and remind yourself of what you have written about yourself.

These are just a few suggestions for how this passage could be used—add your own.

'I remembered one morning when I discovered a cocoon in the bark of a tree, just as a butterfly was making a hole in its case and preparing to come out. I waited a while, but it was too long appearing and I was impatient. I bent over it and breathed on it to warm it. I warmed it as quickly as I could and the miracle began to happen before my eyes, faster than life. The case opened, the butterfly started slowly crawling out and I shall never forget my horror when I saw how its wings were folded back and crumpled; the wretched butterfly tried with its whole trembling body to unfold them. Bending over it, I tried to help it with my breath. In vain.

It needed to be hatched out patiently and the unfolding of the wings should be a gradual process in the sun. Now it was too late. My breath had forced the butterfly to appear, all crumpled, before its time. It struggled desperately and, a few seconds later, died in the palm of my hand.

That little body is, I do believe, the greatest weight I have on my conscience. For I realize today that it is a mortal sin to violate the great laws of nature. We should not hurry, we should not be impatient, but we should confidently obey the eternal rhythm.'   *Zorba the Greek* by Kazantzakis

Unequal opportunities

Aims   Awareness raising of the equal opportunities issue
Materials Paper strips in two different colours to make armbands

Procedure
1 Divide into equal groups. Each group is given, or chooses, a colour and makes armbands.
2 Each group then invents a competitive game for the whole group to play. The group writes the rules for its own game so that its own group members are bound to win *without looking unfair.*
3 Everyone joins in playing each group's game in turn.
4 The facilitator encourages everyone to experience and discuss whatever they feel at the end.

The power exercise

Aims   To explore the topic of Power, and to relate it to ourselves and the community and society around us.
        To find out how to take power and how to hand it over.
Materials Copies of the 'Power' statements (from Handy and Aitken, 1986)—or elicit these from the group.

Procedure
1 Read and discuss the four definitions of power.
2 Working in pairs, identify examples of each of these:
  a) in your own life   b) in your school   c) in society.
3 In small groups, share ideas about:
  ● where you get your own power
  ● how you use it
  ● how you get more
  ● how you hand it over
  ● how you enable other people to take power for themselves
  ● how you can give it away and get it back
4 Devise an activity or a game about Power, to use with one of your classes or groups you already work with.

Resource power: Comes to you usually from above. You are the person who controls the resources, therefore you can command respect and attract followers (eg, revolutionaries need guns and ammunition to start a rebellion).

Position power: again, usually appointed to you from above. You are in a position to command respect and wield power, just because of your job title or roles that you play.

Expert power: usually awarded to you from below, from people who are not experts. You know a lot about a certain subject or field, therefore people look to you to tell them what to do and how to do it.

Personal power: conferred by people who look up to you in some way. Your record of accomplishments, your charisma, your connections to other great people, cause people to consult you and ask you to take responsibility for them.

Principles profile

Aims   To identify needs with regard to implementing a student-centred approach.
(Can be used as a whole staff, working party or individually)
Materials Copies of the 'Principles Profile'.

Procedure
1 Discuss each of the student-centred principles in turn, note down current strengths and identified needs.
2 Go on to write an action plan of how you intend current strengths to be utilised and needs to be met.

The Principles	What I already have
1 When we value the learner, we increase her self-esteem and her openness to learning.	
2 The most effective learning is 'owned' by learners who are consistently regarded as responsible for themselves.	
3 Maximum growth of the learner occurs when she herself carries out the planning, organisation, implementation and evaluation of the learning.	
4 Much effective learning is achieved through doing.	
5 Learning can best take place in a safe, supportive environment.	
6 Learning which involves the whole person, not just the mind if the learner but the feelings also, is the deepest and most permanent.	
7 A learner's affective and cognitive growth are enhanced by positive interaction with other learners.	
8 The most socially useful learning is the learning of the process of learning, a continuing openness to experience and incorporation into oneself of the process of change.	
9 Creativity is increased in an environment marked by fun, humour, spontaneity, risk, and intuition.	

© Donna Brandes and Paul Ginnis, Basil Blackwell 1990.

What I need	What my school has	What my school needs

Professional pillars

Aims   A recording tool
Either   to *specify targets* (intended achievements) as a whole school with regard to a
          student-centred approach.
Or   to *review progress* as a whole school in respect of taking a student-centred
          approach.
Materials Copies of the pillars sheet representing Climate and Responsibility.

Procedure

1 Brainstorm 'What we intend to build.' If appropriate, categorise these ideas so that
   pairs or small groups can take responsibility for considering one of the categories. The
   concepts of climate and responsibility could form two broad headings and further
   groupings could be made within each of these.
   Repeat for 'What we have built.'
2 In pairs or small groups discuss and record 'How we will achieve it'. This could be
   taken in two stages, first in respect of personal changes and then considering whole-
   school changes. The degree of personal disclosure will depend on the level of trust
   within the group.
   Repeat for 'How we have achieved it.'
3 The suggestions from each of the working groups could be collated onto one sheet and
   presented to the whole group. The task of prioritising and making agreements as to
   who is going to implement the changes and what support they might require could
   form the agenda for a follow-up session.
   or
   The record from the small groups could be collated and used to:
   ● celebrate the achievements and to note from these what were the key factors in this
     success;
   ● go on to set new targets.

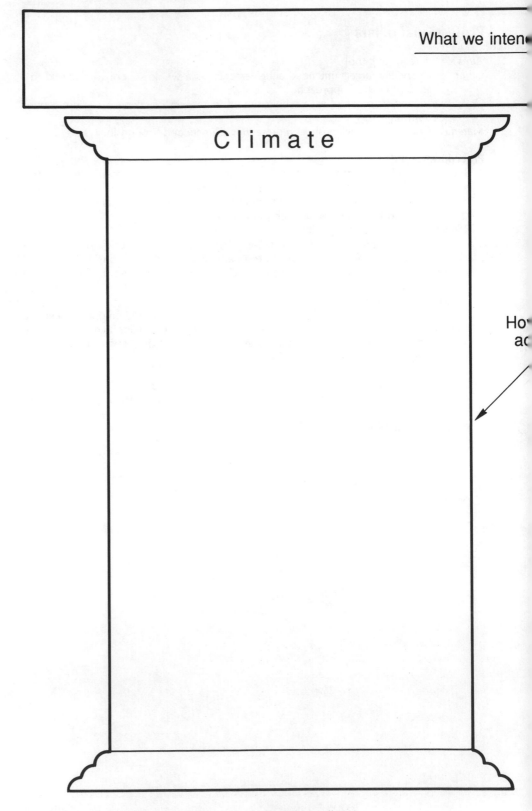

What we inten

Climate

Ho
ac

chieve /build

Responsibility

vill
it

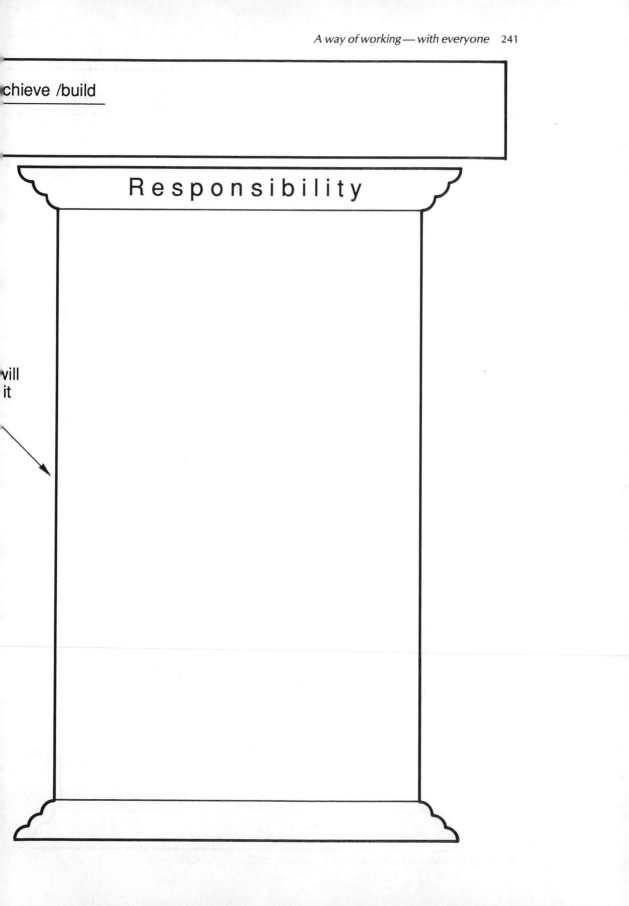

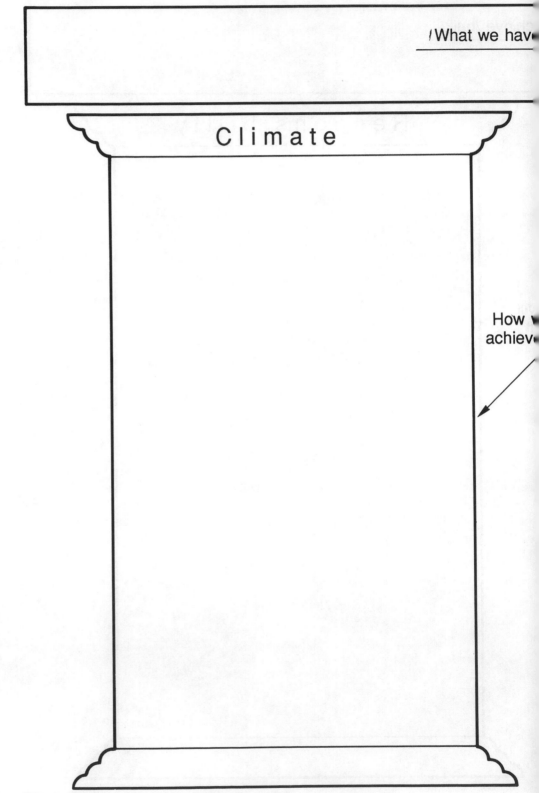

What we hav‹

Climate

How ‹
achiev‹

chieved /built

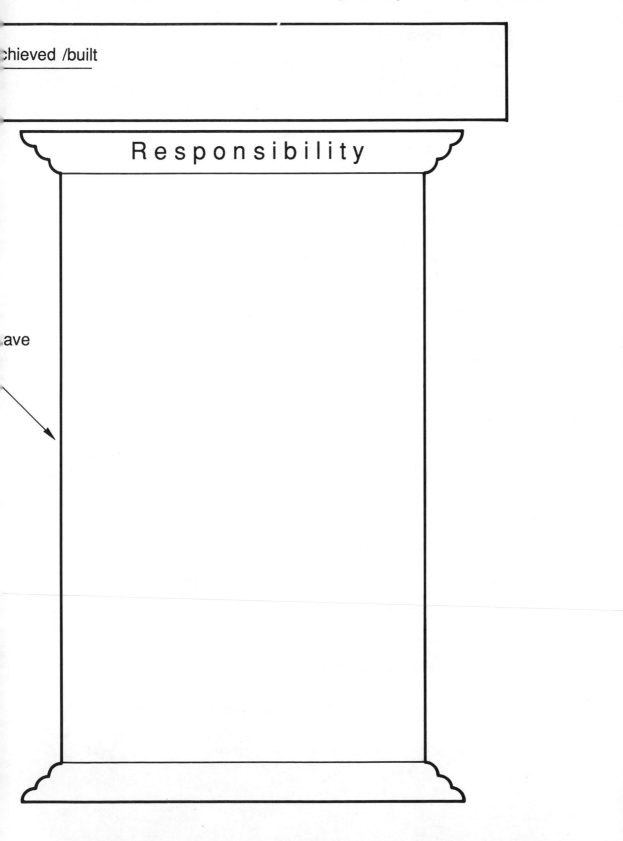

Responsibility

ave

When all's said and done

Aims   Agenda setting for a course or series of meetings
            Trust building
Materials Paper and pens

Procedure
1 Each person folds his sheet into eight rectangles.
2 In each space write one word taken from a list such as:

change	have	feel	want
be	know	start	see
understand	do	take home	make

3 In each rectangle, complete the sentence:

   'When all's said and done, I would like to feel, change, make . . . .'

4 Rank the sentences in order of importance (1–8).
5 The group mingles, sharing their needs. When two people find a common need, they sit down together and discuss it.
6 Whole group joins up and using a round individuals state their two top needs. These could be recorded and displayed for ease of reference throughout the course. If appropriate, the whole group could vote to indicate their priorities as a group.

Extension
Making contracts
Working in pairs, each supports the other in:

• choosing two of the key words or needs to work on.
• defining a continuum for each of these stating the two extremes eg *Context: Induction course for Sixth Form.*

I have no idea of   I have a clear idea
what my skills and   of the options open
interests are and how I   to me related to my
might use these.   skills and interests.

• identifying her current position on the continuum and where she hopes to move to next.
• working out ways of moving towards these personal targets, for example: information to research or people to talk to.
• defining a timescale for action (if appropriate)
• deciding on a review date
Each person signs the contract and the 'owner' keeps it.

To introduce the concept of participatory management

Aims   For Senior staff to state their commitment to developing a more participatory style of management.
                    To introduce the underlying principles of:
                    • ownership
                    • self-esteem

- open communication

To consult colleagues with regard to their support for the proposal of developing a participatory management style, and to proceed with the session according to the weight of opinion.

Materials   OHP and screen, flipcharts, plain A4 paper, felt pens, small stickers, blu-tac.

Furniture arrangement   'U' shape of tables and chairs so that everyone can see each other.

Procedure

Stage 1 — Introduction

1 The (Acting) Headteacher opened the session with an introductory talk which took account of the following points:

- the current factors determining the direction of curriculum and staff development.
- personal commitment to move towards a more participatory style of management.
- asking colleagues to support each other and to work as a team during this period of flux.
- the need for support in terms of facilitation and guidance during this period of development. In this instance, two advisory teachers.

The Head concluded by outlining the programme for the session, the direction of which would be determined by staff opinion regarding the whether or not there was majority assent for the proposal.

2 All other members of the Senior Management team were invited to make their own statement. In turn, each declared their personal support of the ideas and hopes outlined by the Headteacher, adding their own personal viewpoint.

3 The two advisory teachers introduced:

a) the basic principles underpinning the concept of participatory management.

b) the three possible arenas in which they could give support depending on staff opinion:

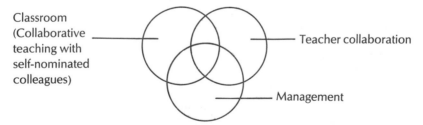

Classroom (Collaborative teaching with self-nominated colleagues) — Teacher collaboration — Management

Stage 2 — Collecting feedback on the proposal

4 A 2D value continuum was used to collect whole staff opinion. This was done as a huge visual graph on the floor. The axes were long pieces of string and the labels were written on large standing cards (like 'A' frames). Each member of staff was given the opportunity to take a cardboard star and anonymously place it on the graph to indicate his opinion.

Figure 2 shows how, in this case, it turned out:

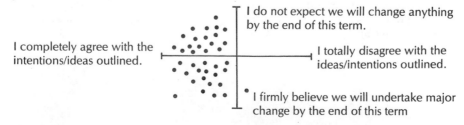

I do not expect we will change anything by the end of this term.

I completely agree with the intentions/ideas outlined.

I totally disagree with the ideas/intentions outlined.

I firmly believe we will undertake major change by the end of this term

As there was strong support for the proposed ideas, the session could proceed with the first step towards a more participatory style. The advisory teachers lead the remainder of the session. This allowed all colleagues to participate fully.

Stage 3 — Identifying priorities
5 Working in small groups (up to 5), colleagues were invited to explain what they felt were the most pressing concerns within the school. There were no constraints regarding what the concerns addressed. The groups worked to a time limit (10 mins). At the end of this time each colleague was asked to note down her own individual priority concern (written large on a sheet of A4), whether or not anyone else in the group supported it.
(During the coffee break, the advisory teachers displayed the concerns around the room, putting similar issues together).
6 The staff reassembled and a prioritising procedure was explained:

- Everyone has 3 stickers to vote with.
- The stickers are used for individuals to (anonymously) indicate priorities.
- The votes can be used flexibly eg all 3 stickers on one concern/2 on one and 1 on another/no votes made.

This method is a device for identifying priorities and is not a win/lose strategy. The concern which receives the most support can be addressed immediately by everyone using a problem-solving approach. In the case of a draw, then a 'play off vote' would be used to determine which would be considered first.

In this instance there was a clear priority: The use of directed time for compulsory meetings and the content of the meetings.

Stage 4 — working together on the priority concern
7 A problem-solving approach was introduced so that all participants understood the procedure:

- clarification of the issue
- all suggestions for solutions collected
- any relevant information offered eg constraints/future changes
- a solution chosen together
- plan of action agreed
- implementation
- evaluation and necessary adjustments

The whole staff worked through the first five stages.

On this occasion the Headteacher could not be present beyond stage 4. She had explained this earlier in the meeting and had asked for two volunteers to meet her later that day to discuss the outcomes of the session with her on behalf of the staff. The two staff reps were able take all the material from the meeting to this discussion.

Stage 5 — the next step
There was agreement that for the following three weeks there would be a whole staff meeting to which everyone would make a commitment. The meeting would have an open and rolling agenda. Any member of staff could propose an item including any of the additional concerns identified but not as yet addressed by the whole staff. Apologies would be given to the meeting. At the end of the third meeting colleagues would review the use of the meeting and decide how to proceed.

In accordance with the requirements of directed time, colleagues would need to work a second session, at some other time during the week. An individual could, however, elect to opt for additional sessions if he so wished. The staff agreed that individuals could choose from a range of options which would be held on the remaining three evenings (ie not Friday):

- Curriculum working groups addressing the National Curriculum and TVE.
- Other workshops or working groups (Lead by staff or INSET providers)
- Individual use of time (in/off site).

Specific strategies used
- 2D value continuum (as a visual graph)
- small group discussion to a set agenda and time limit
- prioritising with 3 votes (stickers)
- a problem solving process

A process for dealing with an issue of whole staff concern

Issue: Wanting to raise staff morale and to increase reassurance, support, and encouragement.

Procedure
1 The colleague who had originally raised this concern introduced the item. She explained how she saw the issue. Other colleagues were invited to add their perceptions.
2 Working in small groups, colleagues discussed ways in which staff morale could be raised and noted these under two headings:
   - Recommendations which could take immediate effect.
   - Recommendations which need further consultation.

(10 minutes)
3 A spokesperson from each group reported back on the recommendations which could take immediate effect. These were noted on a flipchart. The facilitators offered to collect and collate all the issues in the form of a summary chart to help to take the thinking forward.

Follow up:
The next day, each teacher received a personal copy of the summary.

Everyone was invited to add any further thoughts and to make firm proposals for action on an enlarged version of the sheet displayed in the staffroom within the following week.

The facilitators drew up a set of proposals taken from the staffroom chart which they introduced at the next staff meeting. A paper ballot took place and the results were displayed in the form of an action board. In this instance the staff took the following actions:

- set up a staffroom action group of volunteers to address the many issues raised about the staffroom environment and its use;
- set up a social events action group;
- set up two briefings per week to take place in the staffroom in directed time before school;
- senior staff drew up a rota of times when they would make themselves available to any colleagues who wanted to talk with them over any matter.

Processes for collecting feedback

Issue A: Senior teachers wanting feedback from colleagues about their role.

Procedure
1 One of the Senior teachers introduced the item. She explained that the team of Senior teachers were currently discussing the nature and function of their roles in the light of there being a new team member. They hoped to receive feed back from colleagues and offered two prompts:
   - *If I were a Senior Teacher, I would . . .*
   - *My view of the Senior Teacher's role currently is . . .*
   She stressed that the Senior Teachers wanted to be in a listening role and to collect as many viewpoints as possible.
2 The staff divided into equal groups around each of the senior teachers. The Deputy Heads acted as scribes, recording all points on a flipchart. (Time allocated — 10 minutes)
3 The Senior Teachers thanked colleagues for their comments and agreed to report back to the staff on any outcomes of this item after they had discussed the feedback as a group.

Issue B: Curriculum working parties wanting feedback from the whole staff on hearing a report from each working group regarding their progress with regard to the National Curriculum guidelines.

Procedure:
1 Every member of staff was given five slips of paper. Each slip was a different colour representing the five components of the curriculum report back:
   - An introduction giving an overview of current National and local Curriculum themes.
   - Mathematics
   - English
   - Science
   - Early learning
2 As the speaker for each section reported on their work, colleagues noted down any questions, concerns or recommendations on the appropriate colour slip. Each 'reporter' had a 10 minute time limit.
3 After the fifth speaker, the staff posted their slips in the relevant boxes. The coordinator of each working group collected the slips to take to the next meeting of the group for discussion.

A problem-solving process for working on an issue of whole staff concern

Issue: To review the school's system of organising break duties. (This item had been raised at a whole staff meeting where colleagues had voted to refer it to the next Senior staff meeting which would as usual be open to all colleagues.)

Procedure:
The facilitators lead the discussion based upon this model:

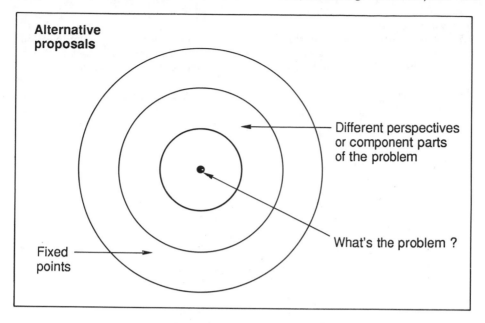

1 *What's the problem?*
   Working within a 10-minute time limit, colleagues, in turn, explained what they each perceived the problem to be. The facilitators wrote up each concern as a component part of the first ring. This helped to build a composite picture of the whole issue to understand how the different aspects of the issue were related. In this way we were able to define the essence of the problem which could then be written into the bull's eye.

2 *What are the things we cannot change?*
   Working again within a ten minute period we listed what we believed to be all the fixed points, for example, the legal requirements of supervision at breaktimes.

3 *What are our alternative proposals?*
   Bearing in mind the ideas and information gathered, we then drew up a range of proposals. In this instance, we realised that we needed additional information about the current pattern of duties. We decided to conduct a staff survey prior to the next staff meeting when this group would report on the thinking so far and consult colleagues with regard to further action.

Information circle

Aims   To pool a group's knowledge and ideas, for example:
- at the start of a learning unit
- in considering possible solutions to a problem
- when revising a topic

Materials A copy of the notes sheet and a pen for each group

Procedure

1 The group divides into 3s or 4s. The groups space themselves around the room forming a circle of groups. Each group is given one copy of the sheet on which to make notes and appoints a recorder.

Information circle

When you get each information sheet note your group number in the margin. Next add any further information your group has. If you think that anything written before may be incorrect, then underline it and note your group number at the end of the line.

Group number	*Information*

2 The issue is clarified, eg
   - ideas for fund raising;
   - revision of photosynthesis;
   - reasons for site location.
3 At the signal to begin, each group notes down its number in the margin and records all the information or ideas it possesses about the given topic. This is done within an agreed time limit, eg 2 minutes.
4 The information sheets are passed on in a clockwise direction. The group again notes its number in the margin, underneath the first group's notes and reads the information they recorded. The new group notes down any further information next to its number. In addition, the new group underlines any information noted by the previous group which is thought to be incorrect.
5 The process continues until each group gets back its original sheet. Each group should then be in possession of a summary of the whole group's thinking. These can be used for the basis of whole group or small group discussion.

Variation

Each group begins the process with a different topic, eg a separate revision topic. In this way, each group will address each topic and on conclusion of the process, there will be a collection of summaries of the whole range of topics.

Boomerang problem solving

(Adaptation of Information Circle)
Aims   To encourage corporate ownership.
            To encourage a creative approach to problem solving
Materials Paper and pens

Procedure

1 The whole group identifies the problem area or topic, for example, disaffection in school.
2 Work in small groups. Each group defines the problem by writing a short and precise situation which illustrates the problem. The situation may fact or fiction.
3 Each group passes its situation onto a neighbouring group. The situation is read, discussed and 'recommended action' is written down.
4 The paper is folded (so that the 'recommended action' is hidden) and then passed on to the next group.
5 The process is repeated until the paper returns to the original group. The group reads all the 'recommended actions' in response to their situation and selects the two most favoured solutions.
6 Each group reads out its 'top two' solutions.

Barriers and boosts

Aims   Building confidence and trust; learning to find creative solutions to problems; self-esteem
Materials Squares of white card, about 6 × 8 inches, or paper; felt pens; (2 cards and a felt pen for everyone)

Procedure

1 Pass out two cards for each person, and pens, and form groups of 5 to 7, sitting in circles around the room.
2 One person in the group volunteers to be the artist for everyone; or else, each person

draws separately for herself. What they are drawing is physical barriers, one to a card, large and clear, such as: a stone wall, or a pit of quicksand.

3 Now, on the second set of cards, people draw 'boosts'; that is, the group designs creative ways of crossing the barriers; like, a trampoline for bouncing over the wall, or a cannon for shooting across the quicksand.

4 Then each person selects a barrier card, and writes on it a description of their own personal barrier, which stops them reaching for their potential; an example might be: 'I can't express my anger to my boss, and it all goes inside and I feel frustrated.'

5 In the small group, one person at a time shares their barrier, and the group generates as many boosts (solutions) as possible. The person with that barrier writes down a solution that he likes, on the barrier card, and so on around the circle.

6 Barriers and boosts can be shared aloud, or displayed on the wall.

Variations:
For participatory management: barriers to effective meetings
For study skills: barriers to effective learning
For history: barriers to peace
For geography: barriers to industrial development
For careers: barriers to good jobs for everyone

Alternative report backs

Aims   To offer interesting ways of sharing the outcomes of group discussions with the whole group.
Materials Paper

Procedure
1 *Two-minute dash*
(5/10 minutes, as appropriate)
At the word 'go', everyone mills around, asking and telling. Each person is to find out as much possible about the learning, ideas, conclusions achieved by others.
When time is up, everyone sits down and does a round of 'The most significant discovery I made was . . . . '

2 *That's draft*
At the end of the work, each small group prepares a statement describing its conclusions or summarising its discussion. Two groups exchange statements, quickly redraft and return them. This process is repeated.

3 *Scrambled 'eads*
When its time to share the learning, re-scramble the groups so that new groups comprise one member from each of the original groups. This can easily be done by giving each group a different colour at the beginning in the form of coloured stickers or cards. The new group ensures that it has each colour represented. Each person then takes a turn to share.

PERSON-CENTRED WRITINGS FOR
READER-CENTRED READERS

We want to invite you to write to us, with us, alongside us.

Send us your thoughts, reflections, feelings,
poems, photographs, answers, cartoons, drawings, essays, students' work,
ideas, critiques, questions, responses.

We can publish your creativity in the new networking newsletter-journal
of the National Association for Student-Centred Learning. To inspire you to
get started . . . we offer here some questions and ideas to think about. Please
write down your ideas and send them to:

Donna Brandes and Paul Ginnis, c/o 22 Vicarage Rd., Kings Heath,
Birmingham, B14 7RA

1 What is your earliest memory of school?
2 What do you wish you had learned in school?
3 Is there anything that happened in school that you feel particularly good
   about?
4 Are there things that you wish had not happened to you in school, or
   that you wish had been different?
5 How do you think it will be possible to integrate alternative learning
   styles with the National Curriculum?
6 How do you respond to the section on Participatory Management?
7 What do you think your own needs/wants are, regarding personal and
   professional development?
8 What do you want to tell us about your experience (positive and negative)
   with a person-centred way of working in any sphere of education?
9 What are your major strengths and skills where SCL is concerned?
10 Please would you take a few minutes, and write a poem, sonnet,
   limerick, song, or fantasy about your thoughts and feelings regarding
   this book, or anything in it. Or draw a picture . . . or send photographs
11 Please send us some disagreement.
12 Please describe your Dream School.

BIBLIOGRAPHY

Aron, A. and Aron, E. N. (1986) *The Heart of Social Psychology*. D. C. Heath and Company, Lexington, MA.

Ashton-Warner, S. (1963) *Teacher*. Bantam, New York.

Baldwin, J. and Williams, H. (1988) *Active Learning: a trainers guide*. Basil Blackwell, Oxford.

Barker, L. L., Wahlers, K. J., Watson, K. W., and Kibler, R. J. (1987) *Groups in Process*. An introduction to small group communication. Third Edition. Prentice-Hall, Englewood Cliffs, NJ.

Barton, L. and Walker, S. (1981) *Schools Teachers and Teaching*. Falmer, Press, Sussex.

Berne, E. (1964) *Games People Play*. Penguin, London.

Berne, E. (1975) *What Do You Say After You Say Hello*? Corgi, London.

Blake, R. and Mouton, J. (1983) (2nd Edition): *Consultation: A Handbook For Individual and Organizational Development*, Addison Wessley, Mass.

Bloom, A. (1987) *The Closing of the American Mind*. How higher education has failed democracy and improverished the souls of today's students. Simon and Schuster, New York.

Bloom, B. S. (ed) (1985) *Developing Talent in Young People*. Ballantine Books, New York.

Blumberg, S. (1983) *Win-Win Administration: How To Manage An Organization So Everybody Wins* Horton and Daughters, Arizona.

Bolam, R. (1988) 'Teacher Appraisal and School Review', *Quality in Schools* NEFR.

Bolton, Gavin M. (1984) *Drama as Education: An argument for placing drama at the centre of the curriculum*. Longman, England.

Boud, D., Keogh, R. and Walker, D., (eds) (1985) *Reflection: Turning Experience into Learning*. Kogan Page.

Boyson, R. (1975) *The Crisis in Education*. The Woburn Press.

Braham, M. (ed.) (1982) *Aspects of Education* Selected papers from the Dartington Conference. John Wiley & Sons, New York.

Brandes, D. (1981) *Hope Street Experience*. Access Publishing, Leeds.

Brandes, D. and Ginnis, P. (1986) *A Guide to Student-Centred Learning*. Basil Blackwell, Oxford.

Brandes, D. and Phillips, H. (1978) *Gamesters' Handbook* I. Hutchinson, London.

Brandes, D. (1983) *Gamesters' Handbook* II. Hutchinson, London.

Brandt, R. S. (ed) *Content of the Curriculum*. 1988 ASCD Yearbook of the Association for Supervision and Curriculum Development.

Brandt, R. (March 1988) '*On Students' Needs and Team Learning: A Conversation with William Glasser*', *Educational Leadership*, 45 No. 6, pp. 39–45.

Brokaw, T. (1987) *NBC News White Paper: To Be A Teacher* Sponsored by IBM.

Brookover, W., (ed) (1982) *Creating Effective Schools: An In-Service Program for Enhancing School Climate and Achievement*. Learning Publications, Inc., Holmes Beach, Florida.

Bruner, J. (1966) *Toward a Theory of Instruction*. Norton, New York.

Button, L. (1974) *Developmental Group Work With Adolescents.* Hodder and Stoughton, London.

Carmegie Ideas for Inner-City Schools Commentary in Chicago Tribune Saturday, March 26, 1988.

Cantor, N. (1947) *The Dynamics of Learning.* Foster & Stewart, Buffalo.

Cardi, J. J. (1984) *Caring and Community: A Study of Professional Norms and Controls in a School.* Dissertation, School of Education, Syracuse University.

Carter, C., and Monaco, J., *Learning Information Technology Skills.* Library and Information Research Report, The British library, Number 54.

Casement, P. (1984) *Learning from the Patient.* Tavistock Publication.

Charles, C. M. (1980) *Individualizing Instruction.* Mosby, St. Louis.

Child, D. (1973) *Psychology and the Teacher.* Second Edition. Holt, Reinhart and Winston, London.

Combs, A. W. (1979) *Myths in Education: Beliefs That Hinder Progress and Their Alternatives.* Allyn & Bacon, Boston.

Coopers and Lybrand, (1988) *Local Management of Schools: A Report to the Department of Education and Science.*

Cronbach, L. J. (1954) *Educational Psychology.* Harcourt Brace Javanovich, Inc.

Daigon, A. and Dempsey, R. A. (1974) *School: Pass at Your Own Risk.* Prentice-Hall, Englewood Cliffs, NJ.

Deal, T. E. (1985) *The Culture of Schools* Leadership: Examining the Elusive.

Delpit, L. (1985) 'Skills and Other Dilemmas of a Progressive Black Educator', *Harvard Educational Review*, Vol. 56 No. 4.

Duck, S. and Perlman, D (eds) (1985) *Understanding Personal Relationships: An Interdisciplinary Approach.* Sage Publications, London.

Duke, D. L. (1984) *Teaching — The Imperiled Profession.* State University of New York Press, Albany.

Educational Achievement: Explanations and Implications of Recent Trends (1986) The Congress of the United States, Congressional Budget Office. U.S. Printing Office, Washington, D.C.

Eisner, E. W. (1985) *The Educational Imagination: On the Design and Evaluation of School Programs.* 2nd Edition. MacMillian, New York.

Fader, D. N., and McNeil, E. B. (1969) *Hooked on Books: Program & Proof* Berkley Publishing, New York.

Glasser, W. (1969) *Schools Without Failure.* Harper and Row Publishers, New York.

Glasser, W. (1987) *The Key to Improving Schools: An Interview with William Glasser.* Phi Delta Kappan, May 1987.

Goffman, E. (1959) *The Presentation of Self in Everyday Life.* Doubleday Anchor Books, New York.

Goodlad, J. I. (1984) *A Place Called School: Prospects for the Future.* McGraw-Hill, New York.

Gordon, T. (1974) *Teacher Effectiveness Training.* McKay, New York.

Graves, Donald H. (1985) *Writing: Teachers and Children at Work.* Heinemann Educational Books, Portsmouth, New Hampshire.

Greer, M., and Rubinstein, B. (1978) *Will the Real Teacher Please Stand Up?* 2nd Edition. Goodyear Publishing, Santa Monica, California.

Greeves, A. 'Alice's Loss in Bakerland', *Education Guardian*, Jan. 10, 1989.

Hadley, H. (1988) *Extending the Principles of Student-Centred Learning into Staff Organisation*, M. Ed. Dissertation, W. Midlands C. H. E.

Handal, G. and Lauvas, P. (1987) *Promoting Reflective Teaching* Open University Press.

Handy, C. and Aitken, R. (1986) *Understanding Schools as Organizations.* Penguin Books, Ltd, Harmondsworth, Middlesex, England.

Hargreaves, D. H. (1967) *Social Relations in a Secondary School.* Routledge & Kegan Paul, London.

Hargreaves, D. H. (1972) *Interpersonal Relations and Education.* Routledge & Kegan Paul, London and Boston.

Hargreaves, D. H. (1978) *What Teaching Does to Teachers, New Society,* March 9, 1978.

Hargreaves, D. H. (1982) *The Challenge for the Comprehensive School, Curriculum and Community.* Routledge & Kegan Paul Ltd., London.

Hazelwood, R., Fitz-Gibbon, C., McCabe, C., (1988) *Student Perception of Teaching and Learning Styles in TVEI.* Evaluation in Research and Education, Vol. 2, No. 2.

Herndon, James (1972) *How to Survive in Your Native Land.* Bantam Books, New York.

Herndon, James (1985) *Notes from a Schoolteacher.* Simon and Schuster, New York.

Hirsch, E. D. Jr. (Dec. 1987/Jan. 1989) *Restoring Cultural Literacy in the Early Grades Educational Leadership* pp. 63–70.

Holt, J. (1972) *Freedom and Beyond.* Penguin Books.

Hord, S. M., Rutherford, W. L., Huling-Austin, L., and Hall, G. E. *Taking Charge of Change.* Association for Supervision and Curriculum Development, Alexandra, Virginia.

Hoskisson, K., and Tompkins, G. E. (1987) *Language Arts Contents and Teaching Strategies.* Merrill Publishing, Columbus, Ohio.

Houston, G. (1984) *The Red Book of Groups and How to Lead Them Better.* Rochester Foundation, London.

Houston, J. (1982) *The Possible Human: A Course in Extending Your Physical, Mental, and Creative Abilities.* J. P. Tarcher, Inc., Los Angeles.

Jackson, P. W. (May, 1977) *Other Voices: Lonely at the Top: Observations on the Genesis of Administrative Isolation.* School Review, pp. 425–432.

Jackson, P. W. (1977) *14. The Promise of Educational Psychology* pp 389–405. Presented as an invited address before Division 15 of the American Psychological Association, August 26, 1977.

Jersild, A. T. (1955) *When Teachers Face Themselves.* Bureau of Publications, Teachers College, Columbia University.

Jessons, D. (1988) 'School Effectiveness and Efficiency', *Quality in Schools, NEFR.*

Johnson, J. (1979) *Use of Groups in School: A practical manual for everyone who works in elementary or secondary schools.* University Press of America, Washington.

Johnson, L., and O'Neill, C. (eds) (1984) *Dorothy Heathcote: Collected Writings on Education and Drama.* Hutchinson, London.

Jones, Richard M. (1968) *Fantasy and Feeling in Education.* Harper and Row, New York.

Jourard, S. N. (1971) *The Transparent Self.* Van Nostrand Reinhold Company, New York.

Joyce, B. and Weil, M. (1986) *Models of Teaching.* Third Edition. Prentice-Hall, Englewood Cliffs, NJ.

Kaufman, Bel (1964) *Up the Down Staircase*. Avon Books, Published by arrangement with Prentice-Hall, Inc., New York.

Kelly, M. J. (1988) *The Manchester Survey of Occupational Stress Among Head-teachers and Principles in the United Kingdom: First Report*. Manchester Polytechnic.

Knowles, Malcolm, (1978) *The Adult Learner: A Neglected Species*. Gulf Publishing Co. Houston.

Kohl, H. R., (1970) *The Open Classroom* A Practical Guide to A New Way of Teaching. Vintage Books, a division of Random House, Inc., New York.

Lehman, J. D. (1982) *Three Approaches to Classroom Management Views from a Psychological Perspective*. Lantham, New York.

Leonard, George B. (1968) *Education and Ecstasy*. Dell Publishing, New York.

Lortie, D. C. (1975) *School-Teacher: A Sociological Study*. The University of Chicago Press, Chicago.

Maeroff, G. I. (1988) *The Empowerment of Teachers* Teachers' College Press, New York.

Maslow, A., (1976) *The Farther Reaches of Human Nature* Penguin.

Mattox, B. A. (1975) *Getting it Together: Dilemmas for the Classroom Based on Kohlberg's Approach*. Pennant Press, San Diego, CA.

Mays, J. B. (1962) *Education and the Urban Child*. Liverpool University Press.

McCollum, J. A. (1978) *Ah Hah! The Inquiry Process of Generating and Testing Knowledge*. Goodyear Publishing, Santa Monica, CA.

Middlebrook, P. (1980) *Social Psychology and Modern Life*. Second Edition. A. A. Knopf & Co., New York.

Miller, R. 'Two Hundred Years of Holistic Education', *Holistic Education*, Vol. 1, Spring, 1988.

Montessori, M. (1964) *The Montessori Method* Schocken Books, New York, pp 86–106.

Montessori, M. (1965) *Spontaneous Activity in Education*. Schocken Books, New York.

Moyles, Janet R. (1988) *Self-Evaluation: A Primary Teacher's Guide*. NFER Nelson.

Mulgan, G. 'Collapse of the Pyramid of Power', The *Guardian*, November 28, 1988.

Munby, S. (1989) *Assessing & Recording Achievement*. (with Paul Phillips and Rose Collinson) Basil Blackwell Oxford.

Musgrave, P. W. (1965) *The Sociology of the School*. Methuen Education, London.

Nelson, B. S. 'Teachers can be trusted to reform their profession.' *Education Week*, Feb. 1987, p.21.

Passons, W. (1975) *Gestalt Approaches to Counselling*. Holt, Rinehart and Winston, New York.

Peter, Laurence J., and Hull, R. (1969) *The Peter Principle: Why Things Always Go Wrong*. Morrow, New York.

Peters, T., and Austin, N. (1985) *A Passion For Excellence: the Leadership Difference*. Random House, New York.

Pluckrose, H. & Wilby, P. (eds) (1980) *Education 2000*. Temple Smith, London.

'Poor Skills Hurt Youth: Job Plan'. *Chicago Tribune* Wednesday, March 23, 1988.

Postman, N. and Weingartner, C. (1969) *Teaching as a Subversive Activity*. Dell, New York.

Proctor, B. (1978) *Counselling Shop*. Andre Deutsch.

Reason, P., and Rowan, J. (1981) *Human Inquiry*. John Wiley and Sons, Chichester.

Renfield, R. (1971) *If Teachers Were Free*. Delta Book Publishing Co., Inc., New York.

Repo, S. (1970) *This Book is about Schools*. Pantheon Books, New York.

Rogers, C. R. (1951) *Client-Centred Therapy*. Houghton-Mifflin, Boston.

Rogers, C. R. (1961) *On Becoming a Person: A Therapist's View of Psychotherapy*. Houghton-Mifflin Company, Boston.

Rogers, C. R. (1983) *Freedom to Learn in the Eighties*. Houghton-Mifflin Boston.

Rosenthal, R. and Jacobson, L. (1968) *Pygmalion in the Classroom: Teacher Expectation and Pupils' Intellectual Development*. Holt, Rinehart and Winston, Inc., New York.

Rubin, L. J. (1974) *Facts and Feelings in the Classroom*. Ward Lock, London.

Sarason, S. B. (1971) *The Culture of the School and the Problem of Change*. Allyn and Bacon, Inc, Boston.

Schmuck, R. A., and Miles, M. B. (eds) (1971) *Organization Development in Schools*. University Associates, Inc., LaJolla, CA.

Schmuck, R. A., and Schmuck, P. A. (1974) *A Humanistic Psychology of Education: Making the School Everybody's House*. National Press Books, Palo Alto, CA.

Schmuck, R. A., and Schmuck, P. A. (1983) *Group Processes in the Classroom*. (fourth edition) Wm. C. Brown Company Publishers, Dubuque, Iowa.

Schutz, W. (1967) *Joy: Expanding Human Awareness*. Grove Press, New York.

Shipman, M. D. (1968) *Sociology of the School*. Longman: London.

Settle, D., and Wise, C. (1986) *Choices*. Basil Blackwell, Oxford.

Sikes, P. J. et al (1985) *Teacher Careers: Crises and Continuities*. Falmer Press, Sussex.

Sikes, P. J., Measor, L., and Woods, P. (1985) Teacher Careers: Crises and Continuities. *Issues in Education and Training Series: 5* The Falmer Press, London.

Simon, S. B., Howe, L. W., and Kirschenbaum, H. (1972) *Values Clarification: A Handbook of Practical Strategies for Teachers and Students*. Dodd, Mead & Company, New York.

Skynner, R., and Cleese, J. (1983) *Families and How to Survive Them*. Methuen, London.

Smith, M. (1975) *When I Say No, I Feel Guilty*. Bantam, New York.

Stone, E. (1970) *Reading in Educational Psychology Learning and Teaching*. Methuen, London.

Teachers' Dispute ACAS Independent Panel: Report of the Appraisal Training Working group. ACAS London, 1986.

Toffler, Alvin (1980) *The Third Wave*. Bantam Books in association with William Morrow & Co. Inc., Toronto.

Wagner, B. J. (1985) *Dorothy Heathcote: Drama as a Learning Medium*. NEA National Education Association, Washington, D.C.

Wakefield, B. (1988) 'Performance Indicators in Secondary Schools', *Quality in Schools*. NEFR.

Watzlawick, P., Bavelas, J. B., and Jackson, D. D. (1967) *Pragmatics of Human Communication: A study of interactional patterns, pathologies, and paradoxes*. W. W. Norton and Company, New York.

Wees, W. R. (1971) *Nobody Can Teach Anyone Anything*. Doubleday Canada Limited: Toronto, Ontario.

Weigand, J. (1985) *Developing Teacher Competencies*. Prentice-Hall, Inc., Englewood Cliff, NJ.

Weil, M.; J., B., and Kluwin, B. (1978) *Personal Models of Teaching Expanding Your Teaching Experience*. Prentice-Hall, Inc., Englewood Cliff, NJ.

Weindling, R. (1988): 'The Process of School Improvement: Some Practical Messages from Research' *Quality in Schools*. NEFR.

Weinstein, G. and Fantini, M. D. Editors (1970) *Toward Humanistic Education: A Curriculum of Affect*. Published for the Ford Foundation by Praeger Publisher, New York.

White, Allan, (1988) 'Student-Centred Learning' unpublished dissertation for the Advanced Diploma in Guidance, Teeside Polytechnic.